Consuming Autobiographies
Reading and Writing the Self in Post-War France

LEGENDA

LEGENDA, founded in 1995 by the European Humanities Research Centre of the University of Oxford, is now a joint imprint of the Modern Humanities Research Association and Maney Publishing. Titles range from medieval texts to contemporary cinema and form a widely comparative view of the modern humanities, including works on Arabic, Catalan, English, French, German, Greek, Italian, Portuguese, Russian, Spanish, and Yiddish literature. An Editorial Board of distinguished academic specialists works in collaboration with leading scholarly bodies such as the Society for French Studies and the British Comparative Literature Association.

MHRA

The Modern Humanities Research Association (MHRA) encourages and promotes advanced study and research in the field of the modern humanities, especially modern European languages and literature, including English, and also cinema. It also aims to break down the barriers between scholars working in different disciplines and to maintain the unity of humanistic scholarship in the face of increasing specialization. The Association fulfils this purpose primarily through the publication of journals, bibliographies, monographs and other aids to research.

MANEY
publishing

Maney Publishing is one of the few remaining independent British academic publishers. Founded in 1900 the company has offices both in the UK, in Leeds and London, and in North America, in Boston. Since 1945 Maney Publishing has worked closely with learned societies, their editors, authors, and members, in publishing academic books and journals to the highest traditional standards of materials and production.

Consuming Autobiographies

Reading and Writing the Self in Post-War France

❖

Claire Boyle

LEGENDA
Modern Humanities Research Association and Maney Publishing
2007

Published by the
Modern Humanities Research Association and Maney Publishing
1 Carlton House Terrace
London SW1Y 5DB
United Kingdom

LEGENDA is an imprint of the
Modern Humanities Research Association and Maney Publishing

Maney Publishing is the trading name of W. S. Maney & Son Ltd,
whose registered office is at Suite 1C, Joseph's Well, Hanover Walk, Leeds LS3 1AB

ISBN 978-1-905981-10-6

First published 2007

Printed in Great Britain

Cover: 875 Design

Copy-Editor: Richard Correll

CONTENTS

THIS BOOK IS DEDICATED
TO MY MOTHER AND FATHER

ACKNOWLEDGEMENTS

This book was chiefly written in Oxford and Edinburgh (and a few more and less interesting places along the way). It has its origins in my doctoral thesis, completed at the University of Cambridge. I must first record my gratitude to the AHRB (as was), which funded me throughout my postgraduate studies, and also to Girton College, Cambridge, for additional financial support. Had I not had that support, the completion of that thesis is just one of a number of things that, as far I can tell, would very likely never have happened.

I count myself especially fortunate to have had my Ph.D. thesis supervised by Dr Emma Wilson. She played a crucial part in helping me develop my ideas on French autobiography, and I could not have wished for more generous advice, encouragement or support during the preparation of my thesis or since. I have many reasons to thank her. Along with Girton College, the Department of French at the University of Cambridge offered a wonderfully stimulating and supportive environment for my research. I am very grateful to the several people there who took the time to discuss ideas with me, especially Sarah Kay and Sarah Cooper, who have readily offered encouragement and advice over a number of years. Further afield, I have had invaluable discussions with Michael Sheringham and Colin Davis, and would like to thank them for their perspectives and guidance, and for supporting my work. My thanks go too to those colleagues at the University of Oxford, particularly at Lady Margaret Hall and Christ Church, who encouraged me in my research and book-writing during my time there; and to my newer colleagues in the School of Languages, Cultures and Religions at the University of Stirling: particularly Elizabeth Ezra, Andrew Ginger and David Murphy for reading portions of the manuscript, and for their readiness to dispense helpful advice. The University of Stirling is also to be thanked for financing a temporary reduction in my teaching commitments, which aided my progress at a vital stage in the preparation of the manuscript.

Chapter 5 of this book includes material previously published in my article 'Writing Self-Estrangement: Possessive Knowledge and Loss in Cixous's Recent Autobiographical Work', in *Hybrid Voices, Hybrid Texts: Women's Writing at the Turn of the Millennium*, ed. by Gill Rye, special edn of *Dalhousie French Studies*, 68 (Fall 2004), 69–77: I am grateful to the editors for permission to re-use this material.

During the life of this project I have been sustained by people whose contributions are all the more precious for being often (although not always) less tangible. For keeping me on an even keel, for their advice in the terminal stages, and for helping me in numerous other ways, I thank Alex Belton, Charlotte Bosseaux, Gavin Cameron, Ruth Cruickshank, Véronique Desnain, Mary Green, Joanna Harris (and Oscar and Tash), Alison Jasper, Anna Morvern, Libby Saxton, and my parents. Special thanks go to Rachel De Wachter: from the start to the finish of this book she found many ways to help me in bringing this project to a successful conclusion, not least through her photographical and other invaluable expertise. Similarly, I record my deep gratitude to Helen Barr, at once my most willing and most demanding reader, for everything she gave to and towards this book. In many places it is the better for her involvement.

Last, but most certainly not least, I thank those who have anonymously read my work for their careful attention and advice, as well as Graham Nelson at Legenda for all his guidance, and for being so empathetic and dependable an editor; and also my copy-editor, Richard Correll, for such meticulous attention to my work.

INTRODUCTION

This is a book about how French autobiography is, or may be, read. In choosing to entitle it 'Consuming Autobiographies', I should state that I am not announcing a work that performs an analysis of autobiography as a product or symptom of the consumer culture that grew up in post-war France.[1] Whilst this would be a rich seam to mine, I shall be more interested here in the potential for the commodification of the autobiographical self than the published work as commodity. This is not, however, to suggest that these two forms of commodification are entirely separate: the cultural climate out of which the published autobiography as commodity emerges so strongly is also the one in which, I shall argue, a particular type of autobiographer fears that to write the self is to run the risk of the self being reified by others — being treated as a thing, an object that others may possess. The particular type of autobiographer I am concerned with is the literary autobiographer, and the literary autobiography I am concerned with is that produced in France in the period from the end of the Second World War until the arrival of the twenty-first century.[2] In this book, I contend that the prospect of being treated as a consumable commodity is one that troubles literary autobiographers — surprising though that may be in the climate in which they write — and that out of a desire for what might be called self-preservation, they are determined to resist such a fate. I argue that these concerns shape the way they engage with autobiography as a genre through their own autobiographical writings in a manner that has gone largely unrecognized.

My use of the term 'autobiographies' in this book's title will also need some explanation. It is often considered that, during the twentieth century, autobiography became an extinct literary genre in France. Describing the vicissitudes of autobiography scholarship over the century, Paul J. Archambault notes a tendency towards its end to proclaim 'the "death of autobiography"': a response to the sustained questioning invited by structuralist and poststructuralist thought of the human subject's ability to know itself, determine itself and fix itself in writing.[3] Paradoxically, this tendency coincides, as the French autobiography scholar Philippe Lejeune reports, with a burgeoning production in France of narratives exploring and exhibiting the self.[4] However, as Mounir Laouyen explains, these increasingly come to be designated with other epithets in preference to the label 'autobiography', reflecting a conviction on the part of literary writers that, in the postmodern era, it has become desirable to signal a rupture with the genre of autobiography, and to 'corroder ses fondements en montrant l'épuisement de sa dynamique créatrice traditionnelle' [corrode its foundations by showing its traditional creative potential to be exhausted].[5] This rupture is often signalled by writers and critics alike (not that I shall want to insist too much on the separation of these two constituencies) through the use of alternative terms for work containing autobiographical content, such as 'self-writing', 'life-writing', '*autofiction*' or '*nouvelle autobiographie*'.

This account of the death of autobiography will come under the spotlight in this book. Here I shall be challenging assumptions that are sometimes made about why it is that writers are reluctant to be associated with the genre of autobiography. Accordingly, in Chapter 1 I go behind the scenes of this distrust expressed in the latter part of the twentieth century toward autobiography as a literary genre, exploring and interrogating the explanations frequently offered for it. In subsequent chapters I pursue readings of works which inhabit a murky territory apparently outwith the realm of autobiography, all published between 1946 and 2000 (the majority published in or after the 1970s). The authors of these works are four prominent twentieth-century writers, representing different poles in the French post-war literary landscape: Nathalie Sarraute (1900–99), Georges Perec (1936–82), Jean Genet (1910–86) and Hélène Cixous (1937–). My readings of their works lead me to question whether the genre of autobiography is really as dead and buried as some would like us to believe. Indeed, this pronounced emphasis on the death of autobiography in texts that otherwise might be categorized as such provides the impetus to this study. What purposes might be served by declaring autobiography dead? Pursuing this question will lead me to ask another: how far does a fear of appearing to offer up one's selfhood for the consumption of others (an anxiety which twentieth-century intellectual preoccupations with the subject's loss of autonomy can only reinforce) influence the standpoint writers take on whether autobiography can continue to survive or not?

Because my aim throughout this book is to explore what lies behind the rejection of the label 'autobiography' that is implied by the pronouncement of its death, I shall be deferring judgement on the question of whether autobiography is dead in the post-war era of French literature. For that reason I shall not be jettisoning references to 'autobiography' as a genre of writing in favour of more recent coinages. This is not to say, I should make clear, that I consider it possible for late-twentieth-century French literary authors to credibly offer the confident, masterful autobiographical self-portraits that previous commentators have found in the work of early autobiographers such as Jean-Jacques Rousseau.[6] Indeed, more acuitive scholars of autobiography have argued against readings which position early autobiographies as straightforward demonstrations of virtuosity and genius; which portray them as personal accounts that reflect their authors' secure conception of a sovereign self, untrammelled by the advent of structuralism and its heirs.[7] For these critics, the distinction between early, self-assured autobiographers and later autobiographers who lack that assurance is not a secure one. Thus I retain the term 'autobiography' (alongside references to self-writing, life-writing and other terms as are contextually appropriate), in the belief that it is a term whose significations are ultimately mobile and supple enough to take account of developments in the genre. Consequently, despite the frequently promulgated image of the genre of autobiography as something somehow fossilized, my references to 'autobiography' — except where the word is preceded with the qualifiers 'conventional' or 'traditional' — are not intended to suggest an ossified or inanimate form of expression.

Declaring autobiography to be dead is, in any case, problematic. The insights of psychoanalysis, structuralism and poststructuralism which were available to post-war writers may have irreparably damaged the notion that the individual human subject can be an authority on itself. Yet this loss of faith in the authoritativeness of any self-written account also coincides with an increasing interest in testimony narratives, as remembering the wartime past instates itself as an ethical imperative amongst writers, politicians, academics and citizens.[8] This interest has also been fuelled by a substantial drive — especially amongst feminist scholars — to seek out and expose the experiences and subjectivities of those marginalized from canonical history and literature by turning to their autobiographical writings.[9] Given this new emphasis on the importance of bearing witness, to insist on the impossibility of testifying to personal experience in writing is a manoeuvre which risks being seen as unhelpful; in the light of the posthumous scandal surrounding the deconstructionist Paul De Man's apparently collaborationist journalistic activities during the Second World War (when he wrote for the pro-Nazi Belgian newspaper *Le Soir*), it may even excite suspicion.[10] To a great extent, this study is about the conflict between these two positions on autobiography: the first being the belief that it is not possible for autobiographers to tell us about themselves; the second being the belief, even demand, that they do. It is in literary autobiography, more than in other forms of the genre, that these views collide.

The essence of autobiography as a genre of writing is that it connects the account that the narrating voice gives of itself — the insights, experiences and reflections that the narrator tells us are his or her own and which explain who he or she is — with a named real-life person, who is the author of the work. Yet the intellectual climate in which modern French authors write makes it very difficult for them to keep faith with the idea that they can actually produce this kind of explanatory account. Indeed, the authors I study here all signal prominently in those of their works that seem to promise it that such an account will not be found there: the reader who hopes to connect with the individual behind the text will be disappointed. Indeed, the theme of estrangement features heavily in these authors' autobiographical narratives, which describe individuals who are estranged from readers, but also from their families and communities. That sense of alienation is often linked to ethnicity, nationality, sexuality or gender, as we find in Perec's and Cixous's treatments of their Jewishness, or Genet's meditations on homosexuality. The issue of gender may not detain Sarraute, but for Cixous her alienation is compounded by expectations attached to gender which she cannot fulfil. Sarraute's insight is that even language, which might be seen as permitting connections to be made between writer and reader, operates as a medium of estrangement, alienating the self from others, and even sometimes from itself.

However, the nub of my argument in this book is that authors do not write their works in such a way as to resist having them labelled as autobiographies simply because they fear that as authors they will be unequal to the task that autobiography seems to impose. I shall argue that there is also a deep aversion to the prospect of *being seen to have written* an autobiography. This manifests itself through the various devices my selected authors use in their texts to dissociate them from autobiography: strategies that betray profound anxieties about the genre. I locate the root of these in what Lejeune, in a seminal work, identifies as the foundation of autobiography: *the perception of an exact correspondence* between the flesh-and-blood person who is the author, and the self that both narrates the text and provides its subject matter.[11]

Questions of perception are at the centre of the argument I make here about autobiography. My thesis in this book is that what generates the discernible anxieties over genre expressed in my chosen corpus of works is fear: fear of being exposed to external perception, and fear of what exactly those external perceptions will be. What emerges as especially troubling is the prospect of a continuous line being formed in those external perceptions, linking back the textual persona encountered in the written work with the real-life individual whose name appears on the book cover. Why should this prospect be so troubling? Certainly, it is a notion that relies on the faithfulness of the textual representation in a way that is quite incompatible, both with the insights into selfhood and representation prevailing in the latter half of the twentieth century, and with those developed by the authors I consider here. My chapters on Sarraute, Perec, Genet and Cixous will show that their works present the establishment of such a link as dubious to say the least. Establishing such a link, however, is what the attribution of a text to the genre of autobiography entitles its readers to do — indeed entails them doing. This provides one explanation for the hostility toward the genre of autobiography which is expressed in the corpus of texts I study, as well as the prevalence of strategies to dissociate these works from autobiography, or to minimize its relevance. The principal aim of these strategies, I shall argue, is to discourage readings in which the textual self is seen as the gateway to the walking, talking self of the author.

The various tactics my chosen authors employ to promote specific attitudes towards autobiography begin to emerge in Chapter 2, along with the idea that the author's selfhood is impenetrable to the reader. Here, through a reading of self-writings by Sarraute, I establish a pattern of relations between writer, genre and reader that, whilst not being exactly reproduced in other cases, nevertheless provides a core architecture for the ideas I develop overall in this book. In this second chapter I analyse Sarraute's writing of the self in the well-known *Enfance*, but also in the later and less acclaimed *Tu ne t'aimes pas* and *Ouvrez*, in the light of Jacques Lacan's theories on the role of the Other in the constitution of the self.[12] I argue that behind Sarraute's rejection of autobiography, and her innovations in writing and conceptualizing the self, there lurks a preference for keeping the self firmly within the self's possession and not acknowledging the extent to which it must always be within another's grasp. Achieving this requires surreptitiously fending off the reader. The case of Perec, who occupies my attention in Chapter 3, is somewhat different: his autobiographical writings *W ou le souvenir d'enfance* and *Je me souviens* show him to be less defensive about keeping control of his identity than Sarraute, and he does not attempt to enforce the reader's adoption of a specific image of himself.[13] It is suggested that this approach results from traumatic childhood experiences which have dispossessed him of a secure sense of identity. However, an attempt to control the reader's response to his autobiographical projects persists, although the effort is focussed on mobilizing the reader as an active, creative participant in the text, rather than a passive consumer of a particular image of the author that it supplies; the willingness of some readers to restore to Perec a specifically Jewish identity suggests this effort has limited success. In Chapter 4, the theme of readers' identifications with an author is revisited, as Genet's early autobiographical writings *Notre-Dame-des-Fleurs*, *Miracle de la rose* and *Journal du voleur* are examined.[14] Identifications made with Genet by critics as part of a queer theoretical approach are all the more notable as Genet — anticipating Michel Foucault's insights into the ways in which the presence of surveying and inquiring others causes deviant selves to be subjugated — tries (although ultimately in vain) to bar any attempt by the reading other to get close to or identify with his self.

A conflict emerges ever more forcefully as this book progresses between the desire of certain actual readers to claim an author as a speaker for the cause of a group whose voice is marginalized, and the author's efforts in their writings to resist this packaging, to resist having his or her self appropriated, consumed in this way. This is a conflict which moves to centre stage in Chapter 5, where I explore a tension between how Cixous comes to suggest her self should be read and how Cixous is read and related to in some quarters by readers who conceive of themselves as being aligned with her project, often seen as feminist. This tension arises from the increasing emphasis latterly in Cixous's autobiographical work, in such texts as *Hélène Cixous: photos de racines*, *Les Rêveries de la femme sauvage: scènes primitives* and *Le Jour où je n'étais pas là*, on the importance of respecting the impossibility of a full encounter with another, even in the context of a meeting that takes place in the atmosphere of what Cixous calls 'love', which has its roots in her concept of a feminist praxis.[15] Having brought out the tensions between what is invested in autobiography by readers — particularly those engaged in forms of identity politics — and the stance taken towards the genre by those who might be thought to write it, I then proceed to my Conclusion. Here I reconsider what is at stake in the rejection of the affiliation with autobiography in the light of the play of power relations to which autobiographical texts play host. Power relations operate between the writing and reading selves, creating pressure points that coalesce around the recurrent issues of knowledge, estrangement and the appropriation or misuse of the self by others.

Autobiography thus emerges as a site of conflict, with the implicit promises held out by the genre clashing with the more limited vision that individual texts present of their capacity to shed light on the author's person. However, this conflict between texts and a genre framework which they disown as their own is just the first in a series of flash points that I identify relating to autobiography in the works of Sarraute, Perec, Genet and Cixous. The genre of autobiography is not the only target: these are skirmishes in which the reader too becomes embroiled. If autobiography is a site of conflict, then it is the author, in more than one sense, who is at the heart of it. Indeed, I shall argue that the effect of disputing the presence of the genre of autobiography in the texts is not only to put the author at the heart of the conflict, but, more precisely, to *make the author himself (or herself) a point of conflict*.

At this point it becomes clear that the death of autobiography is not the only demise that is uncertain: despite proclamations of the death of the author, as is inevitable in a study devoted to writings of the self, this book is written more in the light of what has been called the return of the author, rather than in the shadow of their passing.[16] To speak of the return of the author is not to sweep under the carpet all the problems that made authors difficult to trace through their writings in the first place. I should therefore make clear that when I refer to authors, particularly to what they might desire or intend, I am not claiming to speak about the conscious or even unconscious desires of an existing (or formerly existing) person: I am referring to the *persona* of a specific author, as it emerges from works written by a living, breathing person of the same name.

This semantic point goes to the heart of the key conflict that I want to explore in this book. I have made clear that in my own thinking about Sarraute, Perec, Genet and Cixous, I separate the *persona* of the author encountered in the text from the *person* of the author encountered only in life. In the course of this book I suggest that if invocations of the genre of autobiography provoke anxieties in the works I examine, it is because there is considerable concern betrayed in these works about the consequences that may ensue if this distinction between the author's *persona* and the author's *person* goes unrecognized — as is likely if the text is read as autobiography. It is in this sense that the author becomes a point of conflict, and at this juncture that the reader becomes implicated in it. Narratives of the self written by Sarraute, Perec, Genet and Cixous assert the limited use of the image of the author they construct as a tool affording insights into the flesh-and-blood person behind the literary work. They also reveal an expectation that readers will be reluctant to accept such viewpoints on autobiographical representation. In consequence, the reader comes to be positioned as an adversary.

These are texts, then, which, whilst imparting an image of their author, also impart an image of the reader. They confer a certain identity (as antagonist) upon the reader — just as the reader confers a certain identity upon the author through the creation of their image of him or her. It is my contention that the fact that such an image of the reader is constructed in these works, the fact that they work hard to stabilize an identity for the reader, has much to tell us about the stability — or the lack thereof — of the author's own identity. The idea that identity has to be negotiated with another, or in another's presence, is a common theme in these texts, particularly the negotiation of an individual's identity in the face of assumptions that may be made about it, or in the face of identifications that others make with an individual based on presumptions about shared identity. However, strangely little is said on a particular instance of this: namely, the negotiation of authorial identity that must take place when an author writes his or her self, a negotiation that must be conducted with the reader through the medium of the text. Instead, as I try to illustrate in what follows, the works I analyse are generally concerned with ensuring that the negotiation of the authorial self's identity is one that happens as far as possible on the author's own terms. Critical to this is persuading readers to accept those terms, and in particular the identity as a reader which the autobiographical narratives I study here enjoin them to assume. Concerned as I shall be with what that identity entails, in this study I shall be particularly attentive to the image of the reader that these works construct.

In these works, the reader is commonly ascribed a consuming desire to acquire intimate knowledge of the real-life author's person, as well as the naïve belief that such knowledge is a commodity that these works can supply, and that the possession of this knowledge will be the end-product of his or her reading. It is in this sense that the author — if this approach to autobiographical works goes unchecked — comes to be considered as a commodity, as an entity that can be grasped as the result of a transaction that takes place through the text. The implication is that, unless corrected, readers will not realize that this commodity is unavailable to them: they will not recognize that what they obtain from their reading is not knowledge of the real-life author, but an image of the author which they themselves will have been instrumental in constructing; an image that can make no safe claim to capture the author outside the text. Instead, they will assume that through the situation, experiences and emotions recorded in the author's narrative, the text provides them with a basis to understand, to the point of being able to identify with, the real-life person of the author.

In response, the narratives I study offer at least implicit and often, through direct narratorial address, explicit criticism of any such agenda that might shape reading, an agenda they present as misconceived. The narrators of these works suggest, with varying degrees of censoriousness, that the aspirations of the reader who treats intimate knowledge of the flesh-and-blood writer as a commodity which can be taken into his or her possession are unrealistic, and unreasonable. Indeed these works frequently go so far as to depict this very desire for the author as unethical. For Sarraute (and to some extent for Cixous), this is because any demands for intimate knowledge of another beyond those which that other consents to are unethical; for Perec, the passive mentality with which the narrative will be approached by a reader who adopts the attitude of a consumer awaiting satisfaction is fundamentally discreditable in its blinkeredness. In the case of Genet, the situation is more complicated, since his penchant for reversing positive and negative values means that for him the unethical becomes ethical. However, his autobiographical writings nonetheless suggest that the reader has no right to demand information from him, nor to identify with him; Cixous's work, in addition to exploring the ethics surrounding the seeking of knowledge, highlights the impossibility of another knowing what the self cannot know about itself.

What emerges very strongly from my extended readings of these authors' works is the considerable extent to which these are works concerned with their own reception. Moreover, they are not just concerned with how the reader will respond to the written work they read, but also with how this reader will relate to the real-life writer behind that work. Embedded in these writings is a discomfort linked with the prospect of the author being an object of the reader's desire. There is particular unease at the notion that reading these texts might be seen as a way to satisfy that desire and to procure the desired object. Unsurprisingly, given the anxiety they arouse, we find readers themselves figure prominently in these works, being treated particularly resonantly in Sarraute's and Genet's writings. These intradiegetic representations of readers enable the texts to model appropriate reader responses and indicate which are inappropriate.

Why should such efforts be made to guide the reading of these texts, and why should it be so important to divert readers from the idea that the text can supply them with the intimate relation with the author that they are deemed to desire? The prospect of readers breathing life into the images of the author which they have garnered from the text — images which will inevitably fail to correspond to the author's self-image — is an alarming one because, I shall argue, it represents a loss of autonomy on the part of the author to determine who his or her self is. I contend that the loss of this autonomy is what the authors I am concerned with want to avoid at all costs. These texts attempt to block any identifications that their readers may make through them with the individuals who are their authors. They also conspicuously deny readers intimacy with the person of the author. Both of these manoeuvres function as a means of forcibly preventing the reader from feeling they have sufficient knowledge and intimacy with the author to manufacture the sort of images of them which, having been animated by the reader, can then take on a life of their own and potentially be more widely circulated. Both these manoeuvres seem designed to prevent the circulation of images which are no longer susceptible to being controlled by the author, even whilst they apparently refer back to, reflect and represent their person.

In my reading then, autobiography appears as a place where the autobiographer experiences a loss of sovereignty over the self — unexpectedly perhaps, for autobiography might be thought to be the arena in which the writing self solidifies, stabilizes its self and its identity. I suggest, however, that autobiography confronts the writing self with the prospect, or indeed the likelihood, of the reverse happening: that is, with the strong likelihood of losing control over who it is. If the author loses sovereignty over the self, it is lost to the reader, who is held responsible for stealing it away as a consequence of harbouring an immoderate appetite, not just for a narrative to read, but for a person to consume. Resisting that loss of sovereignty entails, for my chosen authors (but I would venture to suggest not only for them), trying to convince readers that the means by which they appropriate the authorial self and threaten the author's sovereignty are not available to them, or are at least means which, being ethically dubious, they should not countenance using.

These arguments should thus shed some light on why this book's title refers to 'consuming', rather than 'reading' autobiographies. This is because my chosen authors recognize that the consuming of autobiography pertains not only to how a written work is read, but also to how the author behind the work is related to. In reading the work, the reader constructs a relation with the person they believe to be behind it. The implication behind the handling of the reader in the works that I study is that the reading, and the relating, will be conducted with a certain devouring attitude in keeping with the quality of engagement a reader might be expected to have with a work of 'consuming' interest to him, or her.

This, then, is a book about what is at stake when readers consume autobiography. I will argue that what turns out to be at stake is the author's self, and possession over it; the ability of the author to maintain self-determination. As a book which deals with what reader expectations the genre of autobiography stimulates (or is thought by writers to stimulate), it is also a book which has something to say about what is at stake when the label autobiography is applied, or withheld, from a work of autobiographical character.

Notes to the Introduction

1. Vincent Colonna touches on the sociological backdrop to the vogue he detects in contemporary France for writing (and exhibiting) the self in his *Autofiction et autres mythomanies littéraires* (Auch: Tristram, 2004), pp. 11–19.
2. I do not, however, pretend to offer, as Michael Sheringham has done in his *French Autobiography: Devices and Desires: Rousseau to Perec* (Oxford: Clarendon Press, 1993), a survey of the autobiographical writing of this era in France (a work I hereafter refer to as *Devices*). A still broader survey can be found in Jacques Lecarme and Eliane Lecarme-Tabone, *L'Autobiographie*, 2nd edn (Paris: Colin, 1999).
3. Paul J. Archambault, 'Autobiography and the Search for Transparency', *Symposium*, 51 (1998), 231–46 (p. 244); on the vicissitudes in the way the subject is theorized in modern France, see *Subject Matters: Subject and Self in French Literature from Descartes to the Present*, ed. by Paul Gifford and Johnnie Gratton (Amsterdam: Rodopi, 2000).
4. Philippe Lejeune, *L'Autobiographie en France* (Paris: Colin, 1971), p. 104. Some thirty years later, Colonna is able to confirm that publication trends confirm that this type of writing still finds itself in rude health (see Colonna, p. 11).
5. Mounir Laouyen, 'Préface', in *Les Nouvelles Autobiographies/New Autobiographies*, ed. by Mounir Laouyen, special edn of *Esprit créateur*, 42.4 (Winter 2002), pp. 3–7 (p. 3).
6. There are numerous examples of this kind of reading of Rousseau's work, which present it, in the words of Lecarme, as a 'coup de maître qu'aucun écrivain n'a vraiment approché en maîtrise, en détermination, en audace, et en rigueur' [a masterstroke which no other writer has really come close to in terms of mastery, determination, audaciousness and rigour], Lecarme and Lecarme-Tabone, p. 148. This kind of perspective on autobiographers also informs the studies of James Olney, *Metaphors of Self: The Meaning of Autobiography* (Princeton, NJ: Princeton University Press, 1972) and Roy Pascal, *Design and Truth in Autobiography* (London: Routledge and Kegan Paul, 1960).
7. See, for example, the discussion of Romantic autobiography by Linda Anderson, *Autobiography* (London: Routledge, 2001), p. 53.
8. Issues of commemorating and bearing witness to the past are especially central to autobiographical writings by Georges Perec and Hélène Cixous which I will examine later in this book. Too much has been written on the need or duty to remember the past — an imperative crystallizing itself in France particularly around the experience of World War Two and the Algerian War — for me to give more than an *aperçu* here. In life-writing, Assia Djebar's *L'Amour la fantasia* (Paris: Albin Michel, 1995), provides an instance of an experimental autobiographical text concerned to testify to a collective experience of trauma. Scholarly explorations of memory and the *devoir de mémoire* [duty to remember] include Paul Ricœur, *La Mémoire, l'histoire, l'oubli* (Paris: Editions du Seuil, 2000); and Pierre Nora, *Les Lieux de mémoire*, 3 vols (Paris: Gallimard, 1984–92).
9. I allude here to a vast body of work, and I shall have reason to return to this topic in more detail at a later point in this book. Suffice it to say here that this recognizably feminist endeavour to publicize experiences that have been 'hidden from history' lies behind studies of autobiography such as those collected in Bella Brodzki and Celeste Schenk (eds), *Life/Lines: Theorizing Women's Autobiography* (Ithaca, NY: Cornell University Press, 1988); Suzette Henke's *Shattered Subjects: Trauma and Testimony in Women's Life-Writing* (Basingstoke: Macmillan, 1998); and, in the domain of French studies, Kathryn Robson's *Writing Wounds: The Inscription of Trauma in Post-1968 French Women's Life-Writing* (Amsterdam: Rodopi, 2004).
10. Literary critics were left questioning the extent to which De Man's deconstructionist stance had been strategically developed with a view to exculpating him retrospectively for these activities. On this controversy, see Shoshana Felman and Dori Laub, *Testimony: Crises of Witnessing in Literature, Psychoanalysis, and History* (New York: Routledge, 1992), pp. 120–64; and Seán Burke,

The Death and Return of the Author: Criticism and Subjectivity in Barthes, Foucault and Derrida, 2nd edn (Edinburgh: Edinburgh University Press, 1998), pp. 1–7.

11. Lejeune, *Le Pacte autobiographique* (Paris: Editions du Seuil, 1975). I shall discuss Lejeune's conception of the prerequisites for securing an autobiographical pact in more detail in Chapter 1.

12. Nathalie Sarraute, *Enfance* (1983), in *Œuvres complètes*, ed. by Jean-Yves Tadié and others (Paris: Gallimard, coll. Bibliothèque de la Pléiade, 1996), pp. 987–1145; *Tu ne t'aimes pas* (1989), in *Œuvres complètes*, pp. 1147–1291; *Ouvrez* (Paris: Gallimard, coll. Blanche, 1997).

13. Georges Perec, *W ou le souvenir d'enfance* ([Paris]: Denoël, coll. Gallimard Imaginaire, 1975); *Je me souviens: les choses communes*, I (Paris: Hachette, coll. Textes du XXe siècle, 1978).

14. Jean Genet, *Notre-Dame-des-Fleurs* ([Lyons(?)]: Barbezat-L'Arbalète, 1948); *Miracle de la rose* ([Lyons(?)]: Barbezat-L'Arbalète, coll. Gallimard folio, 1946); *Journal du voleur* (Paris: Gallimard, coll. folio, 1949).

15. Mireille Calle-Gruber and Hélène Cixous, *Hélène Cixous: photos de racines* (Paris: Editions des Femmes–Antoinette Fouque, 1994); Hélène Cixous, *Les Rêveries de la femme sauvage: scènes primitives* (Paris: Galilée, 2000); *Le Jour où je n'étais pas là* (Paris: Galilée, 2000).

16. On the return of the author (arguably never quite deceased) see Burke; this phenomenon is the corollary to the return of the subject described in Gifford and Gratton (eds).

CHAPTER 1

❖

Autobiography
Orthodoxies and Paradoxes

If we assent to the idea that autobiography is a label that can no longer be decently applied to personal narratives with autobiographical qualities, autobiography dies. What does that mean? It clearly does *not* mean that people, even literary writers, stop writing autobiographically: the personal narrative with autobiographical qualities lives on, in twentieth- and twenty-first-century France as elsewhere. Rather, what it means is a change to the frame surrounding that narrative. My major focus in this book is the question of where the impetus to change the frame comes from: this requires not only close attention to what the writers of the autobiographical texts I study have to say about their relationship to the frame, or even yoke, that the genre of autobiography provides; it also requires some exploration of that frame beyond the contours it takes on in the eyes of these writers. Although autobiography may appear to have been dealt a mortal blow, with the apparent demise of the genre and the rise of newer nomenclatures to designate narratives of the self, it does not follow that we need give autobiography as a genre no further thought. Raylene Ramsay argues that 'new autobiographies [...] place the territories of old autobiographies, to use a Derridean term "under erasure" ("sous rature")': meaning that, whilst an attempt may be made to have the genre of autobiography in its traditional form 'struck out', it 'will not be fully erased but [...] still perceptible'.[1] It will be important to cast a critical eye on the implicit and explicit insistences made by Sarraute, Perec, Genet and Cixous that their works *do* change the frame surrounding self-writing. Similarly, it will be important to consider from a point of view that extends beyond the author's necessarily self-interested one what the contours of this frame are, and what it is about this frame that might make changing or discarding it seem desirable, or indeed undesirable. This chapter therefore seeks to provide foundations for my later critique of the relationship Sarraute, Perec, Genet and Cixous have with the genre of autobiography. It does this via an exploration of how autobiography as a genre has been perceived, both in life and death, by critical readers, focussing particularly on the variety and vacillation of expectations attached to what otherwise risks being thought of as a monolithic genre (if we allow ourselves to be excessively influenced by the way it is depicted by modern French practitioners).

Over the course of this book, it will become clear that any one conception of the genre of autobiography is intertwined with a specific conception of how it is to be read: models of autobiography as a genre will be seen implicitly to contain within them models of readerly participation. (This is not to suggest that readers always adhere to such models: the accounts that I give of the reception of autobiography provide ample proof to the contrary.) Thus, in this chapter, I shall be particularly attentive to exploring what critics of autobiography have to say about the possibilities that the genre of autobiography holds out to its readers: what it offers them; what it fails to offer them, or cannot; and what obligations or constraints it places on them. This will provide the starting point for a reflection on what the stance taken towards the genre of autobiography by those who write the self suggests to us about the relationship they have, or wish to build, with their readers.

I. Autobiography in Theory

Autobiography: defining moments

We are confronted with evidence that autobiography is not a monolithic genre with a distinct, readily recognizable identity as soon as we stop to consider what is meant by the term. The existence of autobiography as an object of academic study has been recognized by critics ever since Georg Misch's mammoth *Geschichte der Autobiographie*, which appeared in embryonic form in 1907; albeit that Lejeune, writing in 1975, records a persistent resistance in French universities to the study of autobiography as literature.[2] However, a scholarly consensus as to exactly what autobiography is has never been reached. Misch's understanding of what autobiography is is extremely loose: he applies the description to forms of writing such as ancient Egyptian tomb inscriptions, enabling him to trace back the history of autobiography into antiquity as far as the twenty-eighth century BC, providing the genre with a founding origin, and thus, academic respectability.[3]

The inauguration of what would now be recognized as autobiography study in France came with a far shorter work by Georges Gusdorf, published in 1956.[4] His 'Conditions et limites de l'autobiographie' shares something of Misch's preoccupation with typology, but, although his essay is concerned with the properties of autobiography, Gusdorf remained content to describe the conditions giving rise to autobiography, assuming a common and unproblematic definition of autobiography to exist. The notable features of his essay are that — contradicting Misch — it insists that the genre of autobiography is socio-historically contingent, and is only seen in societies that appreciate the individual as a singular and autonomous being.[5] Crucially, as an early follower of Lacan's, Gusdorf sees the writing of autobiography as a performative act which brings into being a subject that does not pre-exist the text: he dismisses approaches which privilege the factual aspects of the autobiographical narrative and argues for autobiography to be considered as primarily a literary, not historical, document.[6] This is in marked contrast to the traditional scholarly view of autobiography amongst Anglophone critics, according to which autobiography seizes a pre-existing self. The writer of autobiography 'memorializes himself in the form of a book', as John Sturrock puts it; he (the pronoun is used advisedly) is engaged in a 'process of singularization', capturing his own individuality in print, asserting it, and thereby preserving it from anonymity and oblivion.[7] Gusdorf's intervention can thus be seen as already sounding the death knell of autobiography at the point of its birth. Gusdorf anticipates what later passes almost as a truism in literary and academic circles, namely that it is unrealistic and simplistic to imagine that by reading autobiography readers can know the person that the author is: an idea which depends on seeing the autobiography as a reliable repository of knowledge; as a text which itself has possession of the author's identity. This contrasts starkly with the widely-accepted position that '[t]here is no such thing as a "uniquely" true, correct, or even faithful autobiography'.[8]

Only after Gusdorf's article, however, did the assumption that defining autobiography was straightforward come to be contested. Jean Starobinski posited a definition in 1970 that is potentially very wide: autobiography is a self-written biography (biography being the writing of the 'tracé d'une vie' [course of a life]).[9] The ancient Greek roots *autos* + *bios* + *graphē* [self + life + writing] supply an etymologically derived understanding of the term: one that still has the most currency amongst scholars, in particular amongst feminist critics. Importantly, despite his initial effort at definition, Starobinski proceeds to argue that seeking to define autobiography exactly is a useless task, for every writer will wish to impose their own individual style on their autobiography in order to convey their individuality. Efforts to define autobiography were not to cease, however, with rival definitions of autobiography emerging in the 1970s. De Man, for one, took vehement issue with what he considered the sterility of the drive, inspired by a structuralist mindset, to define autobiography as a literary genre, insisting that the body of work concerned itself resists this: 'autobiography lends itself poorly to generic definition; each specific instance seems to be an exception to the norm.'[10] In consequence, for De Man, '[a]ttempts at generic definition seem to founder in questions that are both pointless and unanswerable'; the fact that one of these questions concerns truth and the author's sincerity has, in the light of De Man's own concealed truth, retrospectively somewhat weakened the force of this view.[11]

Notwithstanding such criticisms, these definitions are valuable in highlighting different conceptions of what constitutes the essence of autobiography. For example, in his *L'Autobiographie*, Georges May considers the commitment to delivering the truth (as opposed to supplying only fictions) to be the defining feature.[12] This reflects the widely-held view that the hallmark of a 'genuine' autobiography is its 'intentionality': the author intends at least to impart the truth about him- or herself, even if that truth is more of an ontological 'Truth' about the situation of the autobiographer than it is a verifiably factual account of their life.[13] For May, autobiography is therefore defined, and can be differentiated from other literary genres, on the basis of its non-fictional status. Accordingly, May sets autobiography at one pole of a spectrum of fictionality that he devises, with the novel occupying the opposite pole of fiction. Of the five intermediate categories he identifies, two are occupied by variants of autobiography, which, to differing degrees, each incorporate fiction. In an anticipation of later developments in autobiography studies (in particular the concept of *autofiction*), May's suggestion that there is autobiography and also hybrids of autobiography alerts us to the interesting possibility of there being not just one genre of autobiography, but many.[14]

The most significant contribution to the definition debate comes from Lejeune, whose *Le Pacte autobiographique* of 1975 formulated a definition which radically reconceived autobiography and, for the first time, acknowledged the centrality of the reader to this genre of writing. The insights *Le Pacte autobiographique* contains on the situation of the reader of autobiography will prove crucially important for the arguments that I shall go on to develop in this book.

A product of a structuralist outlook, Lejeune's work argues that 'le genre autobiographique est un genre *contractuel*' [the genre of autobiography is a *contractual* genre]; autobiography is any text that the reader, in reply to an invitation from the author, undertakes to read autobiographically.[15] If this seems a nebulous definition, it is supplemented by a formula that is nonetheless quite precise, setting out the circumstances under which this reading will arise:

> La définition met en jeu des éléments appartenant à quatre catégories différentes:
> 1. *Forme du langage*:
>   *a*) récit.
>   *b*) en prose.
> 2. *Sujet traité*: vie individuelle, histoire d'une personnalité.
> 3. *Situation de l'auteur*: identité de l'auteur (dont le nom renvoie à une personne réelle) et du narrateur.
> 4. *Position du narrateur*:
>   *a*) identité du narrateur et du personnage principal,
>   *b*) perspective rétrospective du récit.[16]
>
> [The definition brings into play elements belonging to four different categories:
> 1. *Form of linguistic expression*:
>   *a*) narrative.
>   *b*) in prose.
> 2. *Subject treated*: life of the individual, history of the development of the self.
> 3. *Situation of the author*: identicalness between the author (whose name refers to a real person) and the narrator.
> 4. *Position of the narrator*:
>   *a*) identicalness between the narrator and the principal protagonist,
>   *b*) retrospective narrative perspective.]

Autobiography thus results, for Lejeune, from the production of a specific type of reader: a reader who consents to read the text as autobiographical. This reading will be invoked by the presence of the textual signals enumerated above. These will most usually emerge, Lejeune suggests, from a mixture of textual and peritextual elements (i.e. information, such as blurb, that surrounds and packages the text) that will establish an *identité* [identicalness] — an exact correspondence — between narrator, writer and protagonist ('*identité*' in French has, amongst others, the mathematical sense described in English as 'congruence').[17] An important (although until now largely undeveloped) implication of Lejeune's thinking is that a vital function of autobiography is to *produce its reader* (that is to say, one who will confer on the text the status of autobiography). Once the reader recognizes the distinguishing features, a *pacte autobiographique* [autobiographical pact] will be concluded and for that reader, the text in question will be an autobiography. Although Lejeune admits that there will be exceptions to this rule — there will be cases of autobiography where this *pacte autobiographique* is absent, as the lack of textual guides allows the reader to be the final arbiter — this constitutes, for him, a formula applicable to the vast majority of autobiographies. What is groundbreaking in *Le Pacte autobiographique* is the way its attempt at definition is combined with a study of those relationships constituted in and by the text: the relationships linking author, narrator, protagonist and reader. The frame Lejeune gives to the genre of autobiography is just one frame out of a number of possibilities, none of which may be adequate: autobiography does not have a distinctive and universally recognizable form (which makes it difficult to establish what exactly is snuffed out if autobiography is dead). It is a frame, however, that beckons us toward interesting vistas. Calling attention to the role of the reader, Lejeune's work offers a point of departure for my examination of the power-relations that operate within autobiographical texts, but which also reach beyond them.

Autobiography: critical reinvigorations

A further question to consider when probing the strange case of the death of autobiography concerns the motive for killing it off. Autobiography has come under sustained criticism for what has been perceived as its ideological bias, particularly from Marxist and feminist quarters. In an issue of *New Literary History* treating autobiography, the predominantly structuralist and empiricist approaches favoured by French scholars came under attack for failing to provide a basis for mounting a critique of the ideology behind the genre.[18] A mistrust emerges towards perspectives on autobiography, such as those taken by critics like Gusdorf or Olney, which privilege its literary qualities, as opposed to its documentary function.[19] For Marxist critics, it is politically imperative that the referential (as opposed to self-referential) function of autobiography continues to be recognized.[20] In Louis A. Renza's eyes, autobiography is diminished when its capacity to tell truths about the world beyond the text is downplayed.[21] What emerges from ideologically sensitive readings of autobiography is that this is a genre for the elite: its authors have historically been drawn from amongst the successful individuals within a society. In an essay on autobiography as a genre in nineteenth-century France, Lejeune suggests that an important factor in the growth of publications in this area at this time was that these published autobiographies reinforced the hegemonic bourgeois values of their society. Middle-class autobiographers typically hold themselves up as a good example, and their works consequently:

> function as a reciprocal insurance system between the 'exemplary' individual (who proves by his example the truth of the official dominant discourse on the balance of value and success) and this discourse itself (which allows the 'exemplary' individual to think that he is completely and individually responsible for his success).[22]

Indeed, according to some critics, the very structure of the autobiographical narrative contributes to the ideological potential of the genre. Unable to accommodate both past and present autobiographical selves into one unified whole, autobiographers frequently mitigate this split between the 'I' who narrates in the present and the 'I' of the past by adopting a teleological approach to narrative construction, whereby the self in the present moment of writing becomes the goal that the narrative, starting out from the self in the past, must reach.[23] The interpretative process involved in this writing is seen by sceptical critics as imposing an artificial, linear narrative structure: one complicit with hegemonic conceptions of selfhood, because the resulting self-portrait presents an equally artificial view of what and how the self is constituted.[24] Furthermore, the frequent tendency to shape the autobiographical narrative around the course of a life, or *bios*, is one that feminist critics in particular have found dubious.[25]

If autobiography is a genre for the hegemonic, exemplary individual, then that individual is male, feminists have argued.[26] Considering the template of autobiography to be ill-adapted to women, feminists have found it important to point up the ideology inherent in autobiography, and, beyond this, to widen its boundaries. They contend that the parameters that circumscribe autobiography make it a genre which is at the least inhospitable, if not downright alienating, to women writers, with the result that it is not a fit home to accommodate women's experience.[27] The conventional teleological model of the autobiographical narrative is most receptive to those lives which are of public significance, having been marked by publicly recognized achievements; such lives have usually been male lives, as women have historically most often led their lives in the private sphere. Accordingly, whilst there is no unified body of feminist autobiography scholarship, a frequent priority for feminist scholars has been to recover the lived experience of women from their autobiographical writings.[28] If the strictures of the genre prevent readers from acquiring knowledge of the female author, then an expansion of the parameters of autobiography is required so that readers can gain access to female subjectivities and experience. Feminists have thus looked beyond conventional autobiography to study other forms of personal writing, which they consider inherently better suited to capturing female experience.[29] New generic terms are employed to describe the writings they turn to, in a move to mark their difference from the ideologically tainted genre of autobiography. Thus feminists who prioritize the recovery of the detail of women's lives look to 'life-writing', whilst those interested in works which capture the essence of the female condition without necessarily documenting a life may be more interested in 'autogynography'.[30]

Feminist analyses of autobiography are particularly important for this study, and not only because it features the work of two women writers, one of whom has been closely identified with the feminist movement. Feminist scholars pioneered a critical approach to autobiography that was sensitive to the genre's asymmetrical relationship to those who held, and those who were marginalized from, positions of power in society; it was they who first identified the extent to which autobiography is bound up in, and can serve, identity politics.[31] Their concerns with the writing of marginality and identity politics — that is, the political ramifications involved in claiming, refusing, silencing or asserting a particular identity — are ones shared by the writers I study here. However, it should be noted that for these writers, addressing their marginalization from the canonical genre of autobiography is not only an issue for women. Finding a means to give voice to a minoritized subjectivity is a problem which affects those of minority sexualities and ethnicities too, as we shall see from some of the autobiographical writings which I explore here (particularly in works by Perec, Genet and Cixous).

Autobiography critics who are concerned with the politics of identity are pulled in different directions, however: for some, engagement with identity politics means rendering visible an identity which has been airbrushed from the collective consciousness; others, meanwhile, consider that it is politically imperative to deconstruct the fixity with which identity tends to be cloaked. These are debates that have been particularly prominent in queer theory; debates which, as we shall see, are fought over the territory of the writing of authors such as Genet. The roots of such debates can be found in feminist responses to autobiography.

However, whilst feminist critiques of different aspects of the genre provide useful avenues of approach to autobiography, and shed helpful light on shortcomings of the genre, encouraging us to keep any laments for its loss in proportion, we should not be blind to the limitations of some of these readings. From within feminist scholarship itself, some anxiety has been expressed about approaches which seem to essentialize women, positing an inherently female subject position that all women are assumed to identify with and share.[32] Another hazard of some feminist strategies for approaching female-authored autobiographical writings is that due account may not always be taken of the nature of textuality, or of other factors that may cloud the transparency of these self-representations.[33] A particular limitation of feminist autobiography scholarship has been its lack of engagement with arguments coming from quite different quarters which advocate killing autobiography off and founding new forms of self-writing in its stead, and its limited engagement with these new forms themselves.

Perhaps the most visible sign of this phenomenon in French literature has been the emergence, dating back to the 1980s, of both *nouvelle autobiographie* [new autobiography] and *autofiction* [autofiction].[34] The proclamation of a *nouvelle autobiographie* resulted from autobiographical forays by writers formerly associated with the *nouveau roman* [new novel]. Just as the *nouveau roman* had brought innovations and a greater self-consciousness to the novelistic form, the *nouvelle autobiographie*, as written by Sarraute, Alain Robbe-Grillet and Marguerite Duras, does the same in the sphere of self-writing.[35] This new autobiographical writing demonstrates a postmodern sensibility, being marked by fragmentation, conspicuous metanarrative elements, and pronounced sensitivity to the textual medium through which it operates. *Nouvelle autobiographie* calls into question the very possibility of a fixed self, and thus of self-representation; giving free play to the invention of the self, rather than trying to distil something of its 'truth'. Rather than representing a pre-existing self, *nouvelle autobiographie* provides, as Ramsay states, a 'critical and unsettling deconstruction of both the [writer's] childhood and [...] [present] selves as products of language'.[36]

In *autofiction*, this deconstruction is taken further, targeting the genre of autobiography itself. Whilst different conceptions of *autofiction* exist (indeed, as with autobiography, a settled definition has proved evasive[37]), a characteristic common to all of them is a certain *deliberate* element of fictionality. This is introduced as a calculated attempt to go beyond and fatally unsettle autobiography, as Marie Darrieussecq observes, and it is a goal already clear in the phenomenon's genesis.[38] For Serge Doubrovsky, credited with inventing the term *autofiction*, the word designates something very specific, growing out of his project to disprove Lejeune's contention that it was impossible to produce a narrative that would be accepted as fiction where a narrator-protagonist is given the same name as the work's author.[39] Doubrovsky did precisely this. Thus, for Doubrovsky, producing *autofiction* involves supplying indicators which suggest that the text is an autobiography, whilst at the same time contradicting these indicators by asserting its fictional status. Whilst discussions within autobiography studies make clear that autobiography and fiction never were necessarily so straightforwardly distinct from each other (to recall, in particular, the work of May), the innovation of *autofiction* is that it involves not just an awareness, but a *celebration* of the fictionalization of the self in writing: in some of its hues, *autofiction* involves authors writing the self without concern for what they perceive it to be, but rather, as they fantasize it.[40] In a reversal of the priorities associated with autobiography, *autofiction* participates in a valorization of the imagination which takes precedence over any commitment to representing an extra-textual reality.

It is for that reason that the development of this mode of writing has not entirely been viewed as positive. In its favour, whereas the genre of autobiography has been seen as steeped in ideology, *autofiction*, according to Doubrovsky, is not. Where autobiography is an elite genre, *autofiction* is open to '[l]es humbles, qui n'ont pas droit à l'histoire' [to the humble, who are not permitted access to history].[41] Against it, there is the objection that narratives labelled *autofiction* represent the indulgence of an excessively exhibitionistic streak on the part of their authors.[42] Further objection is provoked by the perception that *autofiction* abandons truth as a value and allows falsehoods to be published with impunity.[43] Gérard Genette accuses those who write *autofiction* of irresponsibility, considering this form of writing the self to be contemptuous, nothing more than 'autobiographie honteuse' [shameful autobiography].[44]

In Doubrovsky's view, however, in the light of evolutions in how we understand the psychic make-up of individuals in a post-Freudian era, the autofictional approach represents a necessary, honest stance towards the project of writing the self. Citing the force of the internal boundaries imposed by the unconscious that contribute to the fracture of the self and of memory, Doubrovsky argues that the self can neither possess, nor pass on the truth of what it is: as in the psychoanalytical process, gaining insights into the truth of the self always requires the participation of another. Knowledge of the self always requires incorporating the knowledge the other has of the self — thus, without the other's participation, full knowledge of the self is impossible. For Doubrovsky, these epistemological limits on self-knowledge call for a form of self-writing that acknowledges these limits, delivering a manifestly incomplete account, a cluster of truth-nuggets that require assembling by the other who reads them.[45] From this perspective, *autofiction* reveals a kind of truth alongside its fictions of the self: through its fragmentary form, it reveals the contingent nature of truth — as something which, even when it concerns the identity of the writing self, is negotiated between self and other.

The forms of self-writing practised in *nouvelle autobiographie* and *autofiction* do not represent merely an alternative way of writing the self to autobiography: what is distinctive about them is their insistence, through their subversion of autobiography, on the impossibility of autobiography as a genre. With these new forms, French autobiography travels towards a place where the author's identity is not written, or memorialized: it is scrambled. The eruption of these new forms of self-writing presents more than a challenge to an established genre: they challenge the reader too.[46] The appearance of these new modes of writing confronts us acutely with the question of how to read narratives of the self, and how they entitle us to relate — if they do so at all — to the authors behind them.

The reader's role

Doubrovskyan *autofiction* throws down a particular challenge to its readers: if the writing self does not fully possess its own self or its own truth, the corollary is that it cannot set down or impart it to another: the reader cannot take delivery of, or be gifted with, the truth of that self. The model of reader-relations operating in Doubrovskyan *autofiction* dictates that, in order to obtain an understanding of the written self they encounter, the reader must make an active, independent and imaginative contribution to realizing that self. The accent here is on the reader's freedom to interpret, but underlying this is the obligation on the reader to accept the active position pre-ordained for them in Doubrovskyan *autofiction*, and to abandon the idea that the textual self-representation allows the reader access to the person of the author. Paradoxically, within the framework of a constraint (readers have to assemble meaning for themselves), it imposes freedom (readers are at liberty to interpret what they read freely, not merely consume it at it is). Just as the writer's imagination is freed by the absence of any obligation to refer to a genuinely existing individual self, *crucially, so is the reader's*: the reader too is liberated to construct whatever fantasies and fictions of the self they choose. Such an active role may be testing for the reader, but it is important to recognize too the challenges this model of reader-relations imposes on the author. As my readings of Sarraute, Genet and Cixous make clear, it is my judgement that they are uncomfortable with the prospect of their readers exercising this level of imaginative freedom (Perec's case will be seen to be more complicated). This plays no small role in the fact that I do not refer to their works as *autofictions* (and neither do they). For all four of these authors, the transactional nature of identity is, I argue, a problem to negotiate, not a fact of life(-writing) to be embraced.

The Doubrovskyan vision of the reader's role contrasts starkly with the passive position that the reader of autobiography traditionally occupies. For a critic such as Olney, the autobiographer is the definitive authority on the subject of himself, to whom the reader should defer and take as a source of inspiration.[47] This is emblematic of a tendency in autobiography scholarship to conceptualize the autobiography as a work in which the autobiographer, by stabilizing the identity of the writing self, rises above being a mere 'author' (a word endowed in more modern times with only a weak meaning), to assume the archaic quality of *auctoritas*: an authority.[48] Autobiographers have encouraged this view of themselves: the preface to Rousseau's autobiography contains a self-confident assertion on the authority of his self-representation, with the declaration that his *Confessions* present a 'portrait d'homme, peint exactement d'après nature et dans toute sa vérité' [portrait of a man, painted exactly according to nature and in all his truth].[49] Rousseau may, according to Sheringham, need his audience, but it is their deferential attention he needs as he paints his picture, not their assistance.[50] This imputed supreme authority of the autobiographer has particular implications for readers' reception of autobiography. The corollary of the author's might is the reader's passivity: if the author provides a definitive account, the reader's function is not to question anything, but rather to assent to the autobiographer's authority and passively consume the authoritative account of the self that is offered. Strikingly, this particular conception of the autobiographer is one invoked, directly or indirectly, by all the authors I discuss.

Nonetheless, it is notable that late-twentieth-century French authors have tended not to produce readily digestible self-portraits for this sort of consuming reader. Instead, they obstruct passive readings. Obstacles placed in the path of this kind of reading include refusing narratorial integrity by alternating between first and third person narration — a device employed throughout *L'Amant*, Duras's work of *nouvelle autobiographie*. Jean-Paul Sartre's *Les Mots* provides an example of a second, much-used strategy that requires a more active engagement on the part of the audience: this involves denying the readership a linear progression through the narrative, which may be achieved by organizing it achronologically, or at least disrupting its chronology.[51] Such techniques are also abundantly in evidence in the works by Sarraute, Perec, Genet and Cixous that interest me here. What is the function of such obstructions? How do they position the reader? If these four authors discourage a passive approach to reading that consumes the narrative line after line, as it is fed to them, yet at the same time they do not give the reader the licence that Doubrovsky's *autofiction* does, what role *do* they envisage for the readers of their autobiographical texts?

Autobiography theorists disagree on the question of how active a role autobiography ascribes to its reader. According to one view, the reader of autobiography presents a benign audience for the autobiographer. From this perspective, the reader receives the autobiography as a sort of *don contraignant*. This is the type of gift that imposes obligations on the recipient: the act of writing an autobiography is seen as one which requires the reader to read the text deferentially, thus limiting their interpretative autonomy.[52] If a reader defers to an autobiographer admiringly perceived as *auctoritas*, then this reader's hands will inevitably be tied when reading the autobiography in question. Even if it is not expected that the autobiography will provide an *exact* representation of the writer's self, it is likely that such a reader will retain the notion that the text imparts an ontological truth about its author, and such truths the reader (short of rejecting them outright) can only passively accept, being powerless to dispute them.

Lejeune provides an intriguing view of the reader's position with respect to autobiography. His *Le Pacte autobiographique* presents the reader as central to the operation of autobiography as a genre, with the reader of autobiography solemnizing a text's generic status, as a result of being directed by the signals present in the narrative to confer the status of autobiography on to a text. It is in this way that the reader becomes a reader of *autobiography* (it is in this sense that autobiography can be said to produce its own reader). The implication is that the reader is a compliant pawn, whose activity is determined by the qualities that the text exhibits. Yet Lejeune's account is ambiguous, for the reader equally functions as a power-wielding player, without whom the text does not operate. For Lejeune, to accept a text as autobiography is to believe that the self encountered in the text corresponds to that of the living author; it is to believe in the ability of the textual self-portrait to represent the person outside the text. Yet the relation of correspondence between these selves is fundamentally precarious, since it depends on the reader's compliant participation in the autobiographical pact to cement it. What therefore subtends the autobiographical pact is the author's reliance on the reader to act as guarantor for the relationship he or she attempts to establish between the self inside and outside the text. In creating a portrait of the self, the author is thus obliged to write for the other, to play to an audience in a specific way, to obtain the reading desired.

Strenuous efforts on the part of the autobiographer to enforce this pact through the use of various textual devices might suggest the domination of the autobiographer over the reader, and seem to enforce that reader's subservience. What I suggest, however, is that this is not the case. Rather, such efforts indicate the extent to which autobiographers are themselves subsumed to a system — that is, the genre system of autobiography — which denies them ultimate sovereignty to pronounce on what their self is or corresponds to, and designates the reader as the arbiter of this instead. Lejeune depicts the reader's role as being to secure the conditions (that is, to conclude the pact) permitting them to consume the autobiographical self-representation as a copy of the living original. Yet the more profound implication of Lejeune's conceptualization of the genre of autobiography is that the reader's role is to take up their place in an overarching framework which intangibly drives the way the autobiographical self is written, read and understood: a framework which accords the reader a position of power *vis-à-vis* the autobiographer, at the expense of the latter's autonomy over their own self; a framework which consumes the autobiographer's self. It seems, therefore, little wonder if the reader is a figure who provokes the autobiographer's unease, as Sheringham implies, referring to 'the flailing gesticulations of someone [an autobiographer] who is trying to see us but cannot'.[53]

Nonetheless, some of the reactions that we will see against the reader seem disproportionately fierce, particularly in the light of the enduring image of the masterful autobiographer. According to this perspective, the writer never cedes the upper hand to the reader, but remains in control of their text. As Sheringham puts it:

> The writer is [...] the producer, freely able to dictate his or her terms, to switch unpredictably from one thing to another, to change the [...] agenda [...], to adopt a different guise. [...] [I]t is the writer's prerogative to keep us guessing.[54]

Yet Sheringham also points to the possibility that in some cases the reader 'becomes the embodiment of stated or unstated laws'.[55] I suggest that the key to understanding the strength of reactions against the reader lies in comprehending the implications for the autobiographical self of having an intangible regulatory framework, such as the one Lejeune discerns, operating at the core of autobiography: a framework that institutes parameters shaping what selves can be. To do this in turn requires that we understand the similarities between the genre framework governing autobiography, and what such twentieth-century French thinkers as Lacan, Foucault and Louis Althusser have identified as other intangible regulatory frameworks operating in society to constrain the development and conduct of individuals. It is at this point that we need to consider evolutions in thinking about autobiography — particularly in the case of evolutions that suggest that there is no longer any autobiography to be thought about — within the broader context of post-war French thought.

II. Autobiography and Theory

The intellectual environment that has so shaped the thinking and practice of literary autobiography in France since 1945 is one dominated by structuralist and poststructuralist thought. A legacy of structuralism was to call into question the idea of a self capable of understanding and exercising autonomy over itself and its destiny. According to this view, as put forward by Lacan, Foucault and Althusser, the self gave way to a 'subject', which denoted a vision of the human individual not as self-made, but as the product of its immersion in systems which it could not fully understand, but which played a determining role in shaping and constraining the being that it was able to become.[56] Remembered, respectively, for their theorizations of the power of ideology, the symbolic, and discourse, these three thinkers are far from reaching identical conclusions about the nature of these systems. Yet all of them posit that each individual is born into a pre-existing, but invisible, framework of expectations, demands and constraints that shape and modify human behaviour and thought: a framework that proves every bit as influential on our conduct and being as are the conspicuous mechanisms of control in our society, such as traffic lights or speed cameras. The effectiveness of these structures derives from the fact that we internalize their prescriptions — Althusser's famous example of the interpellated subject is of a passer-by who turns around when a policeman calls out in the street, assuming erroneously that they are being called.[57] However, whereas we realize we are subject to controlling mechanisms such as those represented by the police, or immigration officers, we do not recognize (indeed, are conditioned not to recognize) the limits on our autonomy imposed by these intangible structures — and we cannot wholly undo their effect even once our consciousness is raised. Evidently, from this perspective, whatever the human individual has to say about their own development, how they have become who they are, could never tell the whole story. This view only reinforces ideas already popularized by Freudian psychoanalysis, according to which the individual is driven by unconscious motivations of which they have no understanding. Plainly, this emphasis on the inherent limits on the self's capacities — particularly the capacity to know — has particular implications for what quality of insight an author can achieve in his or her autobiography, and these perspectives grew to be highly influential (not least on *autofiction*), notwithstanding the fact that certain prominent structuralists subsequently rowed back from this extreme stance and modified their positions.

With similarly significant implications for the enterprise of writing autobiography was the emphasis both structuralism and poststructuralism placed on language. In each of these currents of thinking, language is recast not simply as a medium for expression, but is attributed a solidity of its own, with linguistic systems, signs and utterances becoming an object of inquiry in their own right. In consequence, the ability of (particularly written) language to refer outside of itself and to impart secure meaning is brought into question, as poststructuralist thinkers advance the view that what language signifies in any particular instance cannot be pinned down, due to the inexhaustible potential which they attribute to language to signify differently. Evidently, from this point of view, the author or producer of language can no longer be looked upon as a guarantor of its meaning; indeed, a central tenet of poststructuralist thought is precisely to deny the possibility of establishing via the text any connection with its flesh-and-blood originator beyond the text. This insistence on a divorce between the text's signification and its creator is the philosophical backdrop for Roland Barthes's famous proclamation of the 'death of the author'.[58]

Clearly, the idea of an inevitable rupture between the author and the text has important implications for autobiography, since this is a genre whose particularity and point of interest lies in the notion that it is 'la biographie d'une personne faite par elle-même' [the biography of a person written by him- or herself].[59] Coupled with the theories of structuralism and psychoanalysis, it would seem almost fatal to it. An incompatibility arises between the apparent purpose of autobiography — to allow the author to make his or her person known to the readership in words of his or her own choosing — and the insight that the text cannot provide a path back to its author, whose self-knowledge in any case would be incomplete. Indeed, authors writing in the latter part of the twentieth century frequently acknowledge this problem in their autobiographical writings, designating autobiography as impossible — that is, affirming that it is impossible to produce an account of their own lives or selves — in the intellectual climate in which they find themselves: a climate influenced not only by the insights of poststructuralism into language, but perhaps even more so by the insights of psychoanalysis into the workings of memory, repression and the unconscious. The words of Barthes in his own autobiographical musings, whilst more explicit than many, are representative of this tendency, which is also present in the authors I study in depth here:

> Ce livre n'est pas un livre de 'confessions'; non pas qu'il soit insincère, mais parce que nous avons aujourd'hui un savoir différent d'hier; ce savoir peut se résumer ainsi: ce que j'écris de moi n'en est jamais *le dernier mot*: plus je suis 'sincère', plus je suis interprétable, sous l'œil d'autres instances que celles des anciens auteurs [...]. [...] Ouverts [...] sur ces différents avenirs, mes textes se déboîtent, aucun ne coiffe l'autre; celui-ci n'est rien d'autre qu'un texte *en* plus, le dernier de la série, non l'ultime du sens: *texte sur texte*, cela n'éclaircit jamais rien.[60]

> [This book is not a book of 'confessions'; not that it is insincere, but because we have today a different understanding than before; this understanding can be summed up thus: what I write about myself is never the last word about

> it: the more I am 'sincere', the more I am susceptible to interpretation, under the gaze of other authorities than those of the ancient authors. Open to these different futures, my texts disassemble themselves, none tops the other; this one is nothing other than one more text, the last in the series, not the ultimate in meaning: *text on text*, it never explains anything.]

Barthes, having declared the extinction of the author, seems here in his *Roland Barthes* to be sounding the death knell for autobiography too. Barthes's text harks back to the confessional heritage of the genre (whose origins are often traced to Rousseau's *Confessions*, if not to Augustine's) as a way of dramatizing the gulf perceived between what ancient authors could do and what the modern author can. There is an insistence in this work that Barthes cannot deliver the personal, let alone confessional, account of his life that the lay understanding of autobiography calls for; he cannot explain himself through his writing. None of this is possible because the author is not an *auctoritas*: he is no authority on himself, and his text can enjoy no privilege over any other insights into the author that may exist, or come into existence, whether these originate from him or from elsewhere. Such is the case for diagnosing the death of autobiography. Certainly the way that Barthes presents his text makes it unrecognizable as autobiography in the mould of 'ancient authors' such as Rousseau: the latter produces a linear, chronological narrative in his *Confessions*, whereas *Roland Barthes* takes the form of a series of alphabetized fragments, combined with various illustrations and a series of annotated photos.

Yet this will prove to be far from an open-and-shut case: this is clear from *Roland Barthes* itself, which does also contain the kind of reminiscences that authors from an earlier age might have included in their confessional works. Furthermore, much as it derides the author's claim to authority over the text, part of what this text relies upon to separate it from autobiography is its prefatory injunction that 'tout ceci doit être considéré comme dit par un personnage de roman' [all of this must be considered as if said by a character in a novel].[61] Of course, the force of this preface derives precisely from the fact that it is the author's pronouncement, and as if to authenticate its origin in the flesh-and-blood writer, the comment is transmitted to us via a facsimile reproduction of what we assume to be Barthes's handwriting. In the very process of declaring autobiography obsolete, Barthes relies on the survival of a notion that is central to it: the authoritativeness of the author's account.

If I have lingered over the paradoxical status of autobiography in *Roland Barthes*, it is because this paradox recurs time and again in the personal accounts of themselves written by other literary authors in this period, including those of Sarraute, Perec, Genet, Cixous and others besides. These texts invoke the genre of autobiography, but they also contain denials that they themselves fit in this genre. Autobiography is always what these texts are not. It seems that in them there is a need to conjure up a certain image of autobiography, and then to establish a relation of alterity with it — for example, by saying that it is dead; and that this occurs in precisely those texts which might otherwise be considered to be autobiography. That is to say, a reliance on there being a recognizable concept of autobiography, a genre called autobiography, manifests itself at the very moment when the possibility of such a genre governing the text in question is rejected.

What, then, is the generic classification of such texts? And what prospects does this contradictory attitude hold for the dead-and-alive place that autobiography seems to have become? No consensus has been reached. On the one hand, both Sheringham and Seán Burke, mindful of the paradoxes I have sketched out above, have insisted that *Roland Barthes* cannot be seen as confirming the death or impossibility of autobiography. They argue that autobiography as a genre must be allowed leeway to adapt to new surroundings without being considered defunct.[62] Sheringham sees no need for the insights of poststructuralism into language and the subject's lack of autonomy to finish off the genre, suggesting rather that these open up new territories for autobiography, promoting its renaissance.[63]

On the other hand, for many there is no question that autobiography is dead and buried. Jacques Lecarme and Eliane Lecarme-Tabone admit as much in their survey of the genre, acknowledging the need to defend their decision to retain the term 'autobiographie' [autobiography] and the concept of a genre of this name in the face of an ideology opposed to it.[64] The perception that autobiography is a genre whose time has expired is reflected in the widespread reluctance amongst commentators to use the term (at least with respect to twentieth-century or contemporary texts), and a corresponding preference for the neologisms we have encountered that have sprung up as alternative designations for autobiographical narratives. As we have seen, these are terms with specific nuances, but what *nouvelle autobiographie*, *autofiction*, self-writing and life-writing have in common is that they each designate a text or a type of writing which is self-consciously 'not autobiography'; which defines itself in opposition to it. The very use of one of these neologisms, to the exclusion of the more established nomenclature, conveys that a certain stance is being taken towards autobiography: namely, that it is obsolescent; that it is not what is being discussed, and what is being discussed is not it. Indeed, commentators who use such terms often do so precisely to insist on this kind of distinction, as can be seen in Laouyen's discussion of 'nouvelle autobiographie' versus 'autobiographie classique' [classic autobiography], to take just one example.[65] These commentators echo the position taken on autobiography in texts such as *Roland Barthes*, and those that I shall study in detail in the chapters which follow. Interrogating this position — that autobiography as a literary genre is dead, and that therefore contemporary literary autobiographical writing cannot be classed as autobiography — is part of my purpose in this study.

What becomes clear is that one thing remains unaffected by the conclusion drawn on whether autobiography as a genre is still extant or not: the *image* at least of autobiography lives on. Irrespective of whether autobiography is thought to have been supplanted by new genres which exist outside of its parameters, or whether these are simply seen as evolutions within the genre, considerable importance is attached to establishing the difference of the text in question from autobiography in the abstract. Writers — and indeed some commentators — of those modern autobiographical texts which might be suspected of being autobiographies seem to have need of an imago of autobiography that passes as common currency, an 'autobiography-ideal' which can be used as a comparator against their text: one that shows what autobiography 'is', so that the text in question can be seen not to be it.

To put it another way, the image of autobiography can be imagined as a straw man that is raised up in each of these texts, only to be knocked down again, finished off seemingly by the arrival of a young pretender to take his place. It is not a matter of autobiography being either dead or not dead: it is a question of autobiography being killed off. But this raises a further question — why does this happen?

It is this last question that originally spurred this study. The textual explorations I make here are designed to address the question of why this pattern should be recurrent in those French literary works in the post-war era which have some resemblance to autobiography, and what, if anything, the manner of the reader's projected response to the autobiographical text has to do with it. Why this need for such texts to proclaim their difference from 'autobiography'? What is achieved by drawing this distinction? Why do authors deny they are writing autobiography by asserting that autobiography is dead? In short, why do they need to kill autobiography off? Insights from disciplines as diverse as psychoanalysis, philosophy and anthropology suggest that when something is killed off, it is because its existence provokes such unease that it cannot be tolerated.[66] The move to kill off autobiography suggests nothing so much as that it is still worryingly alive. The point of departure for my argument in this study comes from considering what is worrying about autobiography not being dead.

Notes to Chapter 1

1. Raylene L. Ramsay, *The French New Autobiographies: Sarraute, Duras, and Robbe-Grillet* (Gainesville: University Press of Florida, 1996), p. 24.
2. Georg Misch, *Geschichte der Autobiographie* (Leipzig: Teubner, 1907–[never completed]), 1: *Das Altertum* (1907): this was later expanded by Misch to constitute a monumental multi-volume work: *Geschichte der Autobiographie*, 3rd expanded edn, 8 vols (Frankfurt-am-Main: Schulte-Bulmke, 1949–69). Only the first volume has been published in English: see Georg Misch, *A History of Autobiography in Antiquity*, trans. by E. W. Dickes, 2 vols (London: Routledge and Kegan Paul, 1950); Lejeune, *Pacte*, p. 312.
3. This is Lejeune's view of the enterprise. See *Pacte*, p. 313.
4. Georges Gusdorf, 'Conditions et limites de l'autobiographie', in *Formen der Selbstdarstellung. Analekten zu einer Geschichte des literarischen Selbstportraits. Festgabe für Fritz Neubert*, ed. by Günther Reichenkron and Erich Haase (Berlin: Duncker & Humblot, 1956), pp. 105–23.
5. It has been suggested latterly that this is a problematic view, which does not allow for the possibility of, for example, North African francophone autobiography. See Driss Aïssaoui, 'Présentation', in *Diversité culturelle et désir d'autobiographie dans l'espace francophone*, ed. by Driss Aïssaoui, special edn of *Dalhousie French Studies*, 70 (Spring 2005), pp. 3–6.
6. Gusdorf likens the process of self-discovery in autobiography writing to the self-discovery that occurs in what Lacan calls the mirror stage. See Gusdorf, p. 109, and, on the mirror stage, Jacques Lacan, 'Le Stade du miroir comme formateur de la fonction du Je' (1949), in *Ecrits*, ed. by Jacques-Alain Miller, 2nd edn, 2 vols (Paris: Editions du Seuil, coll. Points, 1999), 1, 92–99.
7. John Sturrock, 'Theory Versus Autobiography', in *The Culture of Autobiography: Constructions of Self-Representation*, ed. by Robert Folkenflik (Stanford, CA: Stanford University Press, 1993), pp. 21–37 (pp. 25, 27).
8. Jerome Bruner, 'The Autobiographical Process', in Folkenflik (ed.), pp. 38–56 (p. 39).
9. Jean Starobinski, 'Le Style de l'autobiographie', *Poétique*, 1 (1970), 255–65 (p. 255); my translation. Except where otherwise stated, all translations are my own: where I have employed published translations, it is chiefly in the case of French theorists whose work is well-known through these translations to an English-speaking audience.
10. Paul De Man, 'Autobiography as De-Facement', *MLN*, 94 (1979), 919–30 (p. 920).

11. Ibid., p. 919; cf. my remarks about De Man's wartime past in the Introduction.
12. Georges May, *L'Autobiographie* (Paris: Presses Universitaires de France, 1979).
13. On the notion that the autobiographer will endeavour to provide a truthful account, see Pascal, and also Elizabeth W. Bruss, *Autobiographical Acts: The Changing Situation of a Literary Genre* (Baltimore: Johns Hopkins University Press, 1976). For the idea that autobiography communicates an ontological 'Truth', see Olney, 'Some Versions of Memory/Some Versions of *Bios*: The Ontology of Autobiography', in *Autobiography: Essays Theoretical and Critical,* ed. by James Olney (Princeton, NJ: Princeton University Press, 1980), pp. 236–67. For discussions of intentionality, see Sheringham, *French Autobiography*, pp. 1–5; and Anderson, pp. 2–3.
14. May, pp. 188–93.
15. Lejeune, *Pacte*, p. 44 (emphasis Lejeune's).
16. Lejeune, *Pacte*, p. 14 (the layout and italics are Lejeune's).
17. This discussion is based on *Pacte*, pp. 13–46. For an account of the peritext, see Gérard Genette, *Seuils* (Paris: Editions du Seuil, 1987). The term 'congruence' describes, in mathematics, a situation where entities (such as triangles, integers) are considered equal to each other with respect to a defined set of properties. (I am grateful to Alex Belton for sharing his mathematical expertise with me on this point.)
18. See *New Literary History*, 9 (1977), 1–188.
19. I refer to Gusdorf's 'Conditions et limites' and Olney's *Metaphors of Self*.
20. See Irving Louis Horowitz, 'Autobiography as the Presentation of Self for Social Immortality', *New Literary History*, 9 (1977), 173–79 for a Marxist perspective on the ideology of autobiography.
21. Louis A. Renza, 'The Veto of the Imagination: A Theory of Autobiography', *New Literary History*, 9 (1977), 1–26.
22. Lejeune, 'Autobiography and Social History in the Nineteenth Century', in *On Autobiography*, ed. by Paul John Eakin, trans. by Katherine Leary (Minnesota: University of Minnesota Press, 1989), pp. 163–84 (p. 172).
23. See Renza for a discussion of different strategies autobiographers use to deal with this split.
24. On this, see, for example, Bruner.
25. See Julia Watson, 'Toward An Anti-Metaphysics of Autobiography', in Folkenflik (ed.), pp. 57–80.
26. Ever since Estelle C. Jelinek raised the matter in her 'Introduction: Women's Autobiography and the Male Tradition', in *Women's Autobiography: Essays in Criticism*, ed. by Estelle C. Jelinek (Bloomington: Indiana University Press, 1980), pp. 1–20, women's absence from canonical autobiography has received much attention. Shirley Neuman gives a valuable account of relevant discussions in her 'Autobiography and Questions of Gender: An Introduction', in *Autobiography and Questions of Gender*, ed. by Shirley Neuman (London: Cass, 1991), pp. 1 11.
27. On women's alienation from autobiography, see Domna Stanton, 'Autogynography: Is the Subject Different?', in *The Female Autograph: Theory and Practice of Autobiography from the Tenth to the Twentieth Century*, ed. by Domna C. Stanton (Chicago: University of Chicago Press, 1987), pp. 3–20; and Susan Stanford Friedman, 'Women's Autobiographical Selves: Theory and Practice', in *The Private Self: Theory and Practice of Women's Autobiographical Writings*, ed. by Shari Benstock (London: Routledge, 1988), pp. 34–62.
28. On the importance of recovering female experience, the motivation behind their edited volume, see Brodzki and Schenk (eds). Sheringham provides a brief overview of feminist autobiography scholarship in his 'Changing the Frame: Women Writers and the Rise of Autobiography', in *A History of Women's Writing in France*, ed. by Sonya Stephens (Cambridge: Cambridge University Press, 2000), pp. 185–203.
29. Jelinek looks to the diary form as a privileged channel for women's self-expression.
30. Brodzki and Schenk make the argument for the importance of continuing to uncover women's experiences, notwithstanding awareness of the problems inherent in transmission of female subjectivity through written texts. On the concept of 'autogynography', see Stanton, and also Germaine Brée, 'Autogynography', *Southern Review*, 22 (1986), 223–30.
31. On feminism, autobiography, and identity politics, see Leah Gilmore, *Autobiographics: A Feminist Theory of Women's Self-Representation* (Ithaca, NY: Cornell University Press, 1994); also Françoise

Lionnet, *Autobiographical Voices: Race, Gender, Self-Portraiture* (Ithaca, NY: Cornell University Press, 1989).

32. Such concerns are articulated by Stanton, pp. 11–13, and also in T. L. Broughton, 'Women's Autobiography: The Self at Stake?', in Neuman (ed.), pp. 76–107.
33. See the discussion in Sidonie Smith, *A Poetics of Women's Autobiography: Marginality and the Fictions of Self-Representation* (Bloomington: Indiana University Press, 1987), pp. 3–19.
34. The first major study of *nouvelle autobiographie* is that by Ramsay; see also Jeanette M. L. den Toonder, *'Qui est-je?' L'Ecriture autobiographique des nouveaux romanciers* (Bern: Peter Lang, 1999). On *autofiction*, see especially Colonna. Different perspectives on *autofiction* are given by Philippe Gasparini, *Est-il je? Roman autobiographique et autofiction* (Paris: Editions du Seuil, 2004); and Lecarme and Lecarme-Tabone, pp. 267–83. Dervila Cooke makes some informative observations on *autofiction* in her *Present Pasts: Patrick Modiano's (Auto)Biographical Fictions* (Amsterdam: Rodopi, 2005), pp. 49–89. On new forms of autobiographical writing, including *nouvelle autobiographie* and *autofiction*, see Laouyen (ed.).
35. Aside from Sarraute's *Enfance*, key instances of *nouvelle autobiographie* have been located in Marguerite Duras, *L'Amant* (Paris: Editions de Minuit, 1984) and Alain Robbe-Grillet, *Le Miroir qui revient* (Paris: Editions de Minuit, 1984).
36. Ramsay, p. 2.
37. On the definition(s) of *autofiction*, see Colonna, pp. 11–16; 227–28; not all critics draw a distinction between *nouvelle autobiographie* and other innovations in autobiographical writing, such as *autofiction*: see, for example Ramsay; Laouyen refers to *nouvelle autobiographie* interchangeably with postmodern autobiography.
38. Marie Darrieussecq declares, in her 'L'Autobiographie, un genre pas sérieux', *Poétique*, 107 (1996), 369–80, that 'l'autofiction met en cause la pratique "naïve" de l'autobiographie, en avertissant que l'écriture factuelle à la première personne ne saurait se garder de la fiction' [*autofiction* calls into question 'naïve' practices of autobiography, by signalling that factual writing in the first person cannot exclude fiction] (p. 379).
39. See Serge Doubrovsky, *Autobiographiques: de Corneille à Sartre* (Paris: Presses Universitaires de France, 1988), p. 69; Lejeune also gives an account of *autofiction*'s invention in his *Moi aussi* (Paris: Editions du Seuil, 1986), pp. 37–72.
40. In addition to Colonna, see Gasparini, who gives a typology of the autofictional narrative.
41. Doubrovsky, p. 69.
42. See Colonna, p. 13 for these objections to *autofiction*; we might note that such objections read very similarly to those that Gusdorf records as being raised against autobiography.
43. See Genette, *Fiction et diction* (Paris: Editions du Seuil, 1991), and Lecarme and Lecarme-Tabone, p. 279.
44. See Genette, *Fiction*, p. 86, n. 2.
45. Doubrovsky, pp. 61–82.
46. For Darrieussecq, 'l'autofiction [...] met en cause toute une pratique de la lecture' [*autofiction* challenges an entire practice of reading] (p. 379).
47. See, for example, Olney, *Metaphors*, pp. 3–50.
48. On the notion of the author as *auctoritas*, see Bernadette Masters, *Esthétique et manuscripture* (Heidelberg: Winter, 1992), pp. 141–56; and Burke, 'Introduction: Reconstructing the Author', in *Authorship: From Plato to the Postmodern: A Reader*, ed. by Seán Burke (Edinburgh: Edinburgh University Press, 1995), pp. xv–xxx.
49. Jean-Jacques Rousseau, *Les Confessions* (1782), in *Œuvres complètes*, I: *Les Confessions; autres textes autobiographiques*, ed. by Bernard Gagnebin and Marcel Raymond (Paris: Gallimard, coll. Bibliothèque de la Pléiade, 1959), pp. 1–656 (p. 3).
50. Sheringham, *Devices*, p. 49. This need for an attentive audience is underscored by the way Rousseau, p. 656, has his text represent its own reception: it finishes on a vignette of Rousseau coming to the end of reading his manuscript aloud to friends, who greet its end with silence.
51. Jean-Paul Sartre, *Les Mots* (Paris: Gallimard, 1964).
52. Bruss, for example, alert to the power relations operating between reader and writer, argues that autobiography places obligations on its reader. Amongst these is the obligation to accept what is

recorded as true. See Bruss, p. 11. The implication of Lecarme's notion of the autobiography as the author's 'testament' (see Lecarme and Lecarme-Tabone, p. 71) is that the reader's response to it will be constrained in some way, just as the default expectation is that anyone given a last will and testament to read should receive (and act on it) benevolently.

53. See Sheringham, *Devices*, pp. 140–41.
54. Sheringham, *Devices*, p. 141.
55. Sheringham, *Devices*, p. 140.
56. For these thinkers, those systems are, respectively, the symbolic order, discourse and ideology. Their theories will be discussed in more detail as they inform specific readings I make of autobiography in subsequent chapters.
57. See Louis Althusser, 'Ideology and Ideological State Apparatuses (Notes towards an Investigation)' (1970), in *Essays on Ideology* (London: Verso, 1984), pp. 1–60.
58. Roland Barthes, 'La Mort de l'auteur' (1968), in *Essais Critiques*, IV: *Le Bruissement de la langue* (Paris: Editions du Seuil, 1984), pp. 61–67.
59. Starobinski, p. 255. Starobinski's definition of autobiography corresponds with a lay understanding of the term, as evidenced by the fact that this is also the definition of autobiography given in *Le Nouveau Petit Robert* dictionary.
60. Barthes, *Roland Barthes* (1975), 2nd edn (Paris: Editions du Seuil, coll. Ecrivains de toujours, 1995), p. 110, emphasis Barthes's.
61. *Roland Barthes*, p. 5.
62. See Sheringham, *Devices*, p. 200 and Burke; in this they echo Barthes, who himself writes of a need to re-model genres: see *Roland Barthes*, p. 110.
63. Sheringham, *Devices*, p. 21.
64. See Lecarme and Lecarme-Tabone, pp. 7–18.
65. See Laouyen, 'Préface'.
66. See, for example, Sigmund Freud, *Totem and Taboo* (1913), in *The Standard Edition of the Complete Psychological Works of Sigmund Freud*, ed. by James Strachey and others, 24 vols (London: Hogarth Press, 1953–74), XIII (1955), 1–162; Emmanuel Levinas, *Totalité et infini: essai sur l'exteriorité* (Paris: Livre de poche, 1971); and René Girard, *La Violence et le sacré* (Paris: Grasset, 1972).

CHAPTER 2

Sarraute Writing the Self
The Drama of Self-Possession

Nathalie Sarraute's concern with the operations of genre was responsible for the work which contributed most to establishing her literary reputation: *L'Ere du soupçon*.[1] Here she noted the suspicious regard in which the novel was held by both readers and authors, and argued for the need for an evolution in the novel to reflect the sophistication of a readership well-acquainted with existing novelistic techniques. However, this is not the only genre to attract Sarraute's criticism: both in interviews and through her writing of the self, she transmits the message that, in her eyes, the genre of autobiography is similarly a target for suspicion.[2] It is the suspicion that Sarraute directs at autobiography which this chapter will interrogate.

Alongside giving an account of her childhood self, Sarraute uses her autobiographical narrative *Enfance* to draw attention to the inherent problems that, for her, beset the enterprise to produce an account of the life of the self in an autobiography. Language, the medium of autobiography, presents a distinct obstacle to that enterprise: particular obstacles being the interfaces between memory and language, and language and selfhood. If the *writing* of the self is problematic, neither is 'the self' as straightforward a notion as the traditional model of autobiography implies. Indeed, the nature of selfhood as Sarraute conceives it is quite incompatible with autobiography in its conventional form, with the result that the autobiographical text is incapable of seizing the self. Sarraute's response is to renounce the genre of autobiography as a template for writing the self, and to develop alternative modes of self-representation. These are showcased in two works which bring to self-writing Sarraute's general aim to represent 'du jaune sans les citrons' [yellow without lemons], as Valerie Minogue puts it.[3] These works are *Tu ne t'aimes pas*, a literal 'follow-up' to *Enfance*, and *Ouvrez*, the last work published in Sarraute's lifetime, whose narrative can be seen as picking up at the point where *Tu ne t'aimes pas* leaves off.[4] Carrying further Sarraute's long-standing interest in exploring intersubjective selfhood and how to portray it in writing, these two narratives inherit the concerns of the rejected genre of autobiography whilst offering a commentary — an explicit one in the case of *Tu ne t'aimes pas* — on its shortcomings.

In charting Sarraute's departure from autobiography, it will be important to probe the reasons her texts offer for it. In the climate of suspicion which enfolds autobiography in post-war France and provides the backdrop for Sarraute's work, it is the exact nature of the objections voiced — or indeed the ones the author chooses not to voice — that is of interest. In Sarraute's case, the seeds of misgiving toward the genre can be found in an early cycle in her work, where she critiques a tendency she identifies in readers to view literary works and their authors as commodities, which, through reading, they can become acquainted with, possess, show off and exchange at will. These early texts suggest that autobiography is problematic to the author because it encourages or rewards a particular reader response: an unwelcome commodifying approach to the author. However, although this disagreeable spectre is conspicuously raised in earlier works, this is not so in the self-writing Sarraute later produces. The prospect of the reader of autobiography being perceived by the author as a threatening presence is introduced, only to be left undeveloped in the texts where it is most pertinent.

Not directly addressing the relationship between the reading other and the writing self in her self-writing is an especially curious omission for Sarraute to make in what are highly self-reflexive works. These are works, moreover, where the others that the intradiegetic selves encounter receive considerable attention. An interest in transactions between self and other which occur through language is indeed the hallmark of Sarraute's entire *œuvre*, being the substance of the tropisms for which she is so renowned. These are characteristically provoked by an apparently anodyne yet bruising utterance that one speaker makes to another, such as the devastating '"C'est bien... ça..."' ['It's good... that'], the central and oft-repeated utterance of her 1986 play, *Pour un oui ou pour un non*: a remark which for the first of the play's two principal protagonists abruptly reveals an immense gulf in values between them.[5] The tropism thus foregrounds how language operates as an arena staging conflict between a self and its threatening other, demonstrating how such conflicts shake an individual's sense of self to the core.

In autobiography, language functions to communicate something about who the writing self is to the reading other. In common with her other works, Sarraute's self-writing shows language to function, not only as a vehicle for the transmission of information about the self, but also as the medium that betrays misunderstandings the other has about the self. From this perspective, differing ideas on the part of autobiographer and reader about who the self that is written is would seem inevitably to bring the author and reader into conflict, in a clash with the Sarrautean self at the centre. Given Sarraute's reflections on autobiography and her preoccupation with reader response throughout her *œuvre*, her failure to address potentially conflictual relations between the writer of the self and her reader is striking. It is especially remarkable since Sarraute is alert in *Enfance* to the potential for a tug-of-war being fought over the self: Natacha experiences this as she is catapulted back and forth between the homes of her divorced parents in Paris and St Petersburg; the motif recurs as the two narrating voices dispute the veracity of each other's accounts of the history and perceptions of the authorial self. In this light, ignoring the tug-of-war between the reader and the writer over the Sarrautean self begins to look like something more than a mere omission.

This strange silence can be read as a deliberate ploy, allowing Sarraute to avoid the prospect of a battle over the self which she cannot win. This losing battle over the self is, I suggest, what autobiography offers to the writer. In this reading, autobiography is experienced by its author as a site of conflict: moreover, one that does not just record conflict, but which *produces* it. If autobiography engenders conflict, it is because, for Sarraute, it sets up another tug-of-war: one which is waged against the reader, with the autobiographical self as prize. This is the implication of the Lejeunian model of autobiography, which, I suggest, establishes the autobiographical text as a terrain analogous to what Lacanian psychoanalysis calls the symbolic: that is, one where the self must negotiate its identity always in sight of an other, and where it can never satisfactorily achieve self-possession and a secure sense of its identity — because the other always has the last word on who the self is.

Psychoanalytic theories on the workings of the symbolic provide useful insights into Sarraute's treatment of self-other relations in the domain of self-writing, particularly on the question of how the Lacanian subject responds to being subjugated to the Other.[6] A Lacanian perspective offers an intriguing explanation for the curious silence Sarraute maintains about the threat of the reader in her autobiographical writing, seeing in her disregard of the reader a measure of the degree of threat readers pose; and a measure of her determination to resist it. This explanation causes us to see in a rather different light the critical stance Sarraute takes on conventional autobiography, and on the other who encroaches on the self. In the first instance, it is to this critical stance itself that we must turn, considering the grounds Sarraute lays out in her self-writing for regarding the genre of autobiography with suspicion. The first of these concern the difficulties posed by memory and language in the project to capture the self in writing.

The Unpossessable Self

Ever since Rousseau's admission that on occasion a 'défaut de mémoire' [defect of memory] might have caused him to embroider his narrative, it has been recognized that the imperfections of memory threaten the accuracy of autobiographers' accounts of their lives.[7] In *Enfance*, however, it is not the remembering which causes the narrators difficulties, but rather, how to represent their recollections. The opening lines of *Enfance* refer to the enterprise to '"*[é]voquer* tes souvenirs d'enfance"' ['"*evoke* your memories of childhood"']: thus from the outset Sarraute frames her endeavour in such a way as to downplay the importance of accurately communicating the detail of the memories.[8] The treatment of memory throughout the work will consolidate our impression that, despite being 'evoked', Sarraute's memories remain in some way beyond the narrative of *Enfance*.

Echoing Sigmund Freud's theories on the condensation, displacement and censorship our unconscious memories are subject to before they can be expressed, Sarraute's narrator emphasizes that her memories are not innocent fragments, which have lain dormant for years, but can then be disinterred intact and forced to yield up their truths by archaeologists of the mind.[9] There is a risk that to give voice to the memory is really to create it, and that her 'memories' may retroactively transform people and places into what they were not: the narrator hesitates to recount the episode where her step-mother told her '"ce n'est pas ta maison"' ['it's not your house'] for fear of distorting it: 'En effet, je craignais qu'en revivant cela, je ne me laisse pousser à faire de Véra et de moi des personnages de contes de fées...' [In fact, I feared that in re-experiencing that, I should allow myself to be pushed into making Vera and myself into characters from fairy tales].[10] Sarraute also raises the issue of the repression of painful memories in the seventeenth fragment of *Enfance*.[11] Here, the child Natacha is rebuffed by her mother with the words '"Laisse donc... femme et mari sont un même parti"' ['Stop it... man and wife are on the same team'] as she tries to join in a high-spirited rough-and-tumble episode between her mother and her step-father. This rejection, the second voice suggests, was highly upsetting to her, as if 'elle t'avait repoussée violemment...' [she had violently pushed you away]. The two voices then dispute the import of the incident, with the first voice reluctant to accept the painful gloss the second narrator puts on the event:

> — Je venais m'immiscer... m'insérer là où il n'y avait pour moi aucune place.
> — [...]
> — J'étais un corps étranger... qui gênait...
> — Oui: un corps étranger. Tu ne pouvais pas mieux dire... C'est cela que tu as senti alors et avec quelle force... Un corps étranger... Il faut que l'organisme où il s'est introduit tôt ou tard l'élimine...
> [...]
> — Non, tu vas trop loin...
> — Si. Je reste tout près, tu le sais bien.[12]

> ['I was coming and intruding, insinuating myself somewhere where there was no place for me. I was a foreign body... an irritating presence...'
> 'Yes, a foreign body. You couldn't put it better. That's what you felt then and so strongly. A foreign body... sooner or later the organism in which it has introduced itself must eliminate it.'
> 'No, you're going too far.'
> 'No I'm not. I'm staying very close to what happened, as well you know.']

In keeping with a Freudian view on memory, Sarraute stresses the unreliability of these recollections, thus sounding a note of caution to the reader by indicating how susceptible her autobiographical account is to inaccuracies. Sarraute's closeness to the theories of classical psychoanalysis is only momentary, however: elsewhere in *Enfance* she suggests that the tendency for autobiographical discourses to be overlaid with the discourse of psychoanalysis presents yet a further barrier to the accurate representation of the self's past in writing, because it supplies ready-made narratives which guide interpretative desire and frame the recall of the subject's past. This desire may well obstruct, rather than supply, an accurate understanding of the self. This is shown in the twentieth fragment where Natacha's creative writing efforts are rebuffed by her mother's friend's remark that '"avant de se mettre à écrire un *roman*, il faut apprendre l'orthographe"' ['before setting out to write a *novel*, you must learn to spell'].[13] The narrators observe how the recollection became privileged because it fitted so easily into a ready-made interpretative framework:

> — [...] C'était si commode, on pouvait difficilement trouver quelque chose de plus probant: un de ces magnifiques 'traumatismes de l'enfance'...
> — Tu n'y croyais pas vraiment ?
> — Si, tout de même, j'y croyais... par conformisme. Par paresse.[14]

['It was so convenient, it would be difficult to find something more convincing: one of these magnificent "childhood traumas".'

'You didn't really believe that?'

'Yes, all the same, I did believe it... out of conformism. Out of laziness.']

Ultimately, this popular psychological interpretation is presented as inadequate and distorting of the incident: a desire to make sense of an occurrence, what stimulates its recall, in fact does more to distance those who read the resultant interpretations from the interpreting self than it does to bring them closer to it.

Out of this ambivalence towards psychoanalysis as a tool to understand memory, it becomes clear that, for Sarraute, the obstacle to producing an account of her past in writing lies in the interpretation of events rather than in recalling them. A distinction is made between what is accessible to the autobiographical self, and what is accessible to her reader. It is no failure of memory that brings the text to a halt; rather, our reading experience is arbitrarily curtailed with the principal narrator's choice to cease narrating, to retain her experience for herself, and no longer to share the memories that give access to the self: 'Je ne pourrais plus m'efforcer de faire surgir quelques moments, quelques mouvements qui me semblent encore intacts, assez forts pour se dégager de cette couche protectrice qui les conserve' [I would not be able anymore to force myself to conjure up certain moments, certain movements which seem to me still intact, strong enough to detach themselves from this protective layer which preserves them].[15]

This remark highlights the fundamentally asymmetrical relationship of the autobiographer and her reader to the text, on which they depend in unequal measure to understand the autobiographical self. Sarraute's exploration in *Enfance* of memory and its textual representation constitutes a reflection on autobiography as a genre. Alongside the childhood recollections, a metanarrative emerges which seeks to establish the inadequacy of the narrative of childhood as a repository of the history of the self. Sarraute thus imbues her writing of the self with doubt about the ability of the autobiographical text to convey accurately the autobiographer's identity to the reader. The nature of memory and recollection provides only one explanation for this inadequacy: *Enfance* suggests that language and the extent of its capacity to (do more than) represent plays a considerable part too.

If memories are distorted by the interpretations the remembering subject imposes on them, language, through which these memories are filtered for the outsider, contributes to this distortion: for Sarraute, the process of utterance itself causes infelicities to occur in the transmission of memory. The dialogic, self-conscious narration of *Enfance* draws attention to the way that Sarraute's memories are shaped by the choice of words in which they are expressed, words that do not always satisfactorily render the original perception of incidents being recollected. This is illustrated by the episode where the narrator recounts a sensation that might be called 'joie' [joy] at being with her father and step-mother in the Jardin du Luxembourg, yet 'joie' is not an adequate term: 'il n'est pas capable de recueillir ce qui m'emplit, me déborde, s'épand, va se perdre, se fondre dans les briques roses' [it is not capable of mustering what it is that fills me up, spills out of me, spreads out, will lose itself, melt into the pink bricks].[16] Consequently, on the same page, the narrator questions the worth of even attempting a description: 'pourquoi vouloir faire revivre cela, sans mots qui puissent parvenir à capter, à retenir ne serait-ce qu'encore quelques instants ce qui m'est arrivé...' [why desire to bring back that experience without the words which might manage to capture, to retain, if only for a few more seconds, what happened to me?]? Because readers have no way to access the memories featuring in *Enfance* beyond the distorting language in which they are expressed, their understanding of the autobiographical self will inevitably be limited. By contrast, the author enjoys access to a pre-linguistic space in her head where her memories survive intact, unspoilt: 'c'est encore tout vacillant, aucun mot écrit, aucune parole ne l'ont encore touché, il me semble que ça palpite faiblement... hors des mots... [...] je voudrais, avant qu'ils disparaissent...' [it's still completely precarious, no written or spoken word have yet touched it, it seems to me that it pulsates weakly... beyond words... I would like, before they disappear...].[17]

Such references to memories as existing separately from language, as resistant to being translated into words, invoke Julia Kristeva's concept of the semiotic.[18] In its first sense, this is the pre-linguistic realm of plenitude which precedes accession to Lacan's symbolic order — the patriarchal order of discipline we all inhabit following socialization and the acquisition of language. Unlike the symbolic order, characterized by absence, including the absence of any other relation with objects than that which occurs through language, the semiotic does not know this lack.[19] In its second sense, the semiotic is a 'marque distinctive, trace, indice, [...] empreinte' [distinctive mark, trace, index, [...] imprint] manifesting inside the symbolic order: something foreign to this order, a residual trace of this realm of plenitude that we have also known.[20] The subject thus continues to be affected by the semiotic even after its entry into the symbolic order, primarily through music and language, where these traces erupt. A semiotic quality in language can be identified where one finds 'un *hétérogène* au sens et à la signification' [a *heterogeneousness* to meaning and signification]: the semiotic presents itself as what makes an appeal to the human subject above and beyond the signifying function that is at the heart of language, and therefore, the symbolic.[21] The Kristevan semiotic is thus a two-sided coin, implying both a site of otherness which is inaccessible to language and that language is itself a channel for an otherness it cannot account for.

Sarraute's depiction in *Enfance* of memory existing 'hors des mots' [beyond words] indicates her affinity with Kristeva's idea of a pre-linguistic space; furthermore, Sarraute, like Kristeva, is alert to excessive qualities in language itself which — like her memories — defy being captured through the linguistic medium. Indeed, this concern with 'sous-conversation' [sub-conversation], the import words have beyond signification, has long been recognized as the very hallmark of her *œuvre*.[22] In *Enfance* there is an especially pronounced interest in the materiality of language — and indeed, due to Sarraute's polyglot background, of specific *languages* — and in how words can have meanings in excess of the signified. This is reflected in the very structure of the work: clusters of reminiscences coalesce around a series of linguistic kernels, such as her governess's '"Das tust du nicht"' ['You don't do that']. In addition, memories are often of words themselves, with attention being drawn to the peculiarly intangible emotive qualities that they can have: Sarraute glosses Vera's remark to her childhood self, '"Tiebia podbrossili"', as '"on t'a abandonnée"' ['you've been abandoned'], but emphasizes its untranslatable brutal resonance.[23] Similarly, *Enfance* records a childhood awareness of the differing tonalities which exist inside pairs of French and Russian cognates, such as 'gniev' and 'courroux' [anger]; 'solntze' and 'soleil' [sun].[24] In *Enfance*, then, Sarraute shows language to be clearly infused with the semiotic in Kristeva's sense: 'une modalité, certes, hétérogène au sens, mais toujours en vue de lui ou en rapport de négation ou de surplus à son égard' [a disposition that is definitely heterogeneous to meaning but always in sight of it or in either a negative or surplus relationship to it].[25] For Kristeva, the semiotic affects language's signifying function, placing language always partially in a relationship of alterity with itself: utterances do not only signify, but, due to the presence of the semiotic, they do more (and less) than this.

In showing that language cannot be a transparent mediator of the autobiographer's self, but has an opacity of its own and acts as a barrier preventing access to that self, *Enfance* once again produces a hierarchization of the author and reader. The reader, whose only access to Sarraute is through language, cannot join Sarraute in her semiotic vision of herself, but must remain at some a distance from the Sarrautean self. As with her treatment of memory, Sarraute's perspective on language strengthens the impression that *Enfance* is a text which, rather than comply with the expectations engendered by the generic template of autobiography, undercuts the assumptions behind this template. The semiotic dimension of language may complicate the written representation of the self, but the semiotic is not only a quality of language: it is also an aspect of selfhood; and of all the shortcomings Sarraute identifies in the conventional autobiographical approach, it is the conflict between the model of selfhood that autobiography implicitly predicates and her own conception of a pluralized selfhood that is most irreconcilable.

We have noted that for Kristeva, the semiotic disposition belongs with the self, but it speaks *through* it; which is to say, it is inaccessible to it. The semiotic thus instates a plurality to selfhood, but also a degree of segmentation: the semiotic can be thought of as what is transported through the liquid of language but is insoluble within it. A semiotic presence in the self thus divides the self into those elements that can be accounted for in language, and those that cannot. Such a conception of selfhood clearly precludes the very possibility of producing a full account of the self in writing. This vision of a self composed of parts, some of which remain out of reach of language, is very similar to the model of selfhood Sarraute develops (albeit that Sarraute, unlike Kristeva, suggests that the self can access its own pre-linguistic core). The notion that the self has multiplicity at its core is one that is developed ever more forcefully as she progresses in her explorations of selfhood from *Enfance* to *Tu ne t'aimes pas* through to *Ouvrez*.

In *Enfance*, the use of two narrators to represent the autobiographical self is the most striking — and a much commented upon — aspect of the work.[26] The idea of a split in the autobiographical self between the writing self in the present and the written self in the past is a familiar one; Sarraute calls attention to this particular split by citing the different name of her childhood self, Natacha Tcherniak. However, her use of dialoguing narrators reveals a more radical inflection of the idea, positing the self as divided even once the diachronic dimension is removed. Yet the impression we gain is not of a self that is split, which implies loss, the breaking of something which was whole. Instead we find a self that is plural, and is more than the sum of its parts. Each of Sarraute's narrating voices contributes to what we might call 'the Sarrautean self' through dialogue with its interlocutor. We note that, unlike the case with the unnamed voices featuring in Sarraute's novels, the speakers narrating *Enfance* are unquestionably not discrete personalities: both narrators have access to the same memory bank, showing that even if there is more than one voice, there is a *shared* subjectivity between them. However, despite their shared subjectivity, the narrating selves do not unify into a single entity, as the rival interpretations of memories proffered by the narrators illustrates. The self in *Enfance* thus emerges as a composite being comprised of separate elements; a self rooted in intersubjectivity and plurality, not an assemblage of discrete fragments.[27] This presentation of two voices, who, even in dialogue together, fall short of substituting for 'the self' in writing is consistent with the idea that *Enfance* is infused with the semiotic, something excessive and beyond representation: it constitutes a refusal to totalize the self or impose limits on what it may be. Because the self is steeped in plurality, always in the process of being formed as a result of the operation of intersubjectivity, it cannot be captured in the text, even by two narrators.

Conceptually autobiography falls down as a vehicle for self-expression and self-exploration at this point, as Sarraute elaborates a conception of selfhood that cannot be fitted into the strictures of the conventional autobiographical narrative with its emphasis on the individual self. Sarraute's unusual narrational manoeuvre thus emphasizes her lack of interest in acquainting readers with 'the autobiographical self', intimating that it is anachronistic to refer to the self in the singular at all. This unorthodox depiction of selfhood in *Enfance* serves as another implicit critique of autobiography. Sarraute's subsequent work develops this theme, making clear that the template of autobiography hinders, rather than helps, the exploration and expression of the self as she conceptualizes it. Further exploration of intersubjectivity will call for a wholly different approach to self-writing, quite divorced from autobiography: this is what we see in Sarraute's later work, where her insights into the constitution of the self become more prominent, and the writing of autobiography is not only eschewed but explicitly critiqued.

In *Tu ne t'aimes pas* Sarraute disaffiliates herself from autobiography, combining a novel approach to representing the self with overt criticism of more conventional approaches.[28] Echoing *Enfance*, *Tu ne t'aimes pas* is episodic in structure and comprises a series of dialogues between unnamed voices; unlike in *Enfance*, this time discussions relate to reactions to the utterances or actions of absent speakers, rather than any experiences which suggest themselves as being personal to the author. Although without any clear autobiographical content (there is also nothing to indicate that any of the narrators are linked to Sarraute), the exploration of self is nonetheless central to this text. At the very beginning of *Tu ne t'aimes pas*, intersubjectivity is posited as the condition of selfhood in an exchange between the narrating voices that recalls the opening of *Enfance*. In the earlier work a sceptical incipient question introduces the narrative, as one voice, referring to the undertaking of the autobiographical enterprise, asks the other '"Alors, tu vas vraiment faire ça?"' ['Well, are you really going to do that?'].[29] For the reader acquainted with *Enfance*, the effect of reprising this device in *Tu ne t'aimes pas* is to reintroduce the concept of a plural selfhood familiar from this earlier work. The difference is that the idea implicit in *Enfance* that the self is steeped in plurality is advanced in the later work as a straightforward matter of fact:

> — 'Vous ne vous aimez pas.' Mais comment ça? [...] Qui n'aime pas qui?
> — Toi, bien sûr... c'était un vous [...] qui ne s'adressait qu'à toi.
> — A moi? Moi seul? Pas à vous tous qui êtes moi... et nous sommes un si grand nombre... 'une personnalité complexe'... comme toutes les autres...[30]

> ['"You don't love yourselves." But what do you mean? Who doesn't love whom?'
> 'You of course... He said yourselves but it was a "you" which was only addressed to you.'
> 'To me? Just me? Not to all of you who are also me... and there are so many of us... "a complex personality"... like all the others...']

The continually re-erupting and reproachful refrain 'tu ne t'aimes pas' [you don't love yourself] reveals itself to be shorthand for a lack of unity in the self, rather than a lack of self-esteem: loving oneself is impossible where the concept of 'oneself' is absent. This conflict provides the core of the narrative, and thus the segments coalesce around an explicit engagement with the question of what comprises the self. Whilst recognizably establishing a kinship with it, *Tu ne t'aimes pas* goes further than *Enfance*, featuring a self represented not by two, but an indeterminate number of voices: this corresponding to this 'self''s perception that there are several selves coexisting within its personality. The narrative emphasizes the richness of this condition: '"Ne sommes-nous pas à nous seuls un monde... des mondes..."' ['Are we not a whole world in ourselves? Worlds even?'].[31] However, confessing to having several selves within isolates the person from the outside world, which, mindful of Jekyll and Hyde, can accept two sides to a personality, but no more: '"Vous vous souvenez de son étonnement... 'C'est peu? [two sides to the personality] Vous en avez donc davantage?'"' ['You remember his surprise? "[Two,] [t]hat's not many? So you have more than that?"'].[32] This turns the spotlight on the arbitrariness of normative identity categories. As an example, Sarraute cites gender identity, an apparently natural state from which our subject feels estranged, in contrast to others who:

> — [...] A chaque étape de leur vie, ils se sentent être des femmes, des hommes...
> — Et rien que cela. De 'vraies' femmes, de 'vrais' hommes... le plus conformes possible aux modèles [*sic*].[33]

> ['At each stage of their life, they feel themselves to be men, women...'
> 'And nothing but that. "Real" men, "real" women... The most exact copies possible of the originals.']

Sarraute suggests that when we assume our identity as a monolithic male or female self, we delude ourselves. The single unitary identity does not come naturally and requires an effort to be performed: '"Vous savez bien avec quel zèle parfois, quel empressement nous réunissons en nous-mêmes ceux d'entre nous qui nous font le mieux ressembler à ce que nous devons sentir que nous sommes..."' ['You know very well with what zeal sometimes, what fervour we bring together in ourselves those of us who best make us resemble what we are supposed to feel that we are'].[34] The lengths to which the multiplicitous subject of *Tu ne t'aimes pas* goes to comply with the injunction to adopt a unitary subjecthood is an index of the pressure the narrative voices perceive to assume a coherent, unified and single identity. Amidst these conflicting notions of the nature of subjectivity, writing the self cannot be a neutral activity. Indeed, through the narrative of *Tu ne t'aimes pas* Sarraute alerts us to the role that self-writing may play in the endeavour to produce an acceptable construction of the self. In their efforts to solidify their identity as a single self, the narrating voices ponder possible strategies besides saying '*je m*'aime' [I love *myself*] (an act imbued with a certain violence, since it suppresses the plurality of voices at work). The example of someone who as a child produced a written 'autoportrait' [self-portrait] inspires them to consider making an image of the self: '"On pourrait 'se raconter'..."' ['We could "tell our story"'].[35] The result is of dubious merit, being likened to a statue, for it fixes the self, and in the process suppresses much of it; the very activity of producing an 'autoportrait' is thus called into question: '"Mais ne lui avait-il pas fallu éliminer [...] tout ce qui se présentait en lui et qui n'était pas digne de faire partie de sa construction, qui aurait pu abîmer sa statue?"' ['But didn't he have to eliminate everything in himself which wasn't fit to be a part of his construction, which could have damaged his statue?'].[36]

Here we see how Sarraute's elaboration of a pluralized concept of selfhood evolves beyond a pure meditation on selfhood to critique specifically the self-representation autobiography offers: a critique which it is difficult to avoid reading as a retrospective commentary on the generic affiliation of *Enfance*. *Tu ne t'aimes pas*, then, is a work which offers a new way of conceptualizing the self and self-writing, whilst criticizing accepted notions of what the self is and how to write it. It thus raises the question of what form of textuality is appropriate to play host to the self. *Enfance* had already drawn attention to the limitations of autobiography for providing an understanding of the person of the author; what *Tu ne t'aimes pas* reveals is that these problems originate in autobiographical discourse itself, and the desire behind it. Readers of *Tu ne t'aimes pas* are sensitized to the potential for self-writing to be complicitous with a discourse that denies full expression to the pluralized self, instead forcing all subjectivity into the straitjacket of isolated singularity. The trajectory of intersubjectivity Sarraute pursues from *Enfance* to *Tu ne t'aimes pas* to *Ouvrez* sees her positing ever more forcefully a space in which an intertwining plurality of voices constitute the self. *Tu ne t'aimes pas* signals that, for this self, autobiography, the expression of an individual singular selfhood, no longer makes any sense.

Having presented a case in *Tu ne t'aimes pas* for abandoning autobiography as a template for self-writing, thereafter Sarraute concentrates her efforts on developing an alternative form of writing that can offer an hospitable environment for the pluralized self. This is the achievement of *Ouvrez*, where the plural self is able to express itself without inhibition. In this work very far removed from conventional self-writing, Sarraute moves beyond the pluralized selfhood always succumbing to the pressure to conceal or deny its intersubjective identity to depict an untrammelled intersubjectivity. Unlike the voices in *Tu ne t'aimes pas*, who anxiously perceive their incarnation of selfhood as deviant, in *Ouvrez* there is no sense of vulnerability or exclusion associated with the failure of the self to assume a single, unified subjectivity. *Ouvrez* is a recuperation and celebration of a diffuse subjectivity in which selfhood does not exist at the level of an individual person at all: 'Des mots, des êtres vivants parfaitement autonomes, sont les protagonistes de chacun de ces drames' [It is words, perfectly autonomous living beings, who are the protagonists of each one of these dramas].[37] The difficulty of finding an appropriate language for the representation of a self that will always exceed language is thus dispensed with. Instead, the narrative describes a biological organism, where words are separated into those 'derrière la paroi' [behind the cell wall] and those on the other side. Agency lies with individual utterances, who decide for themselves when they wish to emerge from the other side of the membrane into discourse. In a manoeuvre that is not without a certain significance, Sarraute portrays an environment where it is taken for granted that there is no transcendent self which words refer to or represent, only the selves in words. Unfettered by anxieties over what image of 'the self' will emerge from individual utterances, the selves depicted in *Ouvrez* express themselves — that is to say, produce their utterances — with notable ease. The more radical form of self-writing practised here involves not simply writing autobiography differently, as Sarraute does in *Enfance*; nor in self-consciously renouncing the writing of autobiography, as she does in *Tu ne t'aimes pas*. Sarraute's treatment of selfhood in *Ouvrez* implies that a free hand to explore and write the self requires exiting from any relation with autobiography whatsoever.

With her attention to the shortcomings of the genre of autobiography and her rejection of the conception of selfhood it implicitly favours, Sarraute does more than denaturalize received ideas, or re-draw her relation to a literary genre: her stance also colours the relation with would-be readers of her autobiography. Autobiography's purpose is to acquaint the other who reads with the self who writes, but the possibility of relating what the self is satisfactorily to the other outside that self is precisely what Sarraute denies. In renouncing the template of autobiography, she renounces too the aim to make the autobiographical self known to its audience — a move most graphically illustrated by the total absence in *Tu ne t'aimes pas* and *Ouvrez* of the recognizably Sarrautean self. Even in *Enfance*, references to what the text can point back to, but cannot make accessible — memories and a semiotic space in the self — have the effect of creating a hierarchical relation between the self, who experiences, and the other, who is outside these experiences. Accordingly, even in *Enfance*, the reader is left little room to satisfy their desire for better acquaintance with the writer's self.

It is to the vital third term of autobiography, its reader, that our emphasis will now shift, for there is another factor to consider in Sarraute's renunciation of the autobiography format, beyond the problems she diagnoses with the representation of self in language. This is Sarraute's concern about how the reader will interpret and respond to these representations. Sarraute's abandonment of autobiography (expressed in the change of modality in her self-writing as she moves from *Enfance* to *Ouvrez*) needs to be considered from a different angle: as a response to the reader's approach to autobiography. It is at this point that an element of conflict can be discerned in Sarraute's renunciation of autobiography. Turning to Sarraute's views of the reader-writer transaction, it becomes clear that in autobiography Sarraute locates an unappetizing combination of a self-representation necessarily carrying a weakened sense of an individual identity, and a pushy, covetous reader desperate to find one. This resistance to having the reader consume the autobiographical self from a text which is incapable of possessing it in the first place proves to be a significant but overlooked factor behind Sarraute's reluctance to set her self down in writing.

The Possessive Reader

It follows from Sarraute's lack of faith in the ability of autobiography to seize adequately the autobiographer's self that, for her, the reader of any autobiographical text must inevitably remain distanced from the real person of the autobiographer even after — and indeed due to — reading their autobiography. However, there are indications in Sarraute's earlier works (in particular *L'Ere du soupçon* and *Les Fruits d'or*) that she anticipates that her reader will not share her perception of an unbridgeable chasm between the writing self and the reading other. This divergence in understanding of the autobiographical text's capacities sets up a conflict between reader and author that reflects a more general tension between Sarraute and her readers.

Readers and reception are recurrent preoccupations throughout Sarraute's work, with Sarraute being, according to Ann Jefferson, 'painfully aware of the reader as an other whose rules of engagement and interpretation do not necessarily tally with those that her own writing proposes. The reader's alterity [...] is perceived as a potential threat to [Sarraute's preferred] patterns of sameness and difference'.[38] Certainly, Sarraute's stance towards readers is often combative: frequently, where Sarraute's writings refer to the activities of readers, they portray the reader as an antagonistic, albeit necessary presence to the literary author. In *L'Ere du soupçon*, this trend is already clear. In the essay which lends its title to the volume, Sarraute discusses the sterility of the mid-twentieth-century novel, which continues to employ literary devices that neither reader nor author find credible.[39] What is striking is the extent to which the reader is taken to task for allowing this situation to persist: the presence of the reader is held responsible for diluting authorial ambitions. Choosing not to pursue the implications raised by the phenomenon of an author who is guided less by their own creative impulses than by an anxiety about how their work will be perceived by readers, Sarraute homes in on the latter's shortcomings. In an unflattering comparison with Pavlov's dog, she argues that the reader will attempt at the slightest provocation to create old-fashioned 'characters' from the text, and this holds back the progression of the novel.[40] The readership is ascribed a different and inferior conceptualization of literature to that of the author, and the author's right — even duty — is to break free of the lazy reader's demands and expectations, which impose unfair and limiting requirements on the author's art.[41]

Sarraute's criticism of readers extends to her own. Speaking in 1971 of the reception of her novels from *Portrait d'un inconnu* to *Les Fruits d'or*, Sarraute attacks readers who 'n'y ont vu d'abord que ce que le langage convenu les avait habitués à voir et ce que précisément je cherchais à détruire' [who at first only saw in it what conventional language had familiarized them with seeing and which was precisely what I was seeking to destroy], and she publicly reproaches one critic who does not share her own approach to textual analysis.[42] Against a backdrop of conflictual reader relations, one thing especially that Sarraute seems minded to 'détruire', or destroy, is the tendency which she detects in readers to treat the person of the author as an object of consumption.

Sarraute presents the commodification of the author as the product of a preference for biographical approaches to reading. These are lampooned in her novel *Les Fruits d'or*, where she lays bare the emptiness of metaliterary discourses which grow up around authors and their works.[43] In this novel about a fictitious novel of the same name written by a certain Bréhier, it is suggested that biographical readings emerge out of readers' anxieties over interpretation. This anxiety stimulates what is presented as a wrongheaded desire to amass as much information as possible about the writer, as if being apprised of every last detail of the author's person would provide a failsafe interpretative key to their work. Personal knowledge of the intradiegetic author therefore confers authority on the individual reader, and is vaunted: 'Vous ne connaissez pas Bréhier... C'est tout simple. Ça explique tout' [You don't know Bréhier. It's very simple. It explains everything].[44] Such a reading strategy reduces the author to an information commodity to be consumed; it depends on acquiring familiarity with the author's person, and stimulates in the reader a boundless appetite for knowledge about the author which overrules any ethical concerns, such as a respect for privacy. We note that Germaine Lemaire in *Le Planétarium* — another writer — suffers with fanatical readers, who at one point are described as lying in wait for her outside her home with cameras at the ready.[45] In *Les Fruits d'or*, the lurking, consuming desire of the reader is treated scornfully as Sarraute portrays readers who want to rummage through the sock drawer of the adored intradiegetic author in order to attain a privileged understanding of him. The animated quality of the reader's discourse conveys the frenzy with which he sets about satisfying what is depicted as an immoderate, gluttonous appetite for intimate details about the author:

> Fouillons, flairons, rien ne nous retient... nous [the readers] aimons nous répandre sur tout... journaux intimes, lettres, confidences, fonds de tiroir oubliés, [...] mémoires de domestiques congédiés... Tout nous est bon. Rien n'est sacré pour nous. [...] Aucun tabou. Ceux mêmes dont l'œuvre pourrait tenir en respect ne sont pas épargnés. Bien au contraire.[46]

> [Let's search it out, sniff it out, nothing to stop us. We like to spread ourselves out and cover everything... private diaries, letters, confidences, the forgotten things at the back of drawers, memoirs of dismissed staff... Everything is grist to our mill. For us, nothing is sacred. No taboos. Even those whose work might endow them with respect are not spared. Quite the reverse.]

The discernibly contemptuous tone in this passage on consuming readers conveys a strong sense of disapproval at such a mentality. Here, the seeds of an antagonistic stance towards the genre of autobiography are sown. If readers harbour an impulse to digest all information pertaining to the person of the author as an aid to reading his or her works, then that author's autobiography will assume a particular importance for them, since, according to the traditional expectation of the genre, it will satisfy their craving for information about the author by delivering an authoritative account of his or her life and selfhood. Writing autobiography thus becomes an act intrinsically complicit with that consuming desire. Given Sarraute's clear sensitivity, pre-dating *Enfance*, to this desire for intimate knowledge of the author's person, and her apparent scorn for reading approaches which set up the author as an object of consumption, her refusal to collude with this desire in her autobiographical writing is not surprising.

Indeed, one of the notable aspects of *Enfance* is precisely that it does not give away very much genuine biographical information about its author: in particular, the focus on childhood means the dangerous and dramatic period of Sarraute's life when she lived under a false identity during the Occupation remains untouched.[47] However, Sarraute goes further than simply not telling: she also draws attention to her not telling. Readers cannot fail to be alerted to the way the author withholds the conventional autobiographical narrative from them, especially as Sarraute allows a strong contrast to emerge between the *Enfance* narrative and something much closer to traditional autobiography: the story Natacha's grandmother recounts of her life to her granddaughter, reported to us in the fifty-ninth fragment.[48] Unlike *Enfance* itself, this story provides a detailed and descriptive account of the major events of its narrator's life. By calling attention to the small amount of biographical information she herself reveals, Sarraute makes her obstruction of the reader's attempt to gain intimate knowledge about the autobiographer overt. Her decision in later works of self-writing to present a multiple and essentially anonymized self also has the effect of staving off bounty-hunting readers seeking to mine the depths of the person of the author.

Yet *Les Fruits d'or* shows that the objection to consuming readers is not only directed at the *manner* in which they relate to the writing self, by greedily lapping up information about them; the goal underlying this consumption is also objectionable: namely, their desire to get closer to the author. Sarraute's engagement with the ethics that subtend reading moves beyond the theme of consumption to one of her long-standing concerns: the ethics of intimacy and the opposing drives for proximity and distance.[49] In *Les Fruits d'or*, the gluttonous reader's narration exposes the problem with the reader's desire for intimacy with the author, the source of his appetite for information. This desire, it becomes clear, betrays a will to establish equivalence between them:

> D'eux justement [respected authors], de leur intimité quelque chose de particulièrement délectable se dégage, quelque chose qui nous [...] rassure, nous assure que nous sommes bien tous les mêmes au fond, [...] tous des hommes en fin de compte, bien pareils, malgré ce détail — leur *œuvre*....[50]

> [Precisely from them, from their intimacy, something particularly delicious emerges, something which reassures us, assures us that we are indeed all the

> same underneath everything, all men at the end of the day, quite identical, despite this detail... their *work*.]

The inference is that this desire for equality constitutes undesirable readerly behaviour: we know from *L'Ere du soupçon* of Sarraute's dislike for what she considers a general human trait, an insistent desire to establish intimacy with others that underpins all our social interactions. In 'De Dostoïevski à Kafka' she cites sympathetically the New Zealand writer Katherine Mansfield's feeling of suffocation on being cared for during illness by her companion Ida Baker, referring to the 'sorte de crainte et peut-être un léger dégoût [sort of fear and perhaps a slight disgust for] "this terrible desire to establish contact"' that Mansfield perceived on the part of her carer.[51] Sarraute's own low opinion of this psychological attribute emerges ever more clearly in the essay: she expresses an exasperation with what she calls an 'impossibilité de se poser solidement à l'écart, à distance, de se tenir "sur son quant à soi", dans un état d'opposition ou même de simple indifférence' [impossibility of standing resolutely apart, at a distance, of keeping oneself to oneself, in a state of opposition or even of simple indifference].[52] As in *Les Fruits d'or*, underlying the urge to achieve proximity with another is the search for the same: what Sarraute describes as a 'besoin obsédant de fusion' [obsessive need for fusion].[53] This equates to denying the other's difference; imposing transparency instead of opaqueness; seeking to make of the other something familiar, not foreign. Thus a clear contrast emerges between what is portrayed as a reasonable impulse to situate the self at a distance from others, and 'ce besoin continuel et presque maniaque de contact' [this continual and almost maniacal need for contact], a demand for closeness to another which this essay typifies as excessive, invasive and distorting.[54]

This intolerance of separateness and difference, this insistent will to 'se frayer un chemin jusqu'à autrui, de pénétrer en lui le plus loin possible, de lui faire perdre son inquiétante, son insupportable opacité' [to beat a path to the other person, to penetrate into him as far as possible, to make him lose his worrying, intolerable opacity] is a fault Sarraute explicitly identifies in readers too: in her own audience she berates 'cette tendance à ramener l'inconnu au connu le plus banal' [this tendency to reduce the unknown to the most banal of the known].[55] *L'Ere du soupçon* suggests that the urge which we saw depicted in the intradiegetic readers in *Les Fruits d'or* to gather and consume information about the other results from a drive to gain emotional proximity with others, to be able to identify with their motivations and thought processes — without any regard for their receptivity to this. As *L'Ere du soupçon* reveals, for Sarraute, this striving for intimacy with another is an ethical issue: behind it is an inappropriate, appropriative and invasive desire, which, if indulged, will prove harmful to the person at whom it is directed.

However, *Les Fruits d'or* suggests there is a still more sinister dimension to the desire for sameness. As the excursus of the gluttonous reader in *Les Fruits d'or* continues, it becomes clear that what seems like a desire to get close to others, to find commonality with them, is not really about a search for the same at all. Disregarding the literary achievement of the author ('malgré ce détail — leur *œuvre*...'[56]), the reader adds:

> [...] quant à tout le reste [...] on y trouve souvent tant de faiblesses, tant de paresse, d'incurie, tant d'infantilisme, de perversion, même parfois une telle

> bassesse qu'il nous est difficile, il faut l'avouer, de ne pas éprouver un sentiment bien légitime de supériorité.[57]
>
> [as for everything else... one often finds so many weaknesses, so much laziness, carelessness, so much childishness, perversion, even sometimes such baseness that it is difficult, I have to confess, not to feel a quite legitimate sense of superiority.]

Here we arrive at the root of the problem. The intradiegetic consuming reader in *Les Fruits d'or* reveals that the search for greater knowledge of and intimacy with the author — which has seemed like a deferential gesture that venerates authors, raises them up on pedestals as adored objects — is in fact part of a power struggle which the reader wages against the author. The novel shows how the establishment of sameness between readers and the writer Bréhier as a result of closer contact represents not a state of equality, but the triumph of the readers: they had believed the writer to be superior to them, worthy of idolization, but their thirst for knowledge uncovers that he is no better than they in reality, and so they can justifiably topple him from his elevated position. This perception that a struggle for supremacy underlies relations between self and other mirrors Sarraute's reference in 'De Dostoïevsky à Kafka' to the achievement of intimacy with the other as a bid to 'rétablir le contact, reprendre possession d'autrui' [re-establish contact, take back possession of the other].[58] In Sarraute's conception of reader relations, as depicted in *Les Fruits d'or*, the reader harbours an antagonism toward the writer. A desire for intimate knowledge of another, to perceive another as being the same as the self is not after all a benign, admiring gesture towards that other: it is, on the contrary, a sign of an intending dominance.

Sarraute's visions of how self and other relate to each other have an especial importance with respect to her thinking on autobiography. We note that, in *Les Fruits d'or*, the ammunition used to bring the author down is the information readers have been able to glean about him. Through their interrogations of self–other relations, including the specific dynamics of the reader's relation to the author, these earlier works reveal to us an ethical basis for resisting the reader's drive to secure intimacy and privileged information about the author. Sarraute's writings imply that to supply an autobiography which gives away information about the person of the author is not only to collude with the notion that the author is a commodity for consumption: it also encourages the reader to believe that in taking possession of the author through reading the text, they gain a genuine intimacy and proximity with that author. This is not something the author is likely to encourage: Sarraute, as we have seen, expresses antipathy toward an excessive appetite for contact. We know too from Sarraute's earlier writings that the prospect of having her person used as an object by readers to assert their own dominance is not one she will tolerate lightly: the model of reader-relations Sarraute herself practised and trenchantly advocates in *L'Ere du soupçon* is one in which readers are to become subject to the author's domineering force, rather than the other way round. Referring to the audience's response to the 'indices' [trademarks] of the new, modern style of writing she detects, Sarraute affirms that readers are to be made to 'plonge[r] en eux aussi loin que l'auteur et fai[re] sienne sa vision' [dive into them as far as the author and adopt his vision]; the goal being to do no less than to 'reprendre au lecteur son bien et l'attirer coûte que coûte sur le terrain de l'auteur' [take back from the reader his property and draw him at whatever cost onto the author's ground].[59]

These concerns, combined with Sarraute's willingness to confront the reader, would seem to set the ground for an antagonistic relationship between Sarraute and the reader of autobiography. Sarraute's earlier texts reveal that any autobiographical work of hers has the potential to be marked by a pattern of conflictual reader relations articulated around the use and abuse of the author's self-representation. This occurs when a reader constructs and appropriates images of the author unethically, transforming the author into a possession, a prized commodity which bolsters that reader's standing. In the light of Sarraute's clear hostility towards what she perceives as an appropriative and possessive agenda towards authors amongst readers, and the vehemence of her criticism of readers prior to *Enfance*, we might expect to find an overtly confrontational quality to this text. We may anticipate another ill-tempered tug-of-war, this time over the *extra*-diegetic Sarrautean self, as the author defends her textual self against misuses on the part of the reader to which she does not consent.

There is evidence of these concerns in *Enfance*, and it goes beyond Sarraute's conspicuous refusal to cooperate with a readerly appetite for biographical detail. In *Enfance*, we find the ethics of contact and intimacy foregrounded once more, both within and outwith the reader relation. The desirability of respecting the intimate territory of others is shown in an episode where the child Natacha is trying to solicit a declaration from her father of his love for her. Natacha is rewarded (both with words and a balloon) for taking pains not to encroach on his emotions to the point of causing him to feel awkward. This makes possible the utterance she craves to hear:

> 'Mais oui, mon petit bêta, *je t'aime.*'
>
> Alors il est récompensé d'avoir accepté de jouer à mon jeu... 'Eh bien, puisque tu m'aimes, tu vas me donner...' tu vois, je n'ai pas songé un instant à t'obliger à t'ouvrir complètement, à étaler ce qui t'emplit, ce que tu retiens [...].[60]
>
> ['But of course, you daft thing, *I love you.*' Then he is compensated for having consented to play my game with me... 'And so, since you love me, you're going to give me...' You see, I didn't for a moment dream of making you open yourself up completely, put on display what you have within you, what you keep for yourself.]

Here we are presented with an interaction with the other that, by contrast with the depictions of self–other relations in *L'Ere du soupçon* and *Les Fruits d'or*, is shown to be much more considerate of that other's requirements — in particular, their right to remain 'foreign', not familiar. What is especially significant is that the narration clearly depicts the child actively choosing to prioritize consideration of the other at some cost to herself: although Natacha refrains from forcing an eruption of demonstrativeness from her father, framing the declaration of love in playful terms, she nonetheless has a yearning for such affection, as illustrated by the narrator's wistful observation that 'tu pourras en laisser sourdre un tout petit peu...'

['you can let just a little bit of it spring up...'].[61] This need, however, she forbears from indulging. The narrative makes clear that this considerate course of action is far preferable to the alternative of goading the father into revealing his innermost self to satisfy an appetite for contact: an option which Sarraute presents here in unfavourable terms, employing — significantly — the vocabulary of commerce and consumption in her reference to putting the essence of oneself on display: 'étaler ce qui t'emplit' [put on display what you have within you]. Whilst the message about encroachment is consistent with that of previous texts, there is notably none of the withering commentary on excessive appetites for knowledge of the other which earlier writings more readily put forward. Yet the further recurrence of this theme in *Enfance* suggests it has a significance belied by the subtlety with which it is treated (the narrators, for example, do not directly discuss it). Significantly, the disagreeableness of the unilateral demand for intimacy is revisited in the context of the reader–writer relation. Sarraute incorporates into her autobiographical narrative the scenario of an author's reluctance to share intimacies with her readership. This comes in the episode where the child Natacha is set the task of writing an assignment on 'mon premier chagrin' [my first sorrow]:

> — De retrouver un de mes chagrins? Mais non, voyons, à quoi penses-tu? Un vrai chagrin à moi? vécu par moi pour de bon... et d'ailleurs, qu'est-ce que je pouvais appeler de ce nom? Et quel avait été le premier? Je n'avais aucune envie de me le demander... ce qu'il me fallait, c'était un chagrin qui serait hors de ma propre vie, que je pourrais considérer en m'en tenant à bonne distance...[62]
>
> [To re-live one of my sorrows? Certainly not, really, what are you thinking of? A real sorrow of my own? That I really experienced? And besides, what could I call by this name? And which had been the first? I had no desire whatsoever to ask myself these questions... what I needed was a sorrow which lay outside my own life, which I could contemplate whilst keeping myself at a good distance from it.]

In this episode, the failure to deliver a genuine autobiographical narrative has nothing to do with the inadequacies of the autobiographical form. It is clear in Natacha's response to this homework task that she has a desire not to reveal to her audience the full extent of her own history, questioning her prospective audience's prerogative to make her ask herself a question which she is not unable to answer, but rather, is unwilling to be asked.

Confronted with what she considers to be the improper desire of another to learn more about herself, Natacha uses self-writing as a device, not to supply the information sought, but to the opposite effect: supplying misinformation by providing an entirely spurious account of her first sorrow. The child insists on the need for distance, and imposes it between herself and her readership: not only by misleading her audience about her personal history with a false trail, but also by covertly betraying the autobiographer's pact, which relies on there being a commitment on the part of the author to providing an account of his or her life as it was really lived. By staging this refusal on the part of Natacha even to attempt to remember her 'premier chagrin' in response to an invasive reader who desires to acquire intimate information about the writer, Sarraute models a relation between writer and reader which cannot fail to have resonances for the reader of Sarraute's own autobiographical narrative.

Although the concern with the ethics of proximity and distance is maintained into this text, these issues receive noticeably subtle treatment in *Enfance*. Only muted and oblique criticism is offered on matters of reception in which the reader of autobiography may be implicated: this despite Sarraute's readiness elsewhere to criticize and deride bad readers, and her advocacy of a confrontational approach to readers in *L'Ere du soupçon*. Here we do not find the confrontational approach adopted by some of Sarraute's contemporaries, such as Genet. However, Sarraute's failure to resort to the fierce direct address to the reader that can be found elsewhere in twentieth-century French autobiographical writing does not equate to an author rowing back from directing reader response: it merely reflects the fact that she adopts a different strategy to influence her readers. Instructive on this point is the resolution of the problem caused by the unwelcome demand made on Natacha in the 'premier chagrin' episode. Here no direct remonstration is made with the intrusive reader who encroaches on to Natacha's private territory, although as bystanders we readers of *Enfance* are keenly aware of the antipathy this intradiegetic reader's conduct provokes. Instead of detailing her objections to recounting her first sorrow, the narrator eschews aggressive tactics in favour of the subterfuge of a made-up confession, ostensibly supplying the reader with what is wanted. This response involves Natacha in a more oblique manipulation of the unknowing reader, a manipulation which clearly gives her satisfaction:

> — [...] [C]ela me donnerait une sensation que je ne pouvais pas nommer [...] ... un sentiment...
>
> — De dignité, peut-être... [...] et aussi de domination, de puissance...
>
> — Et de liberté... Je me tiens dans l'ombre, hors d'atteinte, je ne livre rien de ce qui n'est qu'à moi... mais je prépare pour les autres ce que je considère comme étant bon pour eux, je choisis ce qu'ils aiment, ce qu'ils peuvent attendre, un de ces chagrins qui leur conviennent...[63]

> ['That would give me a sensation I couldn't name... a feeling...'
>
> 'Of dignity perhaps... and also of domination, power.'
>
> 'And freedom... I keep myself in the shadows, out of reach, I don't surrender anything of what is mine alone... but I prepare for the others what I consider to be good for them, I choose what they like, what they can expect, one of these sorrows which suits them...']

Les Fruits d'or suggests that at the heart of the reader–writer relation is a power game. This power game continues here, but it is not a contest of brute force. This passage of *Enfance* alerts us to Sarraute's use of more sophisticated strategies against the would-be reader of the autobiographical text to prevent their trespassing onto territory which the author considers they are not entitled to access.

Whilst in *Enfance* we continue to see suspicion and disapproval directed at outsiders — explicitly including readers — who want to get closer to the self, it seems, if anything, that Sarraute is trying in *Enfance* to *avoid* directly confronting her reader over their aims in reading her work, using evasive tactics in her narration so that any potential conflict is situated at one remove from the autobiographical self and its reader. Yet there is no sign that this retreat from confronting her audience over their reading approaches correlates with a softer position on the rights and wrongs of readers seeing the authors of the works they read as possessable commodities, into whose intimacy they are entitled to be taken. On the contrary, Sarraute's willingness to resort to other, more subtle, even manipulative strategies to shape her reader's response to her self-writing suggests that the author's paramount concern is not so much to persuade the reader to adopt a particular ethic when relating to the person of the autobiographer through the medium of the text; what counts is succeeding in keeping her audience at a distance, triumphing over her reader in this tug-of-war played out, rather behind closed doors, over possession of the autobiographical self.

Once we start to consider the possibility that Sarraute may use a whole arsenal of strategies to disarm the potentially encroaching reader of her autobiography, we are then led to reassess the significance of narrative features or devices occurring in *Enfance* in the light of their possible efficacy as measures to fend off readers with potentially excessive designs on the autobiographical self. Particularly deserving of closer scrutiny is Sarraute's relationship with the genre of autobiography, or, more specifically, her detailed critique of autobiography and her renunciation of this form of writing. Genre is important for setting the parameters of reader expectations; from Sarraute's perspective, there is but a small step between the promises associated with the genre of autobiography — which she carefully indicates to us that she will not be fulfilling — and inappropriate readerly desires and the commodification of the author. It may be expected, therefore, that Sarraute's clear hostility towards what she perceives as a potentially appropriative and possessive agenda amongst readers of her self-writing might be reflected, not only in the tone it takes toward the reader, but also in its adherence to the precepts of the genre of autobiography. Declining to provide her audience with a conventional autobiography deprives the consuming reader of the kind of material they seek, and can be viewed as a tactic to fend off these unethical readers, without the need for confrontation. Could we have stumbled across a further explanation, beyond the one the text most obviously offers us, for Sarraute's renunciation of autobiography in its conventional form?

The abandonment of the generic norms of autobiography can be seen as a tactic to influence the way in which Sarraute's readership relates to the person of the author through the text; a tactic which obviates the need to confront the reader directly over their reading strategy. My own reader may wonder why Sarraute would fail to acknowledge this conflict with the reader; why, if Sarraute is genuinely concerned with the reader's reception of her text to the extent that she feels the need to exert influence over it, she would resort to somewhat oblique strategies for doing so; and why, if reader conduct motivates the renunciation of autobiography, Sarraute insists so much on the qualities of selfhood as an obstacle to the writing of conventional autobiography, at the expense of more clearly highlighting the problem of the unduly possessive reader.

It is my contention that the plainly discernible conflict between Sarraute's self-writing and the generic norms associated with autobiography has the function of occluding another conflict: that between Sarraute and the reader of her self-writing, which arises out of suspicions about the motives underpinning this reader's approach to the text. The tug-of-war with the reader over the possession and appropriation of the self must lurk beneath the surface of Sarraute's self-writing, rather than being more openly acknowledged, because for Sarraute victory is not certain. Exploring this hidden battle for the possession of the self will be our next focus.

Conceding Possession

Sarraute's earlier works indicate a certain vulnerability that the author feels on being exposed to the presence of an independent, encroaching and judging reader; the act of writing autobiography, because it conveniently supplies intimate details to the reader which they can make free with, risks heightening this sense of vulnerability to the reading other. Yet amongst the various reservations about autobiography expressed in her self-writing, the threat of the possessive reading other is not directly voiced: instead her text is principally concerned with the nature of the self, presenting this as the motivating factor behind Sarraute's abandonment of the autobiographical template. To what extent, though, is this writing of the self in fact a writing of the other? How far does a rhetoric of the self's multiplicity (and hence unpossessability), along with the dismissal of even the possibility of autobiography, alleviate the discomfort caused by the prospect of a reader's desiring to read autobiography in order to take possession of the autobiographer's self? These questions, which posit writing as in some way palliative, but conversely the written text as a danger area, bring us into the terrain of psychoanalytical interpretation. My proposal will be that Lacanian psychoanalysis — in particular, Lacan's concept of the gaze — lends us a means of answering these questions and understanding some puzzling anomalies in Sarraute's self-writing.

Whilst various psychoanalytical approaches have proved fruitful in studies of Sarraute, caution about this interpretative avenue is sometimes voiced, in the light of the author's own disapproval of the bringing together of literature and psychoanalysis.[64] An example of this is to be found in the work of Emer O'Beirne, who, prior to embarking on her own (in part Lacanian) reading of Sarraute, remarks that 'there can be no easy "mapping" of Lacan's theories onto [Sarraute's] literary work'.[65]

There are, nonetheless, compelling reasons for pursuing a Lacanian reading of Sarraute; and in my view Sarraute's hostility to Lacan is one. Lacan is Sarraute's intellectual contemporary, and there is evidence that she was well acquainted with poststructuralist thought — including that of Lacan; moreover, fictions such as *Entre la vie et la mort*, as well as her critical reflections on narrative, reveal an active engagement with its conclusions.[66] This critical engagement remains in evidence at the end of her career: in its meditations on selfhood *Tu ne t'aimes pas* develops a strongly Lacanian theme. Remarkably, we will find that this is done in such a way as to resist the conclusions on self-constitution that Lacan draws: part of my aim here will be to probe what it is about these conclusions which energizes Sarraute to contest them in this way.

For Lacan, with the onset of relations with others through language, each individual comes to inhabit the symbolic, the order of the Other: this is to be enveloped in a web of requirements that emanate from society and with which the individual must comply.[67] For Lacan this web of demands is central to the process of self-constitution: the Other of the symbolic order shapes and limits the parameters of an individual's selfhood, determining what kind of subject the self is allowed to become. In Lacan's model, the subject of the symbolic, being governed by and dependant on the Other, is inescapably in the Other's possession. A manifestation of this servitude is the ever-present and uncomfortable gaze of that Other, which most often, but not always, the subject will affect not to see.

The theory of the gaze as elaborated by Lacan, and developed by Slavoj Žižek, reveals why being seen by others should be uncomfortable, and yet essential.[68] The gaze of the Other simultaneously confers on the subject a recognized identity, and creates it as a subjugated subject. Its usefulness for this discussion lies in the way it highlights the play of power dynamics operating as the subject is constructed, a construction which, significantly for us as readers of autobiography, is effected through language. For Lacan, each verbal or written utterance cements the subject into the symbolic, the realm of the Other.

On close reading, Sarraute's self-writing displays, but also covers over, an anxiety about how far the self has sovereignty over what it is (perceived to be), and the extent to which the self is determined by external perceptions that it cannot control. In a development with strong implications for relations between writing self and reading other, the other in Sarraute evolves from being a mere nuisance to a threat: once the other who perceives the self is recognized to be determinative of who that self is, this renders the very presence of that other menacing, as the self realizes the limits on its powers of self-possession. Sarraute's treatment of both self and other can be read as an attempt to negate the power of the other's gaze to unsettle the self, and — perhaps surprisingly, given Sarraute's conception of a pluralized self — as a bid to return the self to the self's own possession.

For Lacan, the subject of the symbolic is a *split* subject — that is, one that lacks, desires. One of the ways in which this split may be perceived is in the split Lacan posits between the eye and the gaze; that is, the split between the subject who sees and the object which looks, gazes, at him or her. The gap itself is a manifestation in the visual field of *objet a*, the name given by Lacan to the object we are bound to desire. According to the theory of the gaze, the subject is always already *being* viewed before viewing, and it is unable to account for how it is seen in that view: '*se voyant se voir* — représente un escamotage. Un évitement s'y opère de la fonction du regard' [*seeing oneself seeing oneself* — represents mere sleight of hand. An avoidance of the function of the gaze is at work here].[69]

This psychoanalytical theorization of the gaze differs, then, from the phenomenological and cinematic versions, and from Foucault's conception of the panopticon gaze. In these theories, the gaze is objectifying and gives power to the subject that views (and thus removes it from the person who is the object viewed).[70] Lacan's gaze *subjectifies*: when an individual looks, that looking is anticipated, and part of what is there for him or her to see is the *point de capiton* [quilting point], the stain signifying the Real: that which is beyond the viewer's mastery. Developing

Lacan's image of the stain as a blot, Žižek explains how being confronted with it subjectifies the viewer by proving his or her lack and disempowerment:

> [T]he gaze *qua* object functions like a blot that blurs the transparency of the viewed image. I can never see properly, can never include in the totality of my field of vision, the point in the other from which it gazes back at me.[71]

There is thus a non-coincidence of images between what the subject sees and what the Other sees, even if both look at the self. The gaze directed back at the subject prevents the subject from taking any pleasure in the exercise of observing, an activity that otherwise would be pleasurable, giving the observer a sense of command over what is observed: 'The gaze as object is a stain preventing me from looking at the picture from a safe, "objective" distance, from enframing it as something that is at my grasping view's disposal.'[72] However, the subject is not continually conscious of this lack of mastery: to avoid the subject experiencing unpleasure, the gaze will be overlooked; albeit that this elision of the gaze must momentarily be punctured by awareness of it, in order for the subject to sustain itself as a desiring subject who lacks — that is to say, a functioning subject in the realm of the symbolic.[73]

The notion behind the Lacanian concept of the gaze has not, to my knowledge, been brought to bear in the study of autobiography.[74] Yet the genre is fertile ground for analysis in these terms. Autobiography, after all, involves the self observing itself. Moreover, the autobiographical text generates a situation where the writer's activity of self-contemplation is subjected to the scrutiny of others. Sheringham invokes Harold Bloom's theory of the anxiety of influence to describe a phenomenon that he considers intrinsic to French literary autobiography: an awareness on the part of the writer of the generic tradition into which he is inserting himself. This generates a desire to live up to his autobiographical precursors, whilst at the same time wanting not merely to imitate them, but to assert his individuality: '"*my* life, in *my* autobiography, will not be *mine* if my text is the same as *yours*."'[75] What Sheringham describes here is nothing other than an acknowledgement of the gaze: a case where an autobiographer perceives himself to have been always already seen coming by other writers who have preceded him in his autobiographical forays.[76]

The nature of autobiography means that this function of embodying the gaze of the Other can equally well fall to the reader. Indeed, this is precisely the implication behind Lejeune's concept of the *pacte autobiographique* [autobiographical pact]. Although Lejeune elaborates at length the specific combinations of focalization, narrative content and paratextual apparatus which will create the conditions under which the text will be deemed autobiography, he nonetheless posits the reader as the final arbiter of its generic status. The reader is thus free to confer or deny — perhaps perversely — the text's status as autobiography. The act of writing autobiography may be seen as an attempt to show an other, the reader, who the self is; but the author is never able to assume total mastery and trust that the reader will unconditionally believe in the assertions made. In order for autobiography to be autobiography, the self must always be more than who the self thinks it is; it is also who the reading other thinks it is. Moreover, the writing self is only the author of an *autobiography* if and when the reading other agrees that this is the case. Inherent to Lejeune's model of autobiography is an authorial awareness of the determining power of the scrutiny of the other: the other who will observe the self contemplating itself by reading his or her autobiographical work. Thus, to write autobiography is to invite scrutiny of both self and writing. In this way, the writing of autobiography (or even of self-writing that affirms it is *not* autobiography[77]) reiterates in distilled form the encounter between self and other which takes place in the symbolic: in autobiography as in the Lacanian symbolic, the encounter takes place through language; in each case, despite efforts to assert its identity, the subject's identity is only finally cemented at the point of encounter with the other, and both the identity and the encounter the self is powerless to control.

This description of a self with limited control over its identity and encounters with others is not unfamiliar to Sarraute. In her self-writing, the role of the other in constituting the self is a prominent concern, even if the self and other in question are not the *writing* self and the *reading* other. *Enfance* and *Tu ne t'aimes pas* both explore the determining importance of outsiders' perceptions for deciding what an individual's selfhood is, and the consequently limited control an individual has over their own identity. Indeed, much of the drama animating *Tu ne t'aimes pas* is driven by the narrators' fear of the scrutiny that the other directs towards them. The ideal for them is '[q]ue son regarde nous traverse sans nous voir' [that his gaze should pass through us without seeing us], but this is far from being their experience.[78] Through the course of the fragmentary chapters, the narrating voices' lack of confidence in the validity of their identity manifests itself in their constant concern for whether they are meeting the expectations that others have of them, such as the woman they encounter who invites them on holiday. Accepting the invitation unleashes doubt as they wonder if they will live up to the image the woman has of them, and whether she will regret her invitation: 'Serons-nous à la hauteur?' [Will we be up to the standard?], they ask.[79] A paroxysm of panic sets in as they attempt to select a suitably respectable self, an ambassador, or *délégué*, from amongst their number who will perform for her the version of the self that she desires: 'Il n'y a pas un instant à perdre... il faut qu'un de nos délégués... Ah mais voilà, quel délégué? Qui a-t-elle voulu inviter? Qui désire-t-elle rencontrer? Qu'attend, qu'espère-t-elle?' [There is not a moment to lose... one of our ambassadors must... Ah, but which ambassador? Who did she want to invite? Who does she want to meet? What is she expecting, hoping for?].[80] Judgements made by outsiders such as this woman are invested with such importance that the multiplicitous self uses them as a yardstick of its own worth. The identity the self has in the eyes of others assumes paramount importance, eclipsing any identity it might have for itself.[81]

This motif of a lack of autonomy over one's own identity is also prominent in episodes of *Enfance* where Natacha continually experiences the destabilizing of her identity as a result of encounters with others. Servants, visitors and family members — particularly her mother — call her sense of her own identity into question. What these encounters with adults bring out is a stark difference between how the child perceives herself and how adults do. This is the disturbing and unsatisfactory effect of letters written to Natacha by her mother:

> A qui s'adressent-elles donc, les cartes postales, les lettres que m'envoie maman? A qui croit-elle raconter, comme on raconte à un petit enfant, que là où elle

> passe un mois de vacances les fillettes portent des rubans rouges [...]. Elle ne sait pas qui je suis maintenant, elle a même oublié qui j'étais.[82]

> [So who are they written to, the letters and postcards that Mummy sends me? Whom does she think she is telling, in the way that one tells a small child, that there where she is spending a month on holiday the little girls wear red ribbons. She doesn't know who I am now, she has even forgotten who I was.]

In another episode, Natacha's remark about a peculiarly beautiful doll leads to a stinging rebuke from her mother, which immediately turns upside down the child's perception of herself and marks her out as a 'bad child': '"[u]n enfant qui aime sa mère trouve que personne n'est plus beau qu'elle"' ['a child who loves her mother finds that no one is more beautiful than she is'].[83] Moreover, it is often as a result of being *seen* that Natacha's identity is destabilized: such episodes often involve the child's discomfort at what others — her father's staff, for example — see in her, or see her doing, in incidents which cause the onlooking adult to revise their impression of her.[84] The degree of anxiety caused by this disjunction between self-image and the image others have of that self is shown by Natacha's hope that the activity of writing may alleviate the problem:

> Je ne suis rien d'autre que ce que j'ai écrit. Rien que je ne connaisse pas, qu'on projette sur moi, qu'on jette en moi à mon insu comme on le fait constamment là-bas, au-dehors, dans mon autre vie...[85]

> [I am nothing other than what I have written. Nothing that I don't know about, that they project on to me, that they throw into me without my knowing as they constantly do over there, outside, in my other life.]

What the narrator hopes is that her writing will offer 'sécurité' [security] against the unwelcome awareness she has of the presence of 'ce qu'on perçoit derrière moi' [what they perceive behind me]: an *alter ego* which is not her.[86] What this alerts us to is the possibility that, although writing for Lacan is an activity that can only cement the subject further into the symbolic, there may be an attempt in *Enfance* to use writing as a tool that attempts to neutralize the Other's gaze.

Recourse in *Enfance* to a coping strategy to neutralize onlookers, along with recurrent references to the intradiegetic self's discomfort on being exposed to the scrutiny of another, clearly cast the activity of writing the self for an external audience in an unpropitious light. Moreover, this is a view of autobiographical writing that *Tu ne t'aimes pas*, in its more distanced reflection on autobiography, seems to endorse. Here Sarraute enlarges on the idea that the specific environment created by the genre of autobiography sets the autobiographer up for a particularly uncomfortable outside scrutiny.

In a fragment devoted to self-scrutiny, the activity of self-contemplation — far from being an exercise in narcissism which allows the self to retreat from any relation with outsiders — is presented as driven from the outset by the requirements of an external other that rigorously dissects the self:

> — [...] Connais-toi toi-même, n'est-ce pas? vous le prescrivez... j'en suis capable, vous voyez, je viens me placer auprès de vous, à la distance où vous êtes, et de là je me regarde avec la même impartialité, la même impitoyable

> clairvoyance... J'ai su assimiler vos enseignements, j'ai retenu vos classements, j'applique vos règlements, je suis d'ici, de chez vous, un des vôtres... approchez-vous, tout près... regardons ensemble ce qui est là en moi...[87]
>
> ['"Know thyself," isn't that it? That's what you command... I'm capable of it, you see, I come to place myself alongside you, at the distance from myself that you are at, and from there I look at myself with the same impartiality, the same pitiless clear-sightedness... I have been capable of assimilating your teaching, I have retained your categorizations, I apply your rules, I am from here, from your stable, one of your own. Come close, really close... let us look together at what is there in me...']

The exploration of the self becomes an exercise in proving that the self has successfully internalized the parameters to its identity set by a scrutinizing outsider lying at some distance from that self. In her hesitant narration here, Sarraute lays bare how unsettling the regulatory presence of the external other is that lies at the heart of the autobiographical enterprise; and how its effect is to turn public self-contemplation into an attempt at self-justification. What Sarraute describes here corresponds to the operation of the Lacanian gaze. A reading of this fragment as an acknowledgement of the insistence of the gaze of the other in autobiography is only reinforced as we realize that the acknowledgement manifests at a metanarrative level too. In an apparent recognition that to produce an autobiographical self-portrait is to submit to comparison with one's autobiographical precursors, this fragment presents a riff on the opening of a canonical autobiography (and a text much admired by the author[88]), Rousseau's *Confessions*, in which the narrator declares:

> Je dirai hautement: voila ce que j'ai fait, ce que j'ai pensé, ce que je fus. J'ai dit le bien et le mal avec la même franchise. Je n'ai rien tu de mauvais, rien ajouté de bon [...]. Je me suis montré tel que je fus, méprisable et vil quand je l'ai été, bon, généreux, sublime, quand je l'ai été: j'ai dévoilé mon intérieur tel que tu l'as vu toi-même. Etre éternel, rassemble autour de moi l'innombrable foule de mes semblables: qu'ils écoutent mes confessions [...].[89]
>
> [I will say loudly: this is what I have done, what I have thought, what I was. I have told the good and the bad with the same frankness. I have suppressed nothing bad, added nothing good. I have shown myself just as I was, detestable and despicable when I have been so; good, generous and virtuous when I have been so: I have revealed my core just as you have seen it yourself. Eternal Being, gather around me the immeasurable crowd of my peers: let them listen to my confessions.]

In the light of Sheringham's assertion that autobiographers' relationships with their forerunners are fraught with anxiety, we may construe Sarraute's move to identify her autobiographical precursor here as a defensive measure that weakens the force of any comparison an outsider may make between her work and another's. Such a reading is reinforced by the treatment of the scrutinizing, reading other in *Enfance*.

In *Enfance*, the only acknowledgement that the autobiographical self lays itself open through its writing to the judgemental observation of the other comes at the very beginning, with the suggestion that by writing autobiography the narrators will be seen by others to be participating in a cliché:

> — Alors, tu vas vraiment faire ça? 'Evoquer tes souvenirs d'enfance'... Comme ces mots te gênent, tu ne les aimes pas. [...] Tu veux 'évoquer tes souvenirs'... il n'y a pas à tortiller, c'est bien ça.[90]
>
> ['So, you are really going to do that? "Evoke your childhood memories"... How these words embarrass you, you don't like them at all. You want to "evoke your memories"... there's no dodging it, that's what you want to do.']

This exchange corresponds exactly to what Sheringham would regard as a typical expression of the autobiographer's unease about their work.[91] However, the second narrator's reply quickly brushes aside what others may think: ' — Oui, je n'y peux rien, ça me tente, je ne sais pas pourquoi...' ['Yes, I can't help it, it tempts me, I don't know why'].[92] Nowhere else in *Enfance* is this potential for the writing of autobiography to provoke outside scrutiny of the self and its project raised. Indeed this possibility seems to be banished: the child Natacha resists producing genuine self-writing, as we have seen, and so does not enter the arena of danger. The only scrutinizing presence that the narrators of *Enfance* acknowledge is that which their partner narrator provides: neither of these narrators can be considered to embody the gaze of the other, since both have the same access to the corpus of memories which provide the foundations for the *Enfance* narrative. By splitting the narrating subject into two voices and incorporating into her narration a scrutiny of that narration, Sarraute stages an exposure of the self to the other's gaze. The author draws on the poststructuralist commonplace of the split subject, and institutes a split — but one that fends off the other, rather than expresses servitude to it. In overturning poststructuralist orthodoxy, Sarraute's manoeuvre also points to a desire to keep the other at arm's length from the Sarrautean self.

The discomfort of having the intradiegetic self exposed to the scrutiny of another is a recurrent motif in *Tu ne t'aimes pas* and in the recalled childhood incidents in *Enfance*. However, as the scrutinizing other's gaze touches the writing self of autobiography, not the written self, we see Sarraute draw away from acknowledging the disquiet it causes to the self. Instead of signs of anxiety, we find strategies that disavow the disquieting potential of external scrutiny, for example by simulating it in advance, showing that it is a scrutiny that has been anticipated. This strategy of neutralizing the Other's gaze by attempting to have always already seen it coming, and pre-empting it, corresponds to Žižek's discussion of how the nostalgic gaze functions. In nostalgic viewing mode, the gaze of the Other is obscured by an attempt to replace it with a controlled version of another's gaze: this very attempt, he argues, draws attention to the threatening gaze of the Other and confirms the subject's inscription within the psychoanalytic framework of the symbolic.[93]

In *Enfance* and *Tu ne t'aimes pas*, we find a preoccupation with the other co-existing with Sarraute's meditations on selfhood: a preoccupation which suggests the importance of the onlooking other for solidifying the self's identity. At the same time, the autobiographical self's vulnerability to the other that scrutinizes it (the reader) is downplayed. It is here that oblique defensive strategies are deployed, their role being to refute the autobiographical self's vulnerability to the onlooking other, whilst simultaneously protecting it against that very onlooker. One of these strategies is the author's emphasis on her texts' distance from conventional autobiographical discourse. At first sight this appears simply to be a necessary corollary of Sarraute's idiosyncratic conception of selfhood. Yet this stance on autobiography has a strategic importance, for it insulates a self unsure of itself from the gaze of the reading other, by insisting on the presence of a barrier between them: not a thin, porous one of the kind we find in *Ouvrez*, but an opaque and unbreachable one. We are now left with the question of whether Sarraute's concept of selfhood too might serve a similar strategic purpose.

For Sarraute, the self is steeped in plurality, and has an excessive quality which means that no other can satisfactorily seize what it is: a conception of selfhood which parallels Kristeva's concept of a self always imbued with the semiotic. What is especially significant about Sarraute's development of a theory of selfhood (and language) that could be called Kristevan is the challenge that Kristeva's semiotic presents to the hegemony of the Lacanian Other.

The essence of both Sarraute's and Kristeva's concept of selfhood is that there is an aspect to it which exists beyond language: the semiotic. In this, they both differ from Lacan, for whom the advent of language marks entry into the symbolic order of the Other, and concomitantly, the subject's loss of any relation or selfhood that is not negotiated through language. Kristeva sees the individual's ability to use language as bringing with it the ceaseless potential for the production of utterances marked by semiotic qualities: utterances that, in her view, perform a revolutionary poetic function. In Kristeva's thought, verbal expressions of the semiotic gesture to a realm outwith the signifying system of the symbolic order, thereby disrupting its logic: 'cet hétérogène à la signification opère à travers elle, malgré elle et en plus d'elle, pour produire dans le langage poétique les effets dits musicaux, mais aussi de non-sens qui détruisent [...] les croyances et les significations reçues' [This heterogeneousness to signification operates through, despite, and in excess of it and produces in poetic language 'musical' but also nonsense effects that destroy [...] accepted beliefs and significations].[94] Co-existing with the symbolic, the semiotic, according to Kristeva, is not subsumed under it, and the challenge it presents to the symbolic cannot be neutralized. The semiotic, be it in language or in the self, is exactly the place that the Other cannot touch. As the semiotic impregnates the self through its utterances, the self's capacity to emit these semiotic utterances allows selfhood itself perpetually to occupy a place always partially beyond the bounds of what the symbolic order recognizes as the subject.

The correspondences between Sarraute's vision of language and selfhood and Kristeva's, as revealed by Sarraute's attention to the materiality of language, her references to a pre-linguistic space, and her positing of a pluralized self, allow us to see Sarraute as contesting, in a similar way to Kristeva, the primacy of a Lacanian theory of a self constituted ultimately by its interchanges with the Other through the medium of language. By subscribing to a notion of a self which is traversable by the semiotic, the effect is to undermine the power of the other's gaze, to reject the stranglehold of the symbolic over the subject — which is to say, *the stranglehold of the Other* over what the self can be.

This reading of Sarraute's self-writing as self-writing that tries to write the other (and its gaze) out of the self is supported by Sarraute's aversion in *Enfance*,

Tu ne t'aimes pas and *Ouvrez* to a model of self-constitution that allows the self's identity to become the other's possession: an intolerable situation that only finally comes to be resolved in *Ouvrez*. The problem of the other's influence over the self's identity continues to resurface after *Enfance*, to be finally resolved in *Ouvrez*. Beyond this, the notion that Sarraute's self-writing is designed to protect the self from a threatening other is strengthened by the curiously highly-developed critical engagement with Lacanian notions of selfhood in *Tu ne t'aimes pas*.

In addition to its critique of autobiographical discourse, *Tu ne t'aimes pas* is explicitly concerned with matters that constitute familiar psychoanalytic terrain: a crisis of identity and the question of what constitutes the 'normal', as opposed to lacking, subject. The reproach others direct at the narrating voices, 'tu ne t'aimes pas' [you don't love yourself], isolates them from those around them, who find possession of a unified selfhood an effortless achievement: '[C]hacun d'eux est sain, normal, chacun d'eux s'aime, et nous... on s'aime pas' [Every one of them is healthy, normal, every one of them loves himself or herself, and as for us... we don't].[95] The non-unified subject is portrayed as inadequate, and for the majority of the narrative its difficulties are explicitly attributed to its abnormal lack of 'self-love', in what is difficult not to read — given Sarraute's knowledge of his work — as a sly allusion to Lacan.

Initially, the narrative's engagement with the theories of Lacanian psychoanalysis on the constitution of the self seems to be a dutiful one. Success in being able to love one's own self depends on a process strongly reminiscent of Lacan's mirror stage. In Lacan's thought, this stage is essential in preparing the individual for accession to subjecthood, and involves the infant learning to identify with the images others transmit to it of itself. Unfortunately for the narrating voices, in their case the process goes awry: 'ces images de nous-mêmes que les autres nous renvoient, nous n'arrivons pas à nous voir en elles...' [these images of ourselves that others send back to us, we don't manage to see ourselves in them].[96] However, Sarraute soon challenges the Lacanian view in which completion of the mirror stage is essential for successful accession to full subjecthood. It becomes steadily clearer to the reader of *Tu ne t'aimes pas* that the feeling of inadequacy engendered by this failure to conform to a template of the 'normal' self is misplaced. We recall that Lacan holds that the subject finds knowledge of its own lack an intolerable burden: this is where Sarraute most obviously seems to contest Lacanian theory, for the gradual realization of the multiplicitous self in *Tu ne t'aimes pas* is that in fact it does not lack at all; the multiplicity of the self which has been perceived as a mark of deficiency is exactly the opposite. *This* is the knowledge which has been elided. Sarraute portrays the self here as a site of plenitude, containing not one self, but many: men and women, young and old — yet the pressure to internalize and to perform this template of a single selfhood is such that the full plenitude of the self is denied.[97]

Furthermore, although for much of the narrative it has seemed that this multiplicitous self which occupies the place of the central protagonist is alone in failing to identify with (and thus love) the self as one entity, it transpires that difficulties in integrating disparate elements of the personality into a single subjectivity are more common than we have been led to believe. The voices realize that a group of people are 'reconnaissants' [grateful] to a third 'de s'aimer tant' [for loving himself so much], for this holds the whole group together; whereas 'inversement ce manque d'amour de nous-mêmes... ce manque doit éveiller en eux...' [conversely, this lack of love for ourselves... this lack must arouse in them...].[98]

Sarraute reveals how the presentation of the non-integrated multiplicitous subject as disadvantaged, exceptional and lacking is ultimately a fantasy that must be upheld for the sake of the mass, to underpin the delusion in which it lives. This wider social grouping is threatened by the idea that the non-unified subject who does not 'love' (that is, recognize or accept) its single self can and does exist, for this signals the possibility of an alternative mode of existence not requiring the discipline that the mass customarily accepts. To protect the delusion, the multiplicitous subject of *Tu ne t'aimes pas* must remain a pariah. Sarraute thus asserts the primacy of her own vision of a pluralized, intersubjective selfhood, presenting an alternative narrative of subjecthood that resembles Lacan's as being a collective fantasy, which is upheld for the sake of preserving the fragile identity it confers. Sarraute's portrayal of the multiplicitous self seeing through the charade of the single, unified self is another instance in Sarraute's self-writing where the external other is denied its purchase over the self; in the later *Ouvrez*, where the normality of the multiplicitous self is taken for granted and there is no mention of any possible alternative to this mode of selfhood, the self's liberation from the power of the other is absolute. However, in a telling coincidence, this portrayal in *Tu ne t'aimes pas* of a mass delusion, which has the effect of denying the other its power over the self, closely resembles Lacan's own concept of the fantasy.

In Lacanian psychoanalysis, fantasy is conceived as a coping strategy that aims to transform a hostile environment into a safe one.[99] Fantasy is a structure that sustains the split subject in the symbolic realm, allowing it to maintain some kind of relation with *objet a*, the irretrievably lost object of its desire. Through fantasy, subjects are able to sustain their impression that the system they are subjugated to is a coherent one, which encourages their continued obedience to it.

From a Lacanian point of view, the fantasy here would be Sarraute's suggestion that the multiplicitous subject is *not* the deficient one. This supposition gains some support from the text itself, whose narrative organization contributes to the impression of an outcome that is 'too good to be true'. For the narrating voices, the 'revelation' that others repress the non-self-loving subject to hide their own deficiencies resolves their identity crisis at one stroke — an improbable development, since it involves discounting all the paradigms which have been established over the course of the previous twenty-one fragments (and thereby all the tropistic dramas), all of which have been based on the inadequacy of the multiplicitous subject.

In Lacan's model, creating a fantasy entails dismissing the very circumstance which is most difficult for the subject to accept and the hardest for it to change. In the context of exploring Sarraute's relationship with autobiography, it is especially revealing to note the nature of the problem which the 'revelation' in *Tu ne t'aimes pas*, a commentary on autobiography, very conveniently enables to be swept aside: that of the ever-present and ever-scrutinizing other. Significantly, *Ouvrez* goes even further than *Tu ne t'aimes pas* in this: here, the other cannot encroach on the self, for otherness in the universe of *Ouvrez* is immanent and transitory. As selfhood is located at the level of utterance, any relation of alterity between one utterance and another is only fleeting, dissipating with the termination of the utterance. Most utterances, however, belong to the common 'nous' [us], and operate with reference to the same 'paroi'. Whereas this 'paroi', this cell wall or membrane, might be seen as the location of the other, it is an other without authority. This is despite the fact it controls which utterances may be voiced on any specific occasion, for it is susceptible to being overpowered in its gate-keeping function if the utterances it tries to hold back resist it.[100] It literally has no voice of its own: utterances debate between themselves whether to let a specific utterance through.

Sarraute's manoeuvre of annulling the force of the other appears to be an index of the high degree of turmoil that her self-writing reveals the other's scrutiny causes to the self. This is a turmoil illustrated perhaps most strikingly by comparing the anguish and fretfulness that accompany the performances of selfhood in *Tu ne t'aimes pas* with the quite different portrayal we see of jubilant self-expression in *Ouvrez*. Is it coincidence that what separates these two Sarrautean universes is the position of the other? Whilst the voices in *Tu ne t'aimes pas* feel outcast and rejected from a wider society to which they repeatedly defer, the voices populating *Ouvrez* acknowledge no connection with any others at all beyond the community of utterances in which they participate.

In their narratives, both *Enfance* and *Tu ne t'aimes pas* evince an anxiety on the part of the self about having its identity determined by another who views it from outside. This anxiety can be expected to impact on the author's relation to autobiography, as a genre where the autobiographical self gives itself to be viewed by another. Narrative devices in *Enfance* critique the self-representation offered, and highlight its non-correspondence with the self outside the text, suggesting that the autobiographer is unwilling for her reader to conclude that they have had the autobiographer's self given up to their view. The various observations Sarraute makes on memory, language and the nature of selfhood in the diegesis of *Enfance* offer one explanation for this unwillingness to cede the self to the possession of the reading other. A further and rather different explanation is provided by disapprobatory commentaries in Sarraute's earlier work about unethical desires which push some, including the reader desperate to consume information about a revered author, to breach the privacy of a cherished figure. Such commentaries raise the spectre of the reader as a malevolent presence: one who constructs a sinister and disquieting relation with the author through that author's text.

In the more distilled, depersonalized self-writing Sarraute pursues after and in response to *Enfance*, we find another explanation for this reluctance to expose the self to others. This is an explanation that *Enfance* cannot fully give voice to, and at the heart of it is the hold the other has over the self. Through its concept of the gaze as a disquieting object that the Other disempoweringly directs at the subject of the symbolic order, Lacanian psychoanalysis supplies a mechanism for understanding the reluctance of the autobiographer to offer his or her self for the reader's inspection.

Lacan's notion of the gaze of the Other suggests that the autobiographer has something to fear from the scrutinizing reader: for this unlocatable, unmasterable reader has the ultimate control over the realization of the self which occurs as a result of reading autobiography. Just as Natacha cannot prevent others from projecting a foreign identity on to her, so the autobiographer, despite any number of interventions she may make to correct erroneous readings of her self, is powerless to stop readers from doing the same. The only way the autobiographer has of writing the self whilst defending that self against the reader's projections and the anxiety they provoke is to prevent readers from projecting anything on to the author in the first place. And the only way to restore pleasure and self-mastery to the self-contemplation which is at the heart of autobiographical writing is to ignore the possibility of that self-contemplation being disturbed by the other's presence. This creates contradictory impulses: to rein in the reader on the one hand, and on the other not to show that their presence disturbs. The generic framework of autobiography is what invites readers to make projections on to the autobiographical self. It also endows them with the function of the gazing Other: of being, in their scrutiny of the autobiographical self, always in advance of its own scrutiny of itself. Thus the best way for the author to manage the contradictory impulses and to deal with the difficulty the reader poses; the best way to take back control over the destiny of the written self-image — given that the solution depicted in *Ouvrez* of eradicating the other altogether is not available — is to remove readers from the arena which empowers them to cause trouble: namely, the genre of autobiography. It is in this light that we should reconsider Sarraute's treatment in her self-writing of the nature of selfhood and autobiography: seeing her meditations on these subjects as reflections which distance her from the genre, wrest away the self from the gaze of the other, and restore to it sovereignty over its own selfhood.

Notes to Chapter 2

1. Sarraute, *L'Ere du soupçon: essais sur le roman* (orig. publ. 1956), 2nd edn, in *Œuvres complètes*, pp. 1551–1620. Attracting a lot of attention in literary reviews and from such figures as the already prominent Alain Robbe-Grillet, it was the publication of this volume that brought Sarraute to public notice (see *Œuvres complètes de Nathalie Sarraute*, p. 2041). Sarraute had previously published *Tropismes* (1939), *Portrait d'un inconnu* (1948) and *Martereau* (1953). However, in their first editions, neither *Tropismes* nor *Portrait d'un inconnu* made an impression on critics or the reading public — indeed the left over print run of *Portrait d'un inconnu* was finally sold for the price of the paper (see *Œuvres complètes*, p. 1743). *Martereau* received more attention, but a good amount of it was unenthusiastic (see *Œuvres complètes*, pp. 1787–91).
2. Sarraute's disdain for autobiography is well attested. Revealingly, she remarks: 'Je n'aime pas l'autobiographie. Je n'ai aucune confiance dans les autobiographies, parce qu'on [...] veut se montrer sous un certain jour. [...] C'est toujours très partial — enfin, moi, je n'y crois jamais. Ce qui m'intéresse toujours quand je lis les vraies autobiographies, c'est de voir "ah bon c'est comme ça qu'il voulait qu'on le voie"' [I don't like autobiography. I have no confidence at all in autobiographies, because [their authors] want to show [themselves] in a certain light. It's always very partial — at least, I never believe in them. What always interests me when I read true autobiographies is to see 'Oh, right, that's how he wanted us to see him']. Sarraute, 'Entretien avec Nathalie Sarraute', radio programme, prod. by Jean Montalbetti, broadcast on France-Culture, 5 April 1984. Cited in Lecarme and Lecarme-Tabone, p. 15. See also notes to *Enfance* in *Œuvres complètes*, pp. 1933–35.
3. Valerie Minogue, '*Tu ne t'aimes pas* — Notice', in *Œuvres complètes*, pp. 1958–70 (p. 1960).
4. The notion of *Tu ne t'aimes pas* and *Ouvrez* as being follow-ups to earlier self-writing is in harmony with Sarraute's own view of the genesis of her works: she affirms that her works all

grow out of the ones that come before, cf. her remarks in an interview with Geneviève Serreau, 'Nathalie Sarraute et les secrets de la création', *La Quinzaine littéraire*, 1 May 1968, pp. 3–4, cited in *Œuvres complètes*, p. 1846.

5. Sarraute, *Pour un oui ou pour un non* (1986), in *Œuvres complètes*, pp. 1495–1515.
6. Where referring specifically to the Lacanian Other (Autre) in the context of psychoanalytical theory, I shall indicate this by capitalizing the term, following Lacan's usage. Otherwise I shall not, hence Sarraute's 'other' will always be lower case, even where I am suggesting that the other she perceives or responds to is indeed one that fulfils the function of the Lacanian Other.
7. Rousseau, p. 5.
8. *Enfance*, p. 989 (my emphasis).
9. See Freud, *The Interpretation of Dreams* (1900), in *The Standard Edition*, IV and V (1953), pp. 277–508.
10. *Enfance*, p. 1060.
11. Ibid., pp. 1028–30.
12. Ibid., pp. 1029–30.
13. *Enfance*, p. 1035 (Sarraute's emphasis).
14. Ibid., p. 1035.
15. *Enfance*, p. 1145.
16. *Enfance*, p. 1024.
17. Ibid., pp. 990–91.
18. The semiotic in Sarraute has been explored elsewhere, although not in relation with the discourses of autobiography and psychoanalysis, which is my focus here. For a feminist reading of the Sarrautean semiotic, see Leah D. Hewitt, *Autobiographical Tightropes: Simone de Beauvoir, Nathalie Sarraute, Marguerite Duras, Monique Wittig and Maryse Condé* (Lincoln: University of Nebraska Press, 1990) pp. 65–69; also Ramsay, p. 125.
19. See the discussion of the semiotic by Julia Kristeva, *La Révolution du langage poétique: l'avant-garde à la fin du XIXe siècle: Lautréamont et Mallarmé* (Paris: Editions du Seuil, 1974), pp. 22–30. On the symbolic order, and the significance of the signifier therein, see, for example, Lacan, 'Subversion du sujet et dialectique du désir dans l'inconscient freudien' (1960), in *Ecrits*, II, 273–308.
20. Kristeva, *Révolution*, p. 22; Kristeva, *Revolution in Poetic Language*, trans. by Margaret Waller (New York: Columbia University Press, 1984), p. 25.
21. Kristeva, *Polylogue* (Paris: Editions du Seuil, 1977), p. 158; Kristeva, *Desire in Language: A Semiotic Approach to Literature and Art*, ed. by Leon S. Roudiez (Oxford: Blackwell, 1980), p. 133 (emphasis Kristeva's).
22. Very many commentators on Sarraute's *œuvre* have discussed her focus on tropistic responses. The classic account in English is that of Valerie Minogue, *Nathalie Sarraute and the War of the Words: A Study of Five Novels* (Edinburgh: Edinburgh University Press, 1981).
23. *Enfance*, p. 1089.
24. Ibid., pp. 1134, 1048.
25. Kristeva, *Polylogue*, p. 159; Kristeva, *Desire*, p. 133.
26. See especially discussions by Emer O'Beirne, *Reading Nathalie Sarraute: Dialogue and Distance* (Oxford: Clarendon Press, 1999), pp. 58–75; and Lejeune, who relates the narratorial device to the position of the reader in his 'Paroles d'enfance', *Revue des sciences humaines*, 217 (1990), 23–38; as does Sheringham, *Devices*, pp. 158–64.
27. In its portrayal of the self, *Enfance* thus shows consistency with Sarraute's depictions of intersubjective selfhood in earlier works. On intersubjectivity in Sarraute, see particularly Ann Jefferson, *Nathalie Sarraute, Fiction and Theory: Questions of Difference* (Cambridge: Cambridge University Press, 2000), and also Minogue, *War*.
28. It has been remarked that *Tu ne t'aimes pas* 'deconstruct[s] the discourses of autobiography' by Sheila Bell, 'Orchestrated Voices: Selves and Others in Nathalie Sarraute's *Tu ne t'aimes pas*', in *Narrative Voices in Modern French Fiction: Studies in Honour of Valerie Minogue*, ed. by Michael Cardy, George Evans and Gabriel Jacobs (Cardiff: University of Wales Press, 1997), pp. 13–35 (p. 31).
29. *Enfance*, p. 989.
30. *Tu ne t'aimes pas*, p. 1149.

31. *Tu ne t'aimes pas*, p. 1194.
32. Ibid., p. 1155.
33. Ibid., p. 1164.
34. Ibid., p. 1165.
35. *Tu ne t'aimes pas*, pp. 1165–70 (p. 1167).
36. Ibid., p. 1166.
37. *Ouvrez, prière d'insérer.*
38. Jefferson, *Questions of Difference*, pp. 3–4. Jefferson and Minogue in her *War* are amongst many critics who have offered commentaries on Sarraute's preoccupation with the representation and treatment of readers (usually readers of fiction). My own discussion of specifically autobiographical reader relations in Sarraute is informed particularly by the readings of Jefferson, *Questions of Difference*; Alan Clayton, *Nathalie Sarraute, ou, Le Tremblement de l'écriture* (Paris: Lettres modernes, 1989); and Sabine Raffy, 'Une lecture paranoïaque de l'œuvre de Nathalie Sarraute', in *Nathalie Sarraute, ou l'usage de l'écriture*, ed. by Antoine Compagnon and Philippe Roger, special edition of *Critique*, 656/7 (Jan–Feb 2002), pp. 12–21.
39. Sarraute, 'L'Ere du soupçon' (1950), in *L'Ere du soupçon*, pp. 1577–87.
40. Ibid., p. 1584.
41. Ibid., pp. 1584–85.
42. Sarraute, 'Ce que je cherche à faire', in *Œuvres complètes*, pp. 1694–1706 (pp. 1705, 1706). Sarraute is specifically addressing the reception of *Portrait d'un inconnu*, *Martereau*, *Le Planétarium* and *Les Fruits d'or.* As Jefferson has perspicaciously observed, Sarraute's strong and frequently expressed views on literary criticism and how her own work should be interpreted, together with her frequent unflattering depictions of readers and especially critics, position any academic commentator who deviates from them as a renegade adversary. See Jefferson, 'Nathalie Sarraute: Criticism and the Terrible Desire to Establish Contact', in Cardy, Evans and Jacobs (eds), pp. 37–56.
43. Sarraute, *Les Fruits d'or* (1963), in *Œuvres complètes*, pp. 521–620.
44. *Les Fruits d'or*, p. 608.
45. Sarraute, *Le Planétarium* (1959), in *Œuvres complètes*, pp. 339–519 (p. 452).
46. *Les Fruits d'or*, p. 609.
47. Simone Benmussa, *Entretiens avec Nathalie Sarraute* (Tournai: La Renaissance du Livre, 1999), p. 114 contains a brief account by Sarraute explaining the absence of her wartime experiences from her work. Reflecting Sarraute's public reticence on the subject of her home life, little to date has been published on Sarraute's life during the war, although this is touched on in the unofficial biography by Huguette Bouchardeau, *Nathalie Sarraute* (Paris: Flammarion, 2003). The fullest account, however, is given in the chronology Sarraute helped to prepare for the Pléiade volume of her complete works. See *Œuvres complètes de Nathalie Sarraute*, pp. xxix–xlvi (pp. xxxvii–xxxix).
48. *Enfance*, p. 1117.
49. Jefferson, *Questions of Difference*, demonstrates the central importance of these themes in the context of her discussion of self-other relations and difference in Sarraute's work.
50. Sarraute, *Les Fruits d'or*, pp. 609–10.
51. Sarraute, 'De Dostoïevski à Kafka' (1947), in *L'Ere du soupçon*, pp. 1557–77 (p. 1568).
52. 'De Dostoïevski à Kafka', p. 1568.
53. 'De Dostoïevski à Kafka', p. 1571.
54. 'De Dostoïevski à Kafka', p. 1568.
55. 'De Dostoïevski à Kafka', p. 1568; 'Ce que je cherche à faire', p. 1705.
56. Sarraute, *Les Fruits d'or*, p. 610.
57. Ibid.
58. 'De Dostoïevski à Kafka', p. 1568.
59. *L'Ere du soupçon*, p. 1585; cf. Jefferson's interpretation of these remarks in *Questions of Difference*, pp. 132–44. For Jefferson, this directiveness of the reader is rooted in what she describes as Sarraute's desire for closeness with the reader, or at least a certain type of reader. As is already clear from my reading of *Les Fruits d'or*, I do not share this view that Sarraute's essential desire in respect of her readers is to fuse with them.

60. *Enfance*, p. 1021; emphasis in the original.
61. *Enfance*, p. 1021.
62. *Enfance*, p. 1103.
63. *Enfance*, pp. 1103–04.
64. For comments by Sarraute indicating her disapproval of the recourse to psychoanalytical theories in the domain of literature, see Arnaud Rykner, *Nathalie Sarraute* (Paris: Editions du Seuil, coll. Les Contemporains, 1991), p. 168 and Benmussa, p. 44.
65. See O'Beirne, p. 14. For O'Beirne's psychoanalytical perspective on self–other relations in Sarraute, particularly in *Tu ne t'aimes pas*, see pp. 93–136. Where O'Beirne engages in a Lacanian reading, she posits relations between self and other in Sarraute as being mediated through the imaginary. The implications of this being Sarraute's chosen site for self–other relations are not fully pursued, however. Thus my interest is to consider how Sarraute deals with the threat of the more hostile environment of the symbolic. Other engagements with Sarraute's work from a psychoanalytical perspective can be found in John Phillips, *Nathalie Sarraute: Metaphor, Fairy-Tale and the Feminine of the Text* (New York: Peter Lang, 1994), who performs a Kleinian reading of her work, and in Sabine Raffy, *Sarraute romancière: espaces intimes* (New York: Peter Lang, 1988), pp. 183–247. See also Françoise Asso, *Nathalie Sarraute: une littérature de l'effraction* (Paris: Presses Universitaires de France, 1995).
66. Although Sarraute stated that she found reading Barthes a 'supplice' (*Œuvres complètes*, p. 1843), she demonstrates knowledge of Barthesian thought and terminology in her lectures: see Sarraute, 'Le langage dans l'art du roman', in *Œuvres complètes*, pp. 1679–94; and Sarraute, 'Ce que je cherche à faire'. In an interview with Rykner, Sarraute reveals her acquaintance with Lacan's thought, as well as an indication of her attitude towards it: she admits, for example, that she works in a critique of Lacan into an episode of childish wordplay in *Entre la vie et la mort* (1968), in *Œuvres complètes*, pp. 621–734: she states that the word games with 'Hérault'/'héros'/'erre haut'/'R. O.' etc. which the child indulges in in her novel are included there because, against the backdrop of lots of (in her words) 'Lacanien' puns, she wanted to restore to word games an innocent quality, rather than having them always connotive of a deeper philosophical dimension. See Rykner, p. 162.
67. My discussion of the symbolic order as the order of the Other is based on my reading of Lacan, *Ecrits*, and his *Le Séminaire, Livre XI: Les Quatre Concepts fondamentaux de la psychanalyse*, ed. by Jacques-Alain Miller (Paris: Editions du Seuil, coll. Le Champ freudien, 1973), trans. by Alan Sheridan as *The Four Fundamental Concepts of Psycho-Analysis*, ed. by Jacques-Alain Miller (London: Vintage, 1998).
68. My elaboration of the concept of the gaze and the stain is informed by Lacan, *Quatre concepts*, especially pp. 65–109 and Slavoj Žižek, *Looking Awry: An Introduction to Jacques Lacan through Popular Culture* (Cambridge, MA: MIT, 1991), pp. 91–125.
69. Lacan, *Quatre concepts*, p. 71; Lacan, *Four Concepts*, p. 74.
70. For the phenomenological conception of the gaze, see G. W. F. Hegel, *Phenomenology of Spirit* (1807), trans. by A. V. Miller (Oxford: Clarendon Press, 1977); and Sartre, 'Le Regard', in *L'Etre et le néant: essai d'ontologie phénoménologique*, ed. by Arlette Elkaïm-Sartre, rev'd edn (Paris: Gallimard, coll. tel, 1943), pp. 292–341. The gaze referred to in cinema theory is closer to this phenomenological model than the Lacanian model. On the cinematic gaze, see Laura Mulvey, 'Visual Pleasure and Narrative Cinema' (1975), in *Visual and Other Pleasures* (Basingstoke: Macmillan, 1989), pp. 14–26. I discuss Foucault's theory of the panopticon gaze in Chapter 4 in connection with Genet's prison experience.
71. Žižek, p. 114. Compare with Lacan, *Quatre concepts*, p. 245.
72. Žižek, p. 125.
73. Lacan, *Quatre concepts*, pp. 71–73. Unpleasure is to be understood in Freud's sense, where unpleasure equates to extra disturbance. cf. Freud, *Beyond the Pleasure Principle* (1920), in *The Standard Edition*, XVIII (1955), 1–64.
74. However, see my 'Resisting the Whole Picture: The Gaze, and Reading Autobiographies by Nathalie Sarraute and Georges Perec', in *Seeing Things: Vision, Perception and Interpretation in French Studies*, ed. by Simon Kemp and Libby Saxton (Bern: Peter Lang, 2002), pp. 161–75. O'Beirne, pp. 96–108, discusses the effect of being seen on Sarraute's (fictional) protagonists,

although she seems not to have in mind the Lacanian gaze: the gaze she refers to seems to be objectifying, rather than subjectifying, and is at the disposal of Sarraute's protagonists. See Jefferson, *Questions of Difference*, pp. 99–115 on gender and the gaze in Sarraute.

75. Sheringham, *Devices*, p. 17 (Sheringham's emphasis).
76. The gender-specific pronouns are used deliberately, since the autobiographical precursor is more likely to be male than female, cf. my discussion of women's relation to autobiography in Chapter 1.
77. This likeness between the genre and the symbolic applies even to writings which might be thought of as *non*-autobiography: the author who writes the self, but refuses the label autobiography is still measuring him or herself against the norms of this genre — by wishing to be seen *not* to conform to the autobiographical pact, for example.
78. *Tu ne t'aimes pas*, p. 1226.
79. *Tu ne t'aimes pas*, p. 1192.
80. Ibid., p. 1193.
81. This testifies to an almost Sartrian concern with what the self is *pour autrui*, cf. Sartre, *L'Etre et le néant*, pp. 257–471. This anxiety is a well-developed theme in Sarraute's work, as Celia Britton observes in *The 'Nouveau Roman': Fiction, Theory and Politics* (Basingstoke: Macmillan; New York: St Martin's Press, 1992), pp. 31–36.
82. *Enfance*, p. 1058.
83. Ibid., pp. 1038–46 (p. 1041).
84. See, for example, *Enfance*, pp. 1055, 1076.
85. *Enfance*, p. 1081.
86. Ibid.
87. *Tu ne t'aimes pas*, p. 1287.
88. See Lecarme and Lecarme-Tabone, p. 15.
89. Rousseau, *Les Confessions*, p. 5.
90. *Enfance*, p. 989.
91. Sheringham, *Devices*, pp. 15–17.
92. *Enfance*, p. 989.
93. Žižek, *Looking Awry*, pp. 111–14.
94. Kristeva, *Polylogue*, p. 158; Kristeva, *Desire*, p. 133 (translation modified).
95. *Tu ne t'aimes pas*, p. 1151.
96. *Tu ne t'aimes pas*, p. 1153; cf. Lacan, 'Le Stade du miroir'.
97. *Tu ne t'aimes pas*, p. 1165.
98. *Tu ne t'aimes pas*, pp. 1285, 1286.
99. For accounts of the concept of fantasy, see Lacan, *Quatre concepts*, pp. 168–69; 185–95; and also Žižek, '"I Hear You with My Eyes"; or, The Invisible Master', in *Gaze and Voice as Love Objects*, ed. by Renata Salecl and Slavoj Žižek (Durham, NC: Duke University Press, 1996), pp. 90–126 and 'Fantasy as a Political Category: A Lacanian Approach' (1996), in *The Žižek Reader*, ed. by Elizabeth Wright and Edmond Wright (Oxford: Blackwell, 1999), pp. 87–101.
100. *Ouvrez*, p. 23.

CHAPTER 3

❖

Perec
Autobiography, Possession and the Dispossessed Self

The trauma of Georges Perec's childhood is well-known to anyone acquainted with the author, and indeed much of his literary reputation derives from his attempts to write about it. The fact that this French son of Polish Jews became an orphan as a young boy, as a result of his father being killed on the battlefield and his mother deported from France to Auschwitz under Hitler's genocidal campaign, is understood to be the key to much of his work, from his autobiographical writings — most notably, *W ou le souvenir d'enfance* — to his fictions, such as *La Disparition*.[1] This novel, written entirely without the letter 'e', reminds us that besides his autobiographical writing centred on trauma, Perec is also well known for his involvement with OuLiPo, and his production of texts marked by the deliberate application of systems which constrain their form.

Perec's struggle to write the self and to show how it is touched by the Holocaust, undertaken chiefly and most painfully in *W ou le souvenir d'enfance*, has been explored by a number of Perec scholars, and thus my purpose will not involve recapitulating what is at the core of this text, namely the circumstances surrounding the deaths of Perec's parents and his survival; nor is this the place for an account of Perec's tortuous writing process.[2] It will be my aim instead to consider Perec's relationship to his own identity, a relationship fractured by his traumatic past, and to explore its impact on the evolution of his writing project and his relationship to the genre of autobiography. My discussion will take as its focus the notion of dispossession. This is a quality which indelibly marks Perec's selfhood, and, proving unconquerable, it yields an aesthetic and an ethic that become consciously inscribed in his autobiographical writing endeavour, thus reconfiguring dispossession as a positive value which the reader is asked to adopt.

Embracing dispossession as a positive value means voluntarily abandoning or accepting the loss of something one might otherwise expect to possess, instead of judging that not to possess it is to be divested of an entitlement. In my discussion, I shall describe Perec's self as being 'dispossessed'. Yet it is not only Perec who is divested of a sense of his selfhood: so too, in consequence of his self-dispossession, are his autobiographical texts and their readers. This puts Perec on a collision course with autobiography as a genre. His conspicuous state of dispossession highlights some of autobiography's default assumptions: if it is excessively hopeful to imagine that the author or his self-writing (and, subsequently, his readers) might 'possess' the Perecquian self, they are usually expected to possess a sense of what goes into constituting that self: an expectation encapsulated in the centrality Lejeune accords to the history of the development of the self in his theory of the autobiographical pact.

Lejeune's pact also shows how autobiography is inherently a fusion between self and system: without obeying the genre system, even where there is self-writing, there is no autobiography. Perec's interest in systems of textual constraint predates his major autobiographical works, and thus it is no surprise to see that his sensitivity to what is absent — that which leaves his autobiographical self dispossessed — is combined with scrutiny of what is present: the systems propping up autobiography. Concentrating particularly on the widely-read *W ou le souvenir d'enfance* and the less well-known *Je me souviens*, and, to a lesser extent, the earlier *La Boutique obscure*, this chapter explores the interrelationship between the self and the systemic in Perec's autobiographical writing through the figure of dispossession, which, it will be argued, knits them together.[3]

The nature of the trauma endured during childhood results for Perec in a relationship to his own self marked by dispossession. He can never take possession of his own past, nor of his self in the past, however much he feels driven to seize his self and communicate it in writing. For Perec, the experience of trauma that disrupts his sense of an integrated self is crucial to his sense of selfhood, yet it defies being adequately written about: Perec proves able to devise textual systems permitting him to 'write towards' his self, but he can do no more than that. This will have profound implications for his autobiographical writing, since any self-writing he undertakes, rather than restoring his self to him, must once again be dispossessed of the self behind it. My discussion here concerns Perec's attempts to exit from the melancholic cycle that is instigated by his frustrated desire to write the self: attempts which involve him reconfiguring the autobiographical text, enlarging its scope, to make a virtue rather than a catastrophe out of the dispossession of self. To this end, the conventional expectations set up by the generic system governing autobiography are jettisoned. Explorations of the individual's life and identity are attenuated in favour of wider concerns: in particular, the declining emphasis on attaining a grasp of the writing self permits the author to pay more attention to the notion of the system.

Perec's use of his own textual systems to ease the writing process, and his knowledge of the systemic ideology of the Nazis which resulted in his mother's deportation, leads him to the insight that systems, though often passing unnoticed, play a vital role in life, as in writing — either helping or harming us. It becomes Perec's project to use his self-writing to challenge existing systems, and more profoundly to challenge a climate of conformity and unquestioning subservience to systems. The generic system of autobiography is the foremost system to be attacked in Perec's self-writing, and the autobiographical text dispossessed of its autobiographical self is the weapon used to attack it: any expectation that the autobiographical text will yield sufficient information and insights into its author to enable the authorial self to be satisfactorily grasped will be overturned. Self-possession is not only impossible for Perec; for him, possession of the writing self becomes an undesirable, because unreasonable, goal. Significantly, however, Perec's attacks against the systems governing self-writing take the form of a transgressive praxis, rather than extra-diegetic onslaughts against autobiography. Thus he will invent writing strategies and structures which dispossess the reader of the assumption that reading an autobiographical text will or should supply them with a knowledge of the author which they can securely own.

The attempt to dispossess his readers of knowledge of the autobiographical self is conceived as a constructive contribution — not as a means of outmanoeuvring an undeserving, encroaching reader as we have seen in Sarraute. Perec comes to see the failure of the autobiographical text to remedy the dispossession of his self as a positive quality: it leads him to reappraise the outlook he finds ideologically dubious, according to which autobiographical writing should permit self-possession. Equally, his reorientation of his readers' expectations is designed to have positive consequences. Perec seeks to democratize autobiography by shifting emphasis onto the reader, using his own textual systems to create a space in his self-writing for the reader's non-possessive participation. The first step in persuading readers of autobiographical texts not to envisage knowledge of the writing self as a legitimate commodity for their ownership and consumption is to show them that it is unavailable even to the writing self.

Writing Loss: Memory and Selfhood

It is generally agreed in literary and academic circles that autobiography is, as Lejeune puts it, a text where the author 'met l'accent sur sa vie individuelle, en particulier sur l'histoire de sa personnalité' [emphasizes his or her own life, in particular the story of how he or she developed into his or her present self].[4] Therefore, the genre strongly invites — if not demands — that the author deploy his or her subjective memory in order to produce their work: no objective material evidence is likely to suffice in creating a history of a *personnalité* [self]: the French term suggests something in-between the person, whose existence can be empirically verified and objectively described, and the personality, whose qualities and essence are likely to be subjectively inflected, altering with the gaze of each new observer. However, what Perec's *W ou le souvenir d'enfance* illustrates is that it is not self-evident that this subjective memory will be available: the self may be without the memories that give it knowledge of its own history. For Perec, the fragmentary narrative that emerges in the second of the two strands of interwoven segments (I shall call these the childhood segments, distinguishing them from the W segments of the first strand) reproduces exactly the parlously patchy state of his own memories: reflecting on his childhood memories, his (not quite accurate) affirmation is 'je n'ai pas de souvenirs d'enfance' [I have no childhood memories].[5] Without memories of his past, Perec's capacity to write his individual history is acutely impoverished.

This writer's particularly traumatized history makes him especially susceptible to amnesia, as we shall see. However, Perec's case can be seen as an extreme version of a more general phenomenon: we have already encountered Freud's theory that we all suffer incomplete memories of our childhoods, as an effect of having been socialized and of internalizing paternal law. A symptom of this phenomenon is that events known to have happened, and to have had significant import for the child, will be omitted from the subject's conscious memory, while apparently uneventful happenings will be remembered vividly, functioning as screen memories.[6] This is reminiscent of the presentation of memories in both *W ou le souvenir d'enfance*, where very little is recalled, and *Je me souviens*, where hundreds of memories of trivial incidents are recounted. Freud suggests that our childhood memories are not pure: they are not memories of our childhood as it was, but rather as it has been recorded: 'it may indeed be questioned whether we have any memories at all *from* our childhood: memories *relating to* our childhood may be all that we possess.'[7]

This insight suggests that any attempts to imbue autobiography with the Proustian objective of recapturing times past will tend to flounder. Difficulties in recalling contribute to the problem that Perec calls the *indicible* [ineffable]. For him, the *indicible* is not simply a result of his forgetting, but 'c'est lié à la chose écrite elle-même, au projet de l'écriture comme au projet du souvenir' [it is linked to the written thing itself, to the project of writing just as it is to the project of remembering].[8] The disparity between what took place and written accounts of events is not unusual: it is an ubiquitous obstacle for autobiographers. For this reason, although the Holocaust-induced trauma suffered by Perec presents a specific challenge to the enterprise of producing an autobiographical narrative from memories, making his struggle against the *indicible* especially difficult and poignant, his difficulties with memory and his sense of self are relevant beyond the realm of Holocaust autobiography.

Perec's difficulties in remembering his childhood are so pronounced that he is almost bereft even of screen memories. To compensate for this, the childhood segments attempt to recount the past by narrating memories belonging to others, and to record something of the cultural soundtrack to his childhood. These snippets are, however, haunted by the absence of memories of significant events or happenings:

> Il y eut la Libération; je n'en ai gardé aucune image, ni de ses péripéties, ni même des déferlements d'enthousiasme qui l'accompagnèrent et la suivirent et auxquels il est plus que probable que je participai.[9]
>
> [There was the Liberation; I have retained no image of it, nor of the events leading up to it, nor even of the outpourings of enthusiasm which accompanied and followed it and in which it is more than likely that I participated.]

Similarly, a Xeroxed copy of the declaration of his birth is the 'ultime témoignage que j'aie de l'existence de ma mère' [the last evidence that I have of the existence of my mother]: Perec is obliged to refer to *evidence* of his mother's existence since he has no dependable memories of her.[10] He has one recollection of her, recounted three times, in which she takes him to the Gare de Lyon; but in each case the story is slightly different, implying a failure to recall the event as it happened. Even intimacy and love between Perec and his mother have to be attested by what is interpreted as an affectionate gesture in a photograph, rather than by memories of maternal tenderness.[11]

Theorists of trauma would maintain that it is no coincidence that it is the *significant* details of his childhood which escape Perec's conscious recollection: the pathology behind post-traumatic stress disorder involves the conscious mind failing to register traumatic experiences as they occur.[12] Instead, the unconscious registers them, and may replay them to the subject, who is unable to exert control over the reappearance of the images. As Cathy Caruth reports, rather than possessing its own memories and having in its possession a sense of self, the subject becomes possessed by its trauma, which brings only symptoms of the past, not knowledge: 'a history [of trauma] can be grasped only in the very inaccessibility of its occurrence.'[13] The genocidal events of the Second World War have been shown to leave survivors crippled with exactly this type of symptom.

Conscious memory is not the appropriate tool for a traumatized survivor of the Holocaust to use to access their history, since the events, although in the past, were never processed or mastered in the usual way, never became memories. Instead, the weight of those events continues to be felt in the present, although their manifestations in the present cannot compensate for their absence in the past. Regarding his memory and selfhood, Perec affirms: 'Je ne sais où se sont brisés les fils qui me rattachent à mon enfance' [I do not know where the threads ruptured that attach me to my childhood].[14] This demonstrates at once a lack of recall and a consciousness of the significance of his amnesia, which has led him to try to pinpoint the moment of its inception. Anxiety about being detached from one's childhood becomes all the more comprehensible as we understand that what is lost to the narrator is not only memory, but, since the self is rooted in its childhood, the possibility of understanding his own self:

> Mon enfance fait partie de ces choses dont je sais que je ne sais pas grand-chose. Elle est derrière moi, pourtant, elle est le sol sur lequel j'ai grandi [...]. [...] [L]'enfance n'est ni nostalgie, ni terreur, ni paradis perdu, ni Toison d'Or, mais peut-être horizon, point de départ, coordonnées à partir desquelles les axes de ma vie pourront trouver leur sens.[15]
>
> [My childhood is one of these things about which I know that I do not know much. Yet it is behind me, it is the ground on which I have grown. My childhood is not nostalgia, nor terror, nor paradise lost, nor Golden Fleece, but perhaps a horizon, a starting point, a set of coordinates from which the axes of my life will be able to find their direction.]

Without the framework his childhood would provide, Perec finds it impossible for his texts to live up to the expectation that an autobiography will deliver the comprehensive portrait of its subject implied by the choice of terms used in definitions of the genre as a self-written biography, or the 'histoire d'une personnalité': the story of the author's self.[16] As a result of this, Perec finds his autobiographical endeavours are paralysed. Whenever he attempts to write a text conforming to the traditional expectations, he notes '[c]ette quasi-impossibilité de continuer, une fois émis ce "Je suis né le 7. 3. 36"' [this near total impossibility of continuing, once this 'I was born on the 7. 3. 36' has been emitted].[17]

Perec's consciousness of the inadequacy of his self-writing in the face of the traditional autobiographical model is highlighted in *W ou le souvenir d'enfance* by the childhood segments, where, as I have argued elsewhere, the narrator presents a *negative* autobiographical narrative: that is, one which acknowledges what is conventionally required, but self-consciously fails to deliver it.[18] One segment recounts the *forgetting* of his family history by his relatives.[19] Our narrator insists that his recollections are 'non-liées' [not linked], defying the expectation associated with autobiography that a narrative will link moments together to create a continuum between a past and present self. The prolonged use of negative clauses foregrounds the narrator's inability to say what *was*:

> Henri [...] que j'ai pris l'habitude d'appeler mon cousin bien qu'il *ne* le soit *pas*, *pas plus* que sa mère Berthe *n'*était ma tante, Marc mon oncle, Nicha et Paul mes cousins.[20]
>
> Je *ne* me souviens *ni* de son nom *ni* de son aspect [...].[21]
>
> [Henri, whom I took to calling my cousin, even though he was *not*, *no more* than his mother Berthe was my aunt, *nor* Marc my uncle, *nor* Nicha and Paul my cousins.
>
> I remember *neither* his name *nor* his appearance.]

Since the childhood segments obey Lejeune's rule calling for congruence between author, narrator and protagonist, the reader will recognize the autobiographical mode governing the text, only to be confronted with a narrator who self-consciously and unhappily fails in his task, conveying in direct address to the reader, as well as in the form of his narrative, his unhappiness at failing to produce an autobiographical narrative relating his own history and origins.[22] This despondency is most evident in the eighth segment of *W ou le souvenir d'enfance*, in which autobiographical fragments dating from his adolescence are annotated using footnotes, thus revealing traces of the reworking his narrative has undergone.[23] Perec concludes:

> Quinze ans après la rédaction de ces deux textes [the fragments from adolescence], il me semble toujours que je ne pourrai que les répéter: quelle que soit la précision des détails vrais ou faux que je pourrais y ajouter, l'ironie, l'émotion, la sécheresse ou la passion dont je pourrais les enrober, [...] il me semble que je ne parviendrai qu'à un ressassement sans issue.[24]
>
> [Fifteen years after writing up these two texts, it still seems to me that I shall only be able to reiterate them: however precise the true or false details that I could add to them, the irony, the emotion, the detachment or the passion with which I could package them, it seems to me that I shall only achieve a repetition without end.]

Nevertheless, the gravity of the terror which Perec lived through makes it vital to persist in his endeavour. For trauma survivors, reports Dori Laub, the events of the past are a concerning presence, although the subject cannot master them.[25] Giving testimony assists the traumatized self: as part of the process of freeing oneself from the tyranny of being possessed by the symptoms of trauma, it is imperative to say the unsayable, to narrate the traumatic events and thereby reconstruct them outside the boundaries of the self. Beyond this personal basis for the testimony imperative, Holocaust survivors testify to feeling an ethical imperative in respect of others to try to recover and recount their past. This attitude to living in the aftermath of the

Holocaust corresponds to a strong current in contemporary thought, particularly amongst the Jewish community: it is considered essential that survivors bear witness to what occurred as a memorial to individuals who were lost, as well as the absent circles of relatives and friends; and to the lost sense of cultural identity embodied in the disappeared.[26]

Perec presents his writing — and his writing difficulties — as a memorial to the horrific fate of his parents, suggesting that autobiographical desire is likely to emanate from precisely those life experiences which resist expression:

> Je ne sais pas si ce que j'aurais à dire n'est pas dit parce qu'il est l'indicible [...] je sais que ce que je dis est blanc, est neutre, est signe une fois pour toutes d'un anéantissement une fois pour toutes.[27]
>
> [I do not know if what I would have to say is not said because it is the unsayable. I know that what I do say has a blankness, is neutral, is the sign for once and for all of an extermination for once and for all.]

The author himself makes a close connection between the traumatic nature of the circumstances of his childhood and his desire to tell his story:

> Je n'écris pas pour dire que je ne dirai rien, je n'écris pas pour dire que je n'ai rien à dire. J'écris: j'écris parce que nous avons vécu ensemble, parce que j'ai été un parmi eux, [...] l'écriture est le souvenir de leur mort et l'affirmation de ma vie.[28]
>
> [I do not write to say that I will say nothing, I do not write to say that I have nothing to say. I write, I write because we lived together, because I was one amongst them, my writing is a reminder of their death and the affirmation of my life.]

Perec's answer to the conundrum of how to testify to his experience against the backdrop of the Holocaust's legacy which has dispossessed him of his history and selfhood is to refuse to recount directly the defining events of his life. Instead he will bear witness to the past only by alluding to it, in a manoeuvre Lejeune characterizes as 'parler à côté' [speaking to the side].[29] Through the allegorical technique deployed in *W ou le souvenir d'enfance*, Perec is able to answer an imperative to bear witness to his history; by employing allegory in conjunction with two parallel intercut narratives, he creates a dispossessed text which tells 'towards' his experience, whilst foregrounding the gaps and absences which are central to Perec's relationship to his own past through the text's incompleteness and fragmentation. *W ou le souvenir d'enfance* communicates to the reader not only Perec's history, but also his relationship to that history, and the impact it has had on his sense of identity. Although the attempt to recount childhood memories in the childhood segments proves to be something of a blind alley, *W ou le souvenir d'enfance* nevertheless tells a story of his upbringing. Despite having claimed to be cut off from his childhood self, Perec realizes that his memories of childhood have inadvertently found their way into a story he wrote as a boy: 'cette histoire s'appelait "W" et [...] elle était, d'une certaine façon, sinon l'histoire du moins une histoire de mon enfance' [this story was called 'W' and it was, in a certain way, if not the story, at least a story of my childhood].[30]

The ostensible purpose of the W segments, the apparently 'fictional' half of *W ou le souvenir d'enfance*, is to recount a sea voyage taken by a protagonist named 'Gaspard Winckler' to search for a boy whose identity he has usurped by stealing his name, and who is now feared drowned.[31] Instead of finding the boy, 'Winckler' fetches up on the island of W, and begins to chronicle island life, describing what becomes ever more apparently a brutal and dehumanizing regime. Although the childhood segments are delineated as an autobiographical space, the W segments are the repository for what Perec intuitively knows to be part of his history, although it does not 'belong' to him, and neither memory nor empirical evidence can guarantee its veracity: the story of his mother after she was separated from him and deported. The W segments venture towards the horror of the deportations to concentration camps, thus allowing the *indicibilité* that cloaks the historical events, as well as the enterprise of autobiographical writing, to begin to be surmounted. Beyond this, they are also able to reveal how Perec's experience has the effect of derailing the discovery or recovery of an integrated selfhood which would feature in an autobiographical text.

'Gaspard Winckler' is handicapped in his efforts to help the mother of the missing boy in her search by having almost no knowledge of the other Gaspard. The child is described as deaf-mute — a quality that makes him unable to bear witness adequately — and is in all probability dead, living on only as the adult 'Gaspard Winckler': someone completely unconnected to the 'real' Gaspard. The narrative of the search parallels Perec's own experience of his identity: without memories, and having lost the family with whom he shared his childhood, Perec considers he is cut off from his origins. The adult Georges Perec can perceive no connection with the boy of the same name, who was blind, deaf and dumb to the events going on around him, and when he attempts to interrogate his memories and the material evidence that remains with him from his childhood, he is blown off the course which would lead him to discover who that boy was — which is key to understanding who the adult Georges Perec is. What blows Perec off his autobiographical course is his need to speak about the Holocaust. Yet anything he might say about it is inadequate to represent it, just as we learn in the very last W segment how the narrator's account misrepresented the sporting colony: the reader will have imagined a place where an Olympian standard of sporting achievement is likely to be found, whereas 'le 100 mètres se court en 23"4, le 200 mètres en 51"; le meilleur sauteur n'a jamais dépassé 1,30m' [the 100 metres is run in 23.4 seconds, the 200 metres in 51 seconds; the best jumper has never exceeded 1.30m].[32]

Given the apparent inability to relate his present self to the childhood self, it is no surprise that Perec seems to conceptualize his self as double, if not multiple: there are two Gaspard Wincklers in *W ou le souvenir d'enfance*, and Gaspard Winckler lives out additional existences in Perec's *La Vie mode d'emploi* and the unpublished *Le Condottiere* and *Gaspard pas mort*.[33] Mirroring this recourse to multiple *selves*, Perec makes multiple *attempts to write the self*, in works including *Je me souviens*, *La Boutique obscure* and several unpublished pieces. Emerging from this multiplication of selves and self-writings is the intimation that Perec accepts that the single, integrated self is forever lost to him, and that, consequentially, he must find ways of exploring a pluralized self. His pursuit of writing a fractured selfhood and its multiple faces involves him breaking with the expectations of autobiography and its readers: describing his various autobiographical ventures, he observes, 'chaque projet particulier n'entretient avec ce qu'on nomme ordinairement autobiographie que des rapports lointains' [each project maintains only distant relations with what we ordinarily call autobiography].[34]

The depictions of aspects of Perec's self encountered in *W ou le souvenir d'enfance* exist alongside several other self-representations. These images fit together to give a kaleidoscopic picture of the author, producing an effect akin to one that Doubrovsky describes. Doubrovsky argues that the truth of the subject is not susceptible to a single representation, although it is possible to produce a constellation of written texts, each one representing a different aspect of the author's person. For would-be autobiographers, this makes it easier to write autobiographically in a poststructuralist climate in which achieving a true self-representation in language is considered impossible. The quest for truth in autobiography need not wholly be abandoned, for a process of 'joining the dots' points towards the truth of the writer's selfhood:

> la 'vérité' n'est plus énoncée et installée en un texte privilégié; elle s'éparpille, se répartit entre les textes. Plus exactement, elle se joue (ou se noue) à leur jointure, s'expose à leur entrecroisement, se donne dans leur interface. En somme, le lieu du vrai est *l'entre-deux*.[35]

> [the 'truth' is no longer enunciated and sited in one privileged text, it scatters itself, shares itself out between texts. More precisely, it plays around (or knots itself up) at the point where they join, reveals itself where they intertwine, manifests itself at their interface. In sum, the site of truth is the *in-between*.]

The twin pressures of *indicibilité* and the testimony imperative mean Perec has much to gain from adopting Doubrovsky's emphasis on the in-between, the *entre-deux*, which complements Lejeune's notion of 'parler à côté' [speaking to the side] that we have already encountered. We recall that Doubrovsky's theory of writing the self also implies a mode of reading, and the case for reading for the *entre-deux* in Perec is strengthened by the depiction of the self as multiple, as we have seen it in *W ou le souvenir d'enfance*. This is also the way the self is represented in what Perec terms his 'autobiographie nocturne' [nocturnal autobiography], *La Boutique obscure*.[36] This work takes the form of a dream-diary, and foreshadows *Je me souviens* by presenting its reader with a succession of numbered fragments all written in the first person, which succeed in fracturing the self into many parts rather than unifying it. Not only are the dreaming, dreamt and writing selves separate, occupying different territories between the conscious and the unconscious, but there is nothing to connect any of the 124 selves who write with each other, or with those who dream, or with those who are dreamt. The enumerative structures used here and in *Je me souviens* mean that Perec writes not the self, but *a constellation of selves* who are each distinct entities, not joined in intersubjectivity as the voices in Sarraute's later self-writings are.

As we have seen, conceptualizations of a pluralized selfhood are incompatible with the generally received understanding of the autobiographical self. Lejeune's declaration that autobiography is founded on an exact correspondence of the protagonist's self to the narratorial and authorial ones makes explicit the assumptions of earlier critics, for whom writing autobiography involves the establishment of the subject's unity (and unity of intention), making autobiography the preserve of the unified subject. Autobiography allows no room for the self that is elusive, or fragmented into multiple components. Alternative approaches to autobiography assert that autobiography's function is more performative: not so much to produce a written 'copy' of a real-life 'original', but to *create* a cohesive — even ideal — self.[37] Contrasting with both these models, Perec's autobiographical writings emphasize the incompleteness of the written self-representation, and overtly divorce the written subject called Perec from the living person.

The childhood segments of *W ou le souvenir d'enfance* showcase the inevitability of his failure to deliver the narrative of the individual self that an autobiography is traditionally expected to supply. Perec finds it impossible to deliver an adequate self-portrait in writing if he is to be constrained by the autobiographical convention that calls for a whole picture. Through the allegorized metanarrative on the difficulty of conducting a search for the lost boy, the W segments reveal the struggle with the autobiographical genre which besets the author whose story does not fit. The success Perec has in communicating his message by means of 'parler à côté' in the W segments contrasts starkly with the painful attempts to tell the story of his upbringing in the childhood segments, and shows the inadequacies of the prevailing autobiographical conventions. Perec demonstrates that, for him, any success in writing the self depends on breaking free from the shackles which codify autobiography.

In this, Perec may seem to share common ground with his poststructuralist contemporary, Barthes, whose *Roland Barthes* was published in the same year as *W ou le souvenir d'enfance*. Yet, in contrast to Barthes, killing off autobiographical ambition altogether and writing the self as a fiction is not Perec's objective: his will to commit something of the self's lived experience to the text makes this inappropriate. Finding an appropriate means to satisfy the twin objectives of escaping the manacles imposed by genre and answering the testimony imperative will be difficult, however. For Sheringham, the fetishized autobiography that plainly dismisses the aspiration of creating or representing a whole self is not an indicator of the death of autobiography, and the birth of something new: it merely constitutes a variation on the traditional model.[38] If proclaiming incompletion in autobiographical writing becomes part of the generic model, then Perec's fragmentary autobiography, self-consciously riddled with holes whilst devoid of a whole, risks simply being reabsorbed within the genre.

Despite the difficulties involved, and the need to shake off inappropriate generic constraints, Perec retains an ambition to connect the self, life and writing together faithfully in an autobiographical text. Given the inevitability that writing the self for Perec will be writing the self dispossessed, this looks rather like having one's cake and eating it, and the only way Perec can manage the contradiction is to reconsider what the cake is. Both his personal history and his experience of autobiographical writing lead him to scrutinize the system behind the genre of autobiography and, rather than reject or comply with it, to reconfigure the edifice of autobiography so that there is space for the dispossessed self.

Within *W ou le souvenir d'enfance* there are the seeds that provide Perec with the means to reach beyond the (to him) nonsensical demands of autobiography and to reform it. Thus he is able to write an 'autobiographie critique' [critical autobiography], as Lejeune puts it; in the words of Claude Burgelin, 'Perec oblige l'autobiographie à une sorte de révolution copernicienne, par l'usage qu'il fait de la parodie, de la citation, de la réécriture' [Perec obliges autobiography to undergo a sort of Copernican revolution, through his use of parody, citation, and re-writing].[39] The breakthrough for Perec comes at the point where he discovers that the mode of his *énonciation*, the structures behind his words, can communicate what his words, the *énoncé*, cannot. In this text Perec becomes an innovator of autobiography, searching for new modes of self-writing that, if they cannot say the unsayable (that is, the *indicible*), can at least get near to it by oblique means, using metaphors and allegory to 'parler à côté'. Perec's chosen mode of self-depiction calls for a new conception of autobiography. This also heralds the need to change reading practices, so that a more active reading stance is adopted: one which involves another form of what we might call, to borrow from Žižek, 'looking awry'. Perec's success in finding new ways to write and have read the autobiography dispossessed of its self lies in his willingness to critique systems, but also to make use of them.

Systems and Autobiography

As a writer traumatically dispossessed of his self, Perec finds that the strictures of the conventional autobiographical text leave him with 'rien à dire' [nothing to say], despite the impetus that drives him to 'dire' [say]. This serves as something of an indictment of the generic rules of autobiography, and it leads Perec to produce a negative and melancholic narrative when he attempts to write conventional autobiography in the childhood segments of *W ou le souvenir d'enfance*.

Yet although it is the system behind autobiography which hampers Perec's self-expression, systems also rescue his writing project. As a result of Perec's own self-dispossession, his autobiographical writing too must be dispossessed of the authorial self. Writing in 1979, Perec explains that the only way to write autobiographically was to undertake a 'projet autobiographique détourné' [redirected autobiographical project] based around textual constraints.[40] Having employed formal constraints as a backbone in texts pre-dating *W ou le souvenir d'enfance*, he introduces into this text a number of writing strategies and systems that will ease his struggle to write autobiographically, of which his mode of oblique testimony, 'parler à côté', is one; textual systems are further developed in *Je me souviens*, his only successfully completed autobiographical work following *W ou le souvenir d'enfance*. These formal innovations limit the scope of each self-writing project, build in fragmentation and absence, and thus overtly depart from the aim of producing a complete picture of the self, which is the guarantor of intentionality upon which the system of autobiography is based.

The reduced emphasis on capturing the self in his autobiographical writing stimulates Perec to expand the ambit of his work. His struggles with the system of the autobiographical genre contrast with his success at employing his own textual systems in autobiographical texts such as *La Boutique obscure* and *Je me souviens*, where his self-devised structures evince a generative power which facilitates his self-writing and the process of remembering. As his allegorical treatment of a systematized regime on W testifies, systems also have personal significance beyond the text for Perec. In an iconoclastic gesture which has the side-effect of promoting anamnesis, he confronts the ideological hinterland of systems which admit no gaps. Perec's sensitivity to political and ideological issues predates his autobiographical work: early in his writing career, Perec had already declared his determination to describe and engage with the world beyond what are, to him, the sterile literary concerns of the existentialists and *nouveaux romanciers*.[41] He writes that the task of literary writing is to:

> poser comme base que le monde n'est pas tel quel [...] qu'il n'est nul éternel, nul explicable, nul accessible qu'on ne puisse un jour dominer. Moyen de connaissance, moyen de prise de possession du monde, la littérature devient ainsi l'une des armes les plus adéquates qui, à long terme, permettent de lutter contre les mythes que sécrète notre société.[42]
>
> [posit as a starting point that the world is not just as it is [...] that there is nothing eternal, nothing explicable, nothing accessible that we will not one day be able to master. A means of knowledge, a means of taking possession of the world, literature thus becomes one of the best adapted weapons which, in the long term, makes it possible to struggle against the myths that ooze from our society.]

Systems inside and outside the text, which had been a principal preoccupation of his non-autobiographical publications, thus come to assume a prominence in his autobiographical work. This leads to a more positive mode of autobiographical writing that emphasizes what *can* be written rather than what cannot, and which makes a virtue out of self-dispossession.

In embracing the text dispossessed of self, paradoxically Perec is able to recover more of it. The experience of noting his dreams for the project that was to become *La Boutique obscure* reveals how the activity of writing can generate memories: 'je croyais noter les rêves que je faisais: je me suis rendu compte que, très vite, je ne rêvais déjà plus que pour écrire mes rêves' [I believed I was noting the dreams that I was having: I realized very soon that already I was no longer dreaming except in order to write down my dreams].[43] Although doubt is cast over the authenticity of the resulting dreams, nevertheless the fact of remembering them at all constitutes a triumph over Perec's crippling amnesia. This insight into the generative powers of textual systems is later used to productive effect in *Je me souviens*, in which: 'ce sont des souvenirs qui sont provoqués, des choses oubliées que je vais faire resurgir' [these are memories that are provoked, forgotten things that I will cause to surge forth again].[44]

Although Perec finds greater success in writing his self as a result of accepting self-dispossession, using structuration to draw attention to self-dispossession in the autobiographical text is founded on more than self-interest. Embracing the autobiographical text dispossessed of the self constitutes an extension of his principled views on systematization. An evident enthusiast for language systems, as his association with OuLiPo demonstrates, Perec makes continual recourse to textual systems to provide a backbone to his works, but these are always non-totalizing. Perec harbours a mistrust of totalizing systems, and a political commitment to uncovering their ideological blind spots. This finds expression in his postscript to *W ou le souvenir d'enfance*, where he condemns the late ex-Senator Augusto Pinochet of Chile, connecting his regime to the Nazi administration that is allegorized through the presentation of the sporting colony W:

> J'ai oublié les raisons qui, à douze ans, m'ont fait choisir la Terre de Feu pour y installer W: les fascistes de Pinochet se sont chargés de donner à mon fantasme une ultime résonance: plusieurs îlots de la Terre de Feu sont aujourd'hui des camps de déportation.[45]
>
> [I have forgotten the reasons which, at twelve, made me choose the Tierra del Fuego as the location for W: Pinochet's fascists took it upon themselves to give my fantasy a final resonance: several islets of the Tierra del Fuego are today concentration camps.]

This commentary grounds Perec's vigilance against the threat of dehumanizing systems, as well as his encouragement of greater vigilance in others, in his own life-writing, which is inextricably bound up in the history of atrocities in Europe. Due to the difficulty Perec finds in bearing adequate witness to historical events, he cannot but be aware of epistemological limits, which are made strikingly apparent by the fact that Perec's story of his childhood cannot be made to fit into the autobiographical childhood segments, but must be allegorized in the parallel narrative. The writer is therefore very aware of the importance of things that defy empirical knowledge and logic, and this drives his suspicion of systems. This insight surfaces in the W segments, which testify to the hampering effect that a too rigid instance on positivist modes of thought can have: Otto Apfelstahl narrates the story of the missing Gaspard Winckler, relying on solid documentary evidence of the ship's routine to confirm his suppositions about the fate of the missing person. Apfelstahl rejects the proposition put by 'Gaspard Winckler' that maybe the child Winckler was somewhere he should not normally have been, and this accounts for his absent corpse:

> [Winckler] — Il était peut-être tombé à la mer.
> [Apfelstahl] — C'est très peu probable. Il aurait fallu qu'il soit sur le pont et il n'avait aucune raison d'y être.
> — Mais s'il y avait été quand-même?
> — A trois heures du matin! Qu'aurait-il fait sur le pont à trois heures du matin?[46]
>
> [(Winckler) 'Perhaps he had fallen into the sea.'
> (Apfelstahl) 'It is very unlikely. He would have had to have been on the bridge and he had no reason to be there.'
> 'But if he had been there all the same?'
> 'At three o'clock in the morning! What would he have been doing on the bridge at three o'clock in the morning?']

Apfelstahl's refusal to listen to unsubstantiated hypotheses that rely on chance and illogical behaviour leaves him in an impasse, for ultimately, whilst not disputing its occurrence, he can offer no explanation for Winckler's disappearance. The result is that he must hand on his inquiry to someone else, 'Winckler', who might have more success. Perec illustrates how a restrictive epistemological approach simply has nothing helpful to say to anyone confronted with the inexplicable or the *indicible*, the ineffable. Furthermore, the narrative of life on W suggests that any system founded exclusively on logocentric principles, such as those which hinder Apfelstahl's inquiry, is ideologically dubious, potentially inhumane, and should be regarded with suspicion. Given Perec's aversion to logocentric approaches, deriving partly from their tendency to suggest that there is only one possible and inevitable outcome, and his preference for 'parler à côté' [speaking to the side], it is no surprise to find his views on systems are not advanced didactically. Instead, they are implied through his portrayal of W. Allegorizing the supremacist ideology and organizational mania of the Nazis, the colony of W is portrayed as driven by competitive sporting activity, organized through a highly regimented and elaborate system that exists to produce and regulate sporting encounters:

> Tous les matins [...] un Athlète d'un des villages, désigné la veille au soir par son directeur sportif, part à contresens et défie le premier athlète qu'il rencontre. Trois possibilités peuvent se présenter: ou bien l'Athlète qu'il défie est un Athlète de son propre camp, et les compétitions du jour seront des championnats de classement interne; ou bien il appartient à l'un des deux villages connexes, et ce seront des championnats locaux; ou bien il appartient au village non connexe et ce sera une rencontre de sélection.[47]

> [Every morning, an Athlete from one of the villages, designated the previous evening by his sporting director, leaves in the opposing direction to the others and challenges the first athlete that he encounters. Three possibilities can arise: either the Athlete that he challenges will be an athlete from his own camp, and that day's contests will be internal league competitions; or else he will belong to one of the two adjacent villages, and there will be local competitions, or else he will belong to the non-adjacent village and there will be a qualifying trial.]

Although the encounters brought about by this convention appear innocuous at this stage in the narrative, it is this same regulatory impetus which enables the sickening spectacle of competitive gang-rape known as the 'Atlantiades'. At this point the barbaric lack of respect for human dignity which characterizes the regime governing W emerges, and it is a barbarism that exists not despite *but due to* the colony's logical culture which devises systems to organize the athletes' lives. An undue concern for order and logic, far from serving human interests, harms them. The allegory device is used to denounce the mania for systematization, forming part of a wider scrutiny by Perec of systems everywhere. As will become clear, this wider engagement strengthens the argument for linking the excessively organizational systems operating on W with those of the Nazis, and other systems besides. Perec's flagrant breaches of the rules traditionally seen as governing the genre system of autobiography, rules which inhibit Perec's self-expression, indicate that this system too is one of those deserving criticism.

In spite of this implicit critique of textual systems, the success of *W ou le souvenir d'enfance* nevertheless depends on a textual system: allegory. The use of this particular constraint is especially appropriate for Perec, since it gestures back to the *indicible* [ineffable], the constraint in his life that inspires and threatens his self-writing.[48]

Often systems of constraint are the only motor which drives Perec to write: in *W ou le souvenir d'enfance* the partitioning into segments derives from the original need to produce the text in episodes for serialization in *La Quinzaine littéraire*.[49] Systems that produce formal constraints in Perec's autobiographical writing are thus not mere exercises in textual showmanship: they express in themselves something of Perec's self. They also themselves participate in a critique of systems, demonstrating how systems can be uncoupled from ideological blind spots to facilitate both iconoclasm and anamnesis.

The use of obtrusive systems of textual constraint in Perec's autobiographical texts is an expression of the limits to the endeavour undertaken. Building incompletion in at the outset allows his writing to escape from the negativity of concentrating on its own failure; opening up the remit of the autobiographical text to take in a wider concern about the role of systems lends his autobiographical writing a positive purpose. Perec shifts his emphasis away from trying to recapture what it was like to be himself in the past, instead using separate works, of which *Je me souviens* is one, to develop a multiple self-writing that chronicles those experiences which can be chronicled; for Perec this means privileging daily life. This leads to projects which focus on a single facet of the writer's everyday experience as he remembers it, recording it often over a very protracted time span. Such projects to chronicle the quotidian include listing items of food eaten in the course of one year, places slept in *Lieux où j'ai dormi*, and the personal associations of certain Parisian locations in *Lieux*.[50]

One of the few projects of this type which Perec was able to bring to fruition, *Je me souviens* has a twin purpose. Firstly, it imparts Perec's memories to the reader: it thus fits within autobiographical parameters. However, it also functions as a critique of autobiography and the assumptions brought to it, since its structure and content mean that the text operates at the antipodes of the genre. *Je me souviens* is composed of 479 separate, numbered recollections of things remembered from popular culture or events from the recent past.[51] Each of these recollections is entirely discrete and commences 'je me souviens'. The disconnection extends to its style, which is characterized by bareness and simplicity of expression. The list of memories is de-contextualized, without details which would explain why these particular 479 snippets have been recounted at the expense of others; chronological organization is also rejected, as Perec fails to situate the recollections temporally, even though the original manuscript included dates of composition for each entry. Thus the text, whilst supplying some of the stuff of conventional autobiography, also defies expectations: it refuses to deliver the raw material for any self-portrait, let alone a complete one: its focus on recalling the everyday entails dealing in cultural memories common to many, rather than personal memories unique to the individual. The lack of an interpretative overview to the series of micro-narratives ensures the gaps Perec considers inherent 'au projet de l'écriture comme au projet du souvenir' [to the project of writing just as to the project of remembering] are made prominent in the text.

The bareness of *Je me souviens* might suggest that it impoverishes the genre of autobiography: by subverting the norms of the genre, Perec begs the question of the text's merit. However, Perec detects an ideological bias latent in conventional autobiography, suggesting that the genre is always already impoverished. Without the melancholy of *W ou le souvenir d'enfance*, Perec's eye-catching but simple innovations in *Je me souviens* place a spotlight on what else is present and possible. Perec thus probes into a deep-seated and widely-dispersed value system pervading autobiography, just as his treatment of logocentrism in *W ou le souvenir d'enfance* revealed its ideological underbelly. Paying close attention to tiny and apparently insignificant details from his life is valuable precisely because ideology encourages us to overlook them.

In *W ou le souvenir d'enfance*, the narrator observes that part of his loss comes from having very largely forgotten the seemingly insignificant, yet personally resonant, objects and events that form the fabric of all our existences. These are the backdrop on to which the great events of our lives — love, loss, achievement — are embroidered:

> 'Je n'ai pas de souvenirs d'enfance': je posais cette affirmation avec assurance, avec presque une sorte de défi. L'on n'avait pas à m'interroger sur cette question. Elle n'était pas inscrite à mon programme. J'en étais dispensé: une autre histoire, la Grande, l'Histoire avec sa grande hache, avait déjà répondu à ma place: la guerre, les camps.[52]
>
> ['I do not have any memories of childhood': I put forward this affirmation with confidence, with almost a sort of defiance. I was not to be interrogated on this question. It was not included in my programme. I was excused from it: another history, the Great, History with its great axe, history with a capital H, had already answered in my place: the war, the camps.[53]]

The importance of his own private history, populated with trivial happenings whose full sense is apparent only to him, is confirmed by the commemoration of film stars and other figures from public life in the childhood segments, anticipating the later recourse to this form of life-writing in *Je me souviens*.[54]

Perec's sensitivity to the effects of ideology is already clear in his 1974 essay *Espèces d'espaces*, where he argues for an increased scrutiny of the systems in which we are caught and their implications: '[d]e temps en temps, pourtant, on devrait se demander *où* on (en) est' [yet from time to time, we should ask ourselves *where* we are (with things)].[55] *Espèces d'espaces* performs this task, revealing how our lives and attitudes are shaped by external influences, such as the design of the dwelling in which we live (or the genre in which we write).[56] In order to reveal the lurking fingerprints of ideology, what Barthes would call its 'mythologies', Perec advocates a project reminiscent of Michel de Certeau's *L'Invention du quotidien*.[57] We should pay attention to the fabric of our everyday lives, not simply because in Perec's case everyday life is more easily remembered than life's great events, but also because ignoring this area of life is to collude with the ideological idea that it is without interest: 'car ce que nous appelons quotidienneté n'est pas évidence, mais opacité: une forme de cécité, une manière d'anesthésie' [because what we call the everyday is not transparent, but opaque: a form of blindness, a means of anaesthesia].[58] *Je me souviens* continues the vigilance of *Espèces d'espaces* against the stupor which blinds us to the ideological assumptions behind systems.

The preoccupation with the trivia of everyday life in *Je me souviens* contrasts sharply with the preference that Perec, in common with commentators discussed in this study's first chapter, discerns in autobiography for grand narratives concerned with either great events or great men. That only autobiographies of the elite are valued becomes obvious when we consider the social ranking of the people that write, and publish, autobiography. Perec indicates the ideological pedigree of the genre when he describes the type of recollections included in *Je me souviens*:

> elles [the recollections] ne valaient pas la peine d'être mémorisées, elles ne méritaient pas de faire partie de l'Histoire, ni de figurer dans les Mémoires des hommes d'Etat, des alpinistes et des monstres sacrés.[59]
>
> [They (the recollections) were not worth the effort of being committed to memory, they did not merit being a part of History, nor of featuring in the Memoirs of statesmen, mountaineers or great actors.]

Besides privileging the memories and self-writing of only certain types of individual, autobiography is also dominated by one type of memory, known as episodic memory: this relates to things remembered because the self is personally involved in the memory, as in the recollection of a family holiday, or in Perec's case, 'je me souviens que je n'aimais pas la choucroute' [I remember that I didn't like sauerkraut].[60] These are exactly the memories Perec does not have. In this text he is able to dodge the problem of his amnesia by enlarging the scope of his autobiographical work to include semantic memories, which do not usually become the focus of autobiography.[61] These are what the self remembers but never witnessed, for example a figure in public life known only through the media, such as 'Je me souviens de la Bande à Baader' [I remember the Baader-Meinhof Gang].[62] This tactic allows him not to dwell on the paucity of his episodic memories, without requiring him to entirely leave behind his personal history: the semantic memories may connect back to his lived experience. *Je me souviens* shows that self-writing *can* be produced from such material, and invites us to think about what ideological assumptions prevent this from occurring more often.

For Perec, writing *Je me souviens* is a rebellious act, moving away from the inexorable macro-narrative of 'l'Histoire avec sa grande hache' [History with its big axe and capital H] that so dominates *W ou le souvenir d'enfance*, in favour of creating a plethora of micro-narratives. However, the importance for Perec of producing such micro-narratives as '[j]e me souviens du *Théâtre de Lutèce*, rue de Jussieu' [I remember the *Lutèce* theatre on the rue de Jussieu] goes beyond asserting the existence of his memories, or his independence from literary blueprints, or his determination to interrogate these: a happy side effect of the process is that it encourages remembering.[63] The text produced insulates Perec against future gaps in his remembrance, since his memories are committed to paper; yet in its manner of composition, it leaves intact the gaps between the object remembered and its significance. For the author, this detail ensures that *Je me souviens* takes on a non-totalizing and generative quality: on re-reading it, Perec can fill in his own gaps, his anamnesis prompted by the efforts to fix and chronicle his recollections. Although they may seem inconsequential, these reminiscences keep significant histories alive.

Perec declares he has produced a depersonalized text where the emphasis is on the present moment in which 'je me souviens' [I remember]; the recollections listed are 'surtout pas des souvenirs personnels' [certainly not private memories].[64] Nevertheless, an alert reading of *Je me souviens* reveals that it does contain resonances of Perec's troubled past. The text functions as an index of the traces the past has left on its author, and so the reader of *W ou le souvenir d'enfance* is not surprised to see that under 'Famille (souvenirs de)' in the index composed by the author, there are only two memories catalogued, whilst under 'Guerre mondiale (Seconde)' there are fifteen. One of these is memory no. 168: 'Je me souviens des six-jours au Vel d'hiv' [I remember the six days at the Vel d'hiv]: it takes a well-informed reader, however, to deduce the likely connection and the significance for Perec, one aware that during the Occupation in 1942, 13,000 Jews were rounded up at a Parisian cycling stadium, the Vélodrome d'Hiver, to be deported to Nazi camps.[65] Although *Je me souviens* may reconfigure those parameters of autobiography which unjustifiably suppress certain modalities of writing, 'Histoire' [History], which often dominates conventional form of autobiography, still has its place.

The allusions to acts of Nazi genocide constitute a point of common ground between *Je me souviens* and *W ou le souvenir d'enfance*, and, like the earlier text, *Je me souviens* foregrounds the absence of certain stock features of autobiography which mark the text as dispossessed of the autobiographical self. However, *Je me souviens* goes further than *W ou le souvenir d'enfance* in departing from the autobiographical model and shows none of the melancholy or destructive edge of the earlier work, arising from the failure to seize and write the self satisfactorily. In *W ou le souvenir d'enfance*, departure from the autobiographical model is necessitated principally by the author's failed attempt to conform to it, and this failure then directs Perec to consider broader issues. *Je me souviens*, by contrast, triumphs in its limited endeavour, lack of detail and deviation from the norms of autobiography. Where self-dispossession was an impediment in *W ou le souvenir d'enfance*, in *Je me souviens* the simple, playful and easily reiterable pattern of the liturgical 'je me souviens' [I remember] serves to empty out the author's subjectivity from his self-writing. This device develops further the constellation technique of self-writing present in *W ou le souvenir d'enfance*. Being composed entirely of hundreds of micro-narratives, each with its own distinct 'je' [I], *Je me souviens* conspicuously fails to unify the self's perspectives into one subjectivity through the usual device of a sustained narrative. The text thus enacts structurally the fracturing of a selfhood into multiple parts; and because the self-representation is without narrative, it is also without closure, so the text's portrayal of self is never complete. In this way it is wilfully dispossessed of the autobiographical self. Writing a self-dispossessed text becomes a positive achievement: the fragmentary, partial self-representation is to be embraced, for no one instance of self-writing will be able to offer its reader a complete account of its subject. Innovative structural devices play an essential role in this achievement, creating a text which is at once iconoclastic, and yet permits Perec to express the quality of his selfhood and memory.

With *Je me souviens*, Perec proffers a new model of autobiography. Unlike *autofiction*, it does not discard referentiality, but it reconfigures the self as plural not singular; its representations as endless, not finished; and systems that govern the shape of texts as enabling, rather than disabling. Keeping familiar elements, but conjugating them differently, this new conception of autobiography is one which makes new demands on readers, causing them to reconfigure their approach to autobiography and selfhood too.

Recourse to the strategy of using systems of formal constraint might appear as an inconsistent blind spot in an author who is wary of systems that over-regulate. Yet it is Perec's evident engagement with systems that will do most to impact on readers and alter the reading expectations they bring to autobiography. The development of innovative, highly visible formal constraints, such as the interweaving of alternate segments (*W ou le souvenir d'enfance*), anaphora (*Je me souviens*), and the list form (*Je me souviens* and several shorter works), is self-conscious and draws the attention of Perec's reader to the theme of systems and constraint. One effect of this is to present systems in a critical light: *W ou le souvenir d'enfance* illustrates that the existing generic system is inadequate for Perec's needs; both *W ou le souvenir d'enfance* and *Je me souviens* force the reader to recognize the pitfalls of being content to rely on the established organizational systems without questioning the latent ideologies behind them. Another effect is that a contrast is set up between Perec's own systems, and systems which seek to contain everything within them and allow nothing to fall outside their scope.

What is notable in Perec's use of systems is that the point of their collapse is always built in. The overt incorporation of disruption into his text reproduces the mechanism of the system in such a way as to disrupt it: although *W ou le souvenir d'enfance* is composed in such a way as to end up with precisely thirty-seven chapters (a signature number for Perec), the most discussed chapter, the one which most clearly forecloses on the reader, is the one left unwritten, represented by '(...)' on an otherwise blank page.[66] In being constrained by disruptions caused by gaps and incompleteness, the material of Perec's writing mimetically reproduces life. These gaps illustrate that being without everything, being limited, is not just the definition of being constrained, but is constitutive of both life and writing. Perec's insight corresponds to the Lacanian theory of the quilting point, which marks the point where the disruptive Real incurs into what seems like an ordered world (an incursion Sarraute resists seeing, as discussed in the previous chapter). For Perec, systems must always be able to be breached by the unforeseeable:

> Si je classe, si j'inventorie, quelque part ailleurs il y aura des événements qui vont intervenir et brouiller cet ordre. Je sais par exemple que *Je me souviens* est bourré d'erreurs, donc que mes souvenirs sont faux! Cela fait partie de cette opposition entre la vie et le mode d'emploi, entre la règle du jeu que l'on se donne et le paroxysme de la vie réelle qui submerge, qui détruit continuellement ce travail de mise en ordre, et heureusement d'ailleurs.[67]

> [If I classify, if I catalogue, somewhere elsewhere there will be events that will intervene and scramble this order. I know for example that *Je me souviens* is stuffed with errors, and therefore that my memories are false. That is part of this opposition between life and the user's manual, between the rules of the game that you set yourself and the eruption of real life which submerges, which destroys continuously this work of putting into order, and just as well, moreover.]

It is this essential and healthy space, a space created by life's ability to exceed writing: the space between *W* and *le souvenir d'enfance* [The Memory of Childhood]; between *La vie* [Life] and its *mode d'emploi* [User's Manual] to which Perec's exuberantly conspicuous systems of incomplete self-writing draw the reader's attention. If writing always ultimately finds itself overwhelmed by life, as well as by an unpossessable self, then it follows that autobiography — being the genre of self, life *and* writing — must always be open to free play: just as instituting systems which deny this free play to selves and lives is undesirable, so is instituting systems which circumscribe the writing of them.

Opening up autobiography to free play implies not simply expanding the genre of autobiography until its redefined regulations include the types of self-writing Perec practises, but also attacking the notion that autobiography should possess a fixed generic identity at all: certainly distinctions between autobiography and non-autobiography are thoroughly scrambled in the curiously personal and impersonal, revealing and yet unrevealing *Je me souviens*. Just as Perec emphasizes the instability of his own identity, he seeks to destabilize the edifice of autobiography. However, Perec's success at reconfiguring autobiography will depend on readers' willingness to accept autobiography that does not live up to expectations of the genre: in particular autobiography that, being dispossessed of a whole picture of the autobiographer's self, will no more be able to deliver this to the reader than it can to the author.

Activating Readers

Besides offering a critique of autobiography through his innovative use of textual systems, Perec uses systems to enable his reader to break free of the thrall in which they may be held by the autobiographer: in the first place, by diverting their concerns to matters other than harvesting a sense of the authorial self. Perec's innovations in writing the self are thus designed to precipitate a certain kind of reader response. Autobiography, as we established in the first chapter, is a genre requiring readers' approval and cooperation as a vital part of establishing its generic identity. Sheringham pinpoints a spread of strategies autobiographers use to influence the responses of their readers, ranging from ingratiation to repudiation.[68] In this respect, Perec's efforts to direct the response of his readership to his autobiographical writing do not see him depart from conventional practice in the genre: positing the impossibility of self-representation, Perec shows up the unhelpful limitations of parameters circumscribing what is recognizable as autobiography in a critique that clearly has implications for the reception of his autobiographical work. However, the *direction* in which readers are led is less conventional, as an exploration of the treatment of the reader in *W ou le souvenir d'enfance* and *Je me souviens* will show.

Whereas directive autobiographers in the mould of Rousseau encourage readerly deference to the author as the figure who 'knows best', having unassailable knowledge of the written self, Perec's recognition of his self-dispossession causes him to work in the opposite direction. In *W ou le souvenir d'enfance* and *Je me souviens*, he highlights the lack of authority his writing has to pronounce on the autobiographical self: the self-conscious fragmentation in these two works reveals an inability to supply the last piece of the puzzle which is the person of the author, and indeed the undesirability of setting out to hunt for a piece that will bring completion. Perec's readers are to be dispossessed of the illusion that their reading encounter permits them to grasp or consume the autobiographical self, and of the idea that it can be the goal of a text shown to be dispossessed of that self to allow this. Yet Perec, unlike other writers, does not use the prerogative of the autobiographer's authority to forcefully rebuff readers who maintain these aspirations in a manner that only sustains that prerogative. Perec's tactics are more subtle: he de-centres the authorial self from autobiographical work by introducing a critique of systems into the central ground of the text. This encourages a shift in the reader's focus towards the world beyond the autobiographical self, setting the scene for a scrutiny of political systems, which will ultimately encourage vigilance against all systems, including textual ones.

For Perec, writing is spurred on by ideological concerns and has a political function, as observations in disparate works reveal, including *W ou le souvenir d'enfance*, *Espèces d'espaces*, and *Penser/Classer*. Perec's replacement of an existing generic system with self-devised systems implicitly demystifies the systemic approach and raises the consciousness of readers to the presence of systems and constraints in both writing and life. Most crucially, it leads them to ponder the implications of being constrained by systems. Thus the reader of *W ou le souvenir d'enfance* is sensitized to political questions, namely the presence and import of systems of governance, reflecting Perec's engagement with world affairs. If literature can challenge prevailing ideologies, it is only because the reading process in which it engages its audience has the capacity to alter readers' perceptions and perspectives. Perec does not allow his efforts to influence readers to be restricted to broad comments on organizational systems which implicitly critique modalities of reading, but instead intervenes more directly to ensure changes to reading practice. Yet it is important that readers freely arrive at any new views, and do not simply obediently swallow those of the author — even where these may overturn received ideas. Such an approach would uphold the conventional autobiographical model of a passive reader ingesting the words of an authoritative writer, a trap Perec had previously fallen into in *La Boutique obscure*. In this text, readers' assumptions that self-writing might deliver the key to the writing self are overturned via an insistently defensive treatment of the reader, who is categorically barred from an intimate understanding of the authorial self: Perec remarks that his analyst and he have dismissed the dreams recorded in *La Boutique obscure* as having been dreamt to purpose, invalidating any insight they might provide into the author's psyche.[69] The author does not interpret these dreams, and moreover withholds details of his dreams, to block readers' interpretations.

Whilst this obstruction of interpretative avenues echoes the defensive stance Sarraute takes up against her readers, Perec's commitment to challenging dominant ideologies calls for a different approach to hers: it calls for a writing which stimulates his readers to engage critically with what they read. If an audience is to be activated by their reading experience, readers themselves must instigate an active and inquiring approach to reading. Thus, unlike the self-writings of other authors, Perec's evolves to encourage readers to use their creativity in their interpretations of his self. An effect of emphasizing the value of pursuing creative interpretations of the authorial self is to steer readers towards accepting that they will not discover a definitive truth: in other words, towards accepting their estrangement from the author's person. The use of allegorical technique in *W ou le souvenir d'enfance* can thus be seen as an example of a system being used to undo the reader's reliance on the author.

The use of allegory successfully directs readers to change their reading practice, but non-didactically, providing an interpretative freedom denied to readers of *La Boutique obscure*. By writing allegorically, Perec compels his audience to read actively and become autonomous readers, making their own links between an imaginative work and historical reality. The reader is encouraged to see in the grisly details of life on the sporting colony of W something of the fate of Perec's mother as an inmate of a Nazi concentration camp. The author does connect the two series of segments, through tactics such as naming Gaspard Winckler, the missing centre of the W text, in the childhood strand of the narrative.[70] Yet ultimately it is for the reader to join the dots supplied by each single chapter of the twin-track narrative. By reading in this way, readers undertake the cognate activity to Perec's utterance of the *indicible* [ineffable] by means of 'parler à côté' [speaking to the side of it]. Perec's use of allegory also draws attention to his failure to convey direct information about a self of which he is dispossessed. Thus, in a double-pronged manoeuvre, Perec pushes the readers of *W ou le souvenir d'enfance* towards greater self-sufficiency, and drives them away from dependence on the author, without constraining their creative freedom.

In *Je me souviens* we see a further evolution in Perec's direction of the reader's response to his autobiographical writing. In *W ou le souvenir d'enfance*, despite the reader's consciousness of the barriers to self-writing posed by memory and the written medium, the work nonetheless retains a considerable emphasis on conveying aspects of Perec's self to his readers (albeit imperfectly and obliquely). This enables readers to arrive at an understanding of the author's identity, which allows their sympathy and intimacy with Perec to develop. By contrast, in *Je me souviens* the text would seem to distance the writing self from the reader, rather than bring them together. The focal point in this work is no longer the author, and the text is not organized to facilitate the reader's acquisition of knowledge about him. This is a text that makes demands on its readers, rather than answering their demands of the author. With its bare, decontextualized reminiscences, *Je me souviens* repeats the anti-teleological approach that marks the earlier *W ou le souvenir d'enfance*, resulting in a seemingly random and mystifying list. This alienating effect on readers is produced by such sparsely expressed and apparently obscure recollections as:

> 338
> Je me souviens de 'Suivez le bœuf'. [I remember 'Follow the cow'.]
> [...]
> 385
> Je me souviens du Cardinal Spellman. [I remember Cardinal Spellman.]

The utterance '"Suivez le bœuf"' ['Follow the cow'] remains unattributed to any person or group (it was the slogan of a 1960s French government advertising campaign to promote the consumption of beef), and no indication is given of Cardinal Spellman's significance (he was a leading figure of the American Catholic Church in the mid-twentieth-century, a closet homosexual who was engaged in McCarthyism). The lack of connections between individual reminiscences and the absence of any context means that any understanding the reader is able to reach will not be as a result of the author's assistance, but will depend on the reader sharing the memory with the writer.[71]

The consideration Perec gives to handling his readers derives from the fact that, as readers constitute an integral part of the system of autobiography, reading practices must alter if the ideological underbelly of the genre is to be challenged. Perec's efforts in *Je me souviens* to obstruct the reader from developing an intimate knowledge of the authorial self are consistent with his resistance to producing the kind of autobiography which functions as a key that the reader may possess to the authorial self; a goal which for Perec is unattainable and, given his suspicion of totalizing systems, ethically questionable. From this viewpoint, any aspiration on the part of the reader to gain possession of the authorial self through autobiography must be equally ethically questionable. In the face of the hurdles standing in the way of the autobiographer's complete self-expression, the reader should not expect to consume the autobiographical text as if it were a ready-prepared meal. This suggests that Perec's moves to direct his readers away from aspirations to consume and possess an image of his self are fuelled, not by self-defensive motives, as I argued was the case with Sarraute, but with the wider aim of promoting a more appropriate reading practice. Such an interpretation of Perec's directive stance *vis-à-vis* the reader is supported by the fact that his injunctions to the reader include a positive component, just as his stance on the genre of autobiography includes a positive aspect alongside a negative one: he calls for the rejection of generic norms, accompanied by a reconfiguration of the genre. Perec, then, does not reject his readership outright: readers of *Je me souviens* are held at a distance, but they are not *absolutely* denied the chance to learn about the autobiographical self. Successfully achieving a more intimate knowledge of the author depends, not on swallowing what the text supplies, but *on the individual reader's independent participation*. In common with *W ou le souvenir d'enfance*, the rewards of reading come where the reader makes links not directly prompted by the author. The range of events and phenomena recalled in *Je me souviens* extends from the trivial and parochial to the momentous and the global, so inevitably readers, even from a different generation or country, will find some recollections whose subjects are familiar. A British reader may join Perec in recalling:

> 177
> Je me souviens de Youri Gagarine. [I remember Yuri Gagarin.]
> [...]
> 389
> Je me souviens de Christine Keeler et de l'affaire Profumo. [I remember Christine Keeler and the Profumo affair.]

If readers even occasionally have prior acquaintance with isolated cases, such as these, where the narrator recalls the first man in space and the scandal caused by a British Cabinet Minister's affair with a prostitute, they then may share the knowledge with the narrator, and join in the 'impalpable petite nostalgie' [intangible little wave of nostalgia] which Perec celebrates in his work.[72]

However, Perec's constructive direction of the reader goes beyond rewarding good behaviour. Crucial to his project is persuading readers not only to admire the creativity and ingenuity the author brings to his self-expression, but to unleash their own. Beyond showcasing the remembering and unorthodox self-writing of the autobiographer in which the reader may join in, *Je me souviens* has a broader purpose: 'Ça fonctionne comme une sorte d'appel de mémoire' [It works like a sort of spur to jog the memory], writes Perec.[73] Stimulating readers of *Je me souviens* to remember alongside the author is important: the work 'est en sympathie avec les lecteurs, [...] les lecteurs s'y retrouvent parfaitement' [is in sympathy with the readers, the readers know their way around perfectly].[74] Perec's text is imagined as a pretext to encourage his readers' active creativity, and to unite them as a community of free, thinking individuals, in which he is included but is not the focus. This is made clear in the authorial gloss to the volume:

> Ces 'je me souviens' ne sont pas exactement des souvenirs, et surtout pas des souvenirs personnels, mais des petits morceaux de quotidien, des choses que, telle ou telle année, tous les gens d'un même âge ont vues, ont vécues, ont partagées, et qui ensuite ont disparu, ont été oubliées.[75]
>
> [These 'I remembers' are not exactly memories, and certainly not personal memories, but little slices of the everyday: the things which, in such and such a year, everybody of the same generation has seen, lived through, shared, and which then have disappeared, have been forgotten.]

This collective effort has the advantage of involving the reader actively in the text, combating amnesia as well as the elitism of literary autobiography: aspects of the genre which Perec finds particularly problematic. The constraint of the repetitive list becomes a source of creativity for the reader. It is designed to be iterable, in order to entice readers to repeat Perec's work, and to put into writing their own partial images of their selves.[76] Coaxing the reader to write is what lies behind the inclusion of blank pages following the index; an explanatory note on the first of these reads:

> A la demande de l'auteur, l'éditeur a laissé à la suite de cet ouvrage quelques pages blanches sur lesquelles le lecteur pourra noter les 'Je me souviens' que la lecture de ceux-ci aura, espérons-le, suscités.[77]
>
> [At the request of the author, the publisher has left a number of blank pages at the end of this work on which the reader will be able to note down the '*I remember*'s that will have, let us hope, been spawned by reading those here.]

This coda to *Je me souviens* encapsulates the contradiction Perec brings to his autobiographical writing. We have seen textual systems used to attack systems; an acceptance of memory loss which stimulates remembering; and a tension between alienating readers on the one hand, whilst making possible their identifications with the writing self on the other. Underpinning his treatment of the reader is another significant contradiction: Perec guides the reader toward autonomy and liberation from the straitjacket which comes from placing the author at the centre of a reading of autobiography; yet writing the self, even for Perec, also involves writing the reader: guiding reader response, profiting from the traditional acquiescence of the reader of autobiography to its author.

Given that Perec speaks simultaneously to the unreconstructed aspects of the reader of his autobiographical writing, as well as to those he reconstructs, it is not surprising to find that on occasions readers' responses to Perec themselves embody some of these contradictions, and that they do not necessarily implement the active approach to reading that Perec promotes, whereby readers accept estrangement from the writing self as a consequence of the text's dispossession of the author, and widen their reading ambitions beyond the aspiration to take possession of the autobiographical self.

Amongst a certain audience, Perec's loss of his selfhood, and the consequent failure of his autobiographical work to recover possession of that self, does not cause readers to see the author as a figure they cannot possess an understanding of or identify with due to his failed self-representation. For many Jews, themes featuring in *W ou le souvenir d'enfance* of trauma and rootlessness, and the interest in migration that inspires his later collaborative film project, *Récits d'Ellis Island*, are familiar concerns.[78] '[U]ne seule chose m'était précisément interdite, celle de naître dans le pays de mes ancêtres' [One thing alone was specifically forbidden to me: to be born in the land of my ancestors], writes Perec, on being disconnected from his origins: sentiments having resonance for many of his Jewish contemporaries, who can easily identify with them, in the face of population movements provoked by the Holocaust.[79] The wider prominence of the themes explored by Perec in Holocaust writing makes clear that he describes an experience with which many Jews closely identify, and which, for many, identifies Jewishness. This results in an especially developed autobiographical reading desire amongst Jewish readers for Perec's works.[80] Such readers may not have to reflect deeply to see in the story of Gaspard Winckler, who is disconnected from his own identity, a metaphor for something Perec himself confesses to experiencing. Like Sarraute, who uses an analogy with the cuckoo to describe her sense of being an interloper, Perec too feels estranged from himself, reporting a 'sentiment ténu, mais insistant, insidieux, incontournable, d'être quelque part étranger par rapport à quelque chose de moi-même, d'être "différent", mais non pas tellement différent des "autres" que différent des "miens"' [a slight but insistent, insidious, inescapable feeling of being somehow foreign in respect of something in myself, of being 'different', but not of being so much different from 'others' than different from 'my own'].[81] For Perec, this sense of being different, far from binding him to other Jews, extends to his relation to his own ethnic identity.[82] Growing up in the shadow of the French Occupation, exploring his Jewish origins and culture was impossible for Perec: he was baptized, and — as the episode of the phantom Hebrew letter in *W ou le souvenir d'enfance* ostensibly reveals — forgot any Yiddish or Hebrew he once knew.[83] As a result:

> Je ne sais pas précisément ce que c'est qu'être juif, ce que ça me fait que d'être juif. C'est une évidence [...] médiocre, une marque, mais une marque qui ne me rattache à rien de précis, à rien de concret: ce n'est pas un signe d'appartenance, ce n'est pas lié à une croyance, à une religion, à une pratique, à une culture, à un folklore, à une histoire, à un destin, à une langue. Ce serait plutôt une absence, une question, une mise en question.[84]
>
> [I do not know exactly what it is to be Jewish, what it means to me to be Jewish. It is a banal fact, a mark, but a mark which does not bind me to any precise thing, to anything concrete: it is not a sign of belonging, it is not linked to a belief, a religion, a practice, a culture, a folklore, a history, a destiny, a language. Rather it is more of an absence, a question, a questioning.]

This self-estrangement will inevitably render it difficult for this author to incorporate his ethnicity into his self-writing. However, in the eyes of some readers, if not those of the author, this difficulty cements a connection between him and a wider Jewish community: being dispossessed of one's own identity becomes the very point of identification with the author.[85] This can have implications for the reception of an author's literary production: a sense of ownership of an author's work can stem from a reader's perception that they have a privileged connection with the author and can identify with him. Insofar as autobiography is susceptible to being implicated in identity politics, it is the operation of identifications that brings this about: writing the self may reveal experiences that transcend the individual to the point that a specific community may claim the writing self as its own. When this occurs, autobiography is seen to establish not merely an individual, but a collective identity in the consciousness of the readership. Where Perec is concerned, it is the Jewish community for whom his autobiographical writing has resonances, but my discussion of Genet will show a similar dynamic operating between this author and another group targeted in Hitler's genocide: the gay community. In Perec's case, such identifications with the author have on occasion caused certain readers and critics to assume the position of guardianship over the dead writer's legacy, and — ironically, given Perec's efforts to combat readerly deference to the authority of the writer — to use their identification with the author to buttress their authority as readers.[86]

An example of this phenomenon can be seen in an article by Robert Misrahi, who interprets *W ou le souvenir d'enfance* as an allegory for the terrorist attack on Israeli athletes carried out by the Palestinian Liberation Organization at the 1972 Olympic Games in Munich.[87] Here, Perec is cast as a defender of Israel who condemns Palestinians in a position mirroring what are plainly Misrahi's own allegiances. This reading is worth lingering over as it illustrates the potency of reader identifications, even against a tide of discouragement emanating from the author: once an author takes the decision to write the self, the common ground created with the reader can override any estrangement the author may feel towards a given community. At the crux of Misrahi's essay is an identification made between the author and Perec on the basis of Perec's Jewishness — *W ou le souvenir d'enfance* is seen as 'le roman réflexif qu'un Juif construit' [the reflexive novel that a Jew constructs].[88] It is as a Jew that Perec is criticized by Misrahi for failing, as he sees it, to defend the cause of Israel more courageously in *W ou le souvenir d'enfance*.

We have seen Perec affirm, however, that his Jewishness 'ne m'attache à rien de précis' [does not bind me to any precise thing]. This presumably includes Israel; we note that *La Boutique obscure* features a dream in which the dreaming self decides against uttering 'mes sentiments pro-palestiniens' [my pro-Palestinian sentiments].[89] Prominent Perec scholars do not recognize pro-Israeli sympathies in Perec either: Marcel Bénabou presents Perec as having little interest in Jewish concerns and little knowledge of Jewish culture, and David Bellos details anecdotal evidence of a grudge explaining Perec's anti-Zionist position.[90] It is therefore difficult to see Perec as a defender of Israel. It would seem that Misrahi's identification with Perec on ethnic grounds has led him to construct an identification in the opposite direction, assimilating Perec's politics to his own. However, a shared history, cultural identity or ethnicity will not necessarily guarantee shared political perspectives, and Perec's oblique observations on systems and invitations to readers to assemble meaning for themselves encourage numerous politicized interpretations. W is an indictment of any administration where a systematic operation descends into inhumanity, and, if the practice of reading an individual Perecquian text as a component in a larger constellation is embraced, a number of systems or regimes could potentially become targets of his critique of systems. This becomes clear if we consider Perec's writing on the US Immigration Centre at Ellis Island in conjunction with *W ou le souvenir d'enfance*. Such is the pregnancy of allegory and the potency of the technique of reading *à côté* (what we could also call reading awry) that it would be possible to see in the W narrative an allegory of historical American immigration systems: in an article on Ellis Island, Perec initially depicts the gateway to the USA as a place of noble ideals, calling out, 'give me your tired and your poor'; a place that initially heralded freedom and opportunity for the incoming. However, its prestige diminishes in the course of the piece, until it becomes 'une prison pour les individus *soupçonnés* d'activités anti-américaines (fascistes italiens, Allemands pro-nazis, communistes *ou présumés*)' [a prison for individuals *suspected* of anti-American activities (Italian fascists, pro-Nazi Germans, Communists *or those presumed to be*)].[91] Furthermore, in a degradation from compassion to persecution which resembles uncannily the evolution of the island colony of W, Perec invokes a description of the Statue of Liberty by Franz Kafka, where it is a sword, not a lamp, which she holds aloft.[92] The openness of the textual systems governing Perec's work creates profuse interpretative possibilities, and to assume that Perec intended to criticize the PLO specifically would seem over-hasty.

It may be objected that in Perec's case especially, given the space made in his works for active and creative readings, it is inappropriate for interpretations to be restrained by authorial intention or biographical approaches, so Perec's estranged relationship to Jews and Israel may seem irrelevant to how his allegory is interpreted. Misrahi's is an interesting case of a reading following Perecquian principles without following Perec's direction of the reader. Perec's self-writing incites readers to renounce approaches to autobiography which establish the autobiographer's person as the trophy that the reader wins as a result of reading his text. For Misrahi, however, Perec remains at the centre of the autobiographical text due to the identification the critic makes with the author. This identification engenders an expectation that it is possible to possess an understanding of the author, with the consequence that the reader feels entitled to make claims on Perec. Interpretations based on identifications made with the author through his writing perpetuate the reader's dependent and possessive relation to the autobiographer, and do not take into account Perec's insistence that his autobiography is not sufficiently possessed of his self to allow for this kind of empathetic relationship.

Evaluating responses of this kind to *W ou le souvenir d'enfance* is not straightforward, however: undoubtedly partisan, Misrahi's interpretation of *W ou le souvenir d'enfance* is nonetheless an example of the type of creative, independent and politically engaged reading which Perec invites. On the other hand, this is a reader whose failure to be dispossessed of the notion that the autobiographical text can make the person of the autobiographer knowable to the reader is so complete that he permits himself to form identifications with him.

That readers are not always dispossessed of reading assumptions conventionally associated with autobiography confirms that, despite Perec's reconfiguration of autobiography, his writing nonetheless remains within the parameters of the genre: it has been observed that one property of autobiography is that it provokes the reader to conflate the written self and the living person bearing the same name, even though this supposed encounter with the named author must always be illusory:

> Un auteur, ce n'est pas une personne. C'est une personne qui écrit et qui publie. A cheval entre le hors-texte et le texte, c'est la ligne de contact des deux. [...] [L]e lecteur [...] ne connaît pas la personne réelle, tout en croyant à son existence.[93]
>
> [An author is not a person. He or she is a person who writes and publishes. Straddling the text and the zone beyond the text, the author is the line of contact between the two. The reader does not know the real person, even whilst believing in his or her existence.]

Responses to Perec's self-writing which deviate from those he sanctions raise an interesting problem: given that the position to which Perec attempts to steer his readers is one that involves them eschewing a model of reading where the author directs the reader, Perec's readership can hardly be expected always to follow these directions: encouraging readers not to centre their readings on the author also requires that they do not centre their readings on the author's desire. This is the final vicissitude of dispossession in Perec's autobiographical writing: the text may not fully possess the autobiographical self behind it, but conversely that autobiographical self does not himself possess the text. Perec cannot determine the interpretations readers make of his work; he is dispossessed of control over the self-representation he has created. For Perec, autobiography expresses and brings about a dispossession of self. Ironically, dispossession of self also means allowing the reader not to accept this dispossession of self, but, if they choose, still to treat the autobiographical self as something which can be consumed and possessed. The element of the unexpected, the *imprévu*, which Perec insists should be present in all systems is injected where readers use their freedom to ignore Perec's guidance on how to read his innovatively configured self-writing, and instead apply conventional autobiographical reading practices to it.

Perec's *W ou le souvenir d'enfance* shows that we cannot assume that the author will always be able to provide a key to their own selfhood, nor indeed that selfhood is something for which there is necessarily a key to possess. Although Perec is faced with especially atrocious circumstances, for all of us, certain experiences have been consigned to the unconscious, inhibiting our understanding of, and hence ability to write, ourselves. Perec realizes that the legacy of his trauma has been to dispossess him of his selfhood, yet this dispossession coexists with an imperative to give an account of his traumatized self and not to be silenced. Consequently, Perec must find a way to write the self whilst discarding conventional aspirations to capture a whole picture of the self. His recourse to self-devised textual systems to assist his autobiographical projects is to be seen in the light of his need to escape a situation where dispossession equates to disempowerment, and silence.

Articulating his estrangement from his own identity, Perec adopts a kaleidoscopic approach to self-writing which generates multiple self-portraits: dispossession of the self becomes not only a circumstance, but an ethic to be inscribed in self-writing itself. Thus Perec reconfigures the genre, so that instead of an all too familiar system operating to paper over gaps unnoticed, gaps in the system are celebrated. The use of textual systems which build in absence foregrounds the limits on Perec's ability to write the self, as well as introducing into the autobiographical realm concerns not usually found there, as Perec makes forays into the territory of politics and ideology. With this material Perec offers his reader alternative fare for consumption, since a complete self-representation is off the menu.

A second function, then, of Perec's use of systems is to re-write the reader's response to autobiography according to the ethic of dispossession. Rather than encouraging the reader to be a consumer of information that the autobiographical narrative will supply, his texts favour active reader participation, which may bear fruit in the form of the reader's own self-writing. Yet Perec's work also demonstrates that efforts to use systems self-consciously to critique and reconfigure the institution of autobiography may fail to transform the possessive desire of some readers. Although Perec's innovative self-writing suggests that the reader is bound to remain, like the author, estranged from the Perecquian self, readers may nevertheless find their reading experience characterized by estrangement's opposite, identification. Readers remain the final arbiters of how a text is defined and what it achieves, and work which reconfigures the genre of autobiography is thus consigned by some of its readers to the conventional autobiographical stable.

The importance of the reader's controlling influence is acknowledged implicitly by the efforts made to redirect this influence, proving that at the crux of Perec's autobiographical writing is a power struggle to retain control of identity, be it that of the author, or of the genre: Perec's endeavours to direct his readers show that they are not immune either from another's attempts to control them. The potential for autobiography to be used as a tool by another to exert power over the autobiographical self is of particular concern to Genet, and will be explored in the next chapter. Unlike Genet or Sarraute, Perec is not defensive of a self which he jealously guards as his own: he accepts a lack of control over his self. Where he coincides with other autobiographers is in preferring his readers not to aspire to control it either. Yet losing sovereignty over the self is the price of attempting to break down the monoliths of the masterly Writer and the subservient Reader.

Notes to Chapter 3

1. Perec, *La Disparition* (Paris: Denoël, coll. Gallimard Imaginaire, 1969).
2. See David Bellos, *Georges Perec: A Life in Words* (London: Harvill, 1993); Eleanor Kaufman, 'Falling from the Sky: Trauma in Perec's *W* and Caruth's *Unclaimed Experience*', *Diacritics*, 28.4 (Winter 1998), 44–53; Lejeune, *La Mémoire et l'oblique: Georges Perec autobiographe* (Paris: P.O.L., 1991); Manet van Montfrans, *Georges Perec: la contrainte du réel* (Amsterdam: Rodopi, 1999).
3. Perec, *La Boutique obscure: 124 rêves* (Paris: Denoël, 1973).
4. Lejeune, *Pacte*, p. 14.
5. *W ou le souvenir d'enfance*, p. 17.
6. Freud, 'Screen Memories' (1899), in *The Standard Edition*, III (1962), 299–322.
7. Freud, 'Screen Memories', p. 322.
8. *W ou le souvenir d'enfance*, p. 63.
9. *W ou le souvenir d'enfance*, p. 183.
10. Ibid., p. 36.
11. Noted by Odile Martinez, 'Un trompe-l'œil photographique dans *W ou le souvenir d'enfance*', in *Il senso del nonsenso: scritti in memoria di Lynn Salkin Sbiroli*, ed. by Monique Streiff Moretti, Mireille Revol Cappelletti and Odile Martinez (Naples: Edizioni Scientifiche Italiane, 1994), pp. 531–48.
12. My discussion of trauma and PTSD throughout this chapter, except where otherwise indicated, is based on Felman and Laub; and *Trauma: Explorations In Memory*, ed. by Cathy Caruth (Baltimore: Johns Hopkins University Press, 1995).
13. Caruth (ed.), p. 8.
14. *W ou le souvenir d'enfance*, p. 25.
15. Ibid., pp. 25–26.
16. These are, respectively, the definitions of Starobinski; and Lejeune, *Pacte*, p. 14.
17. Perec, 'Je suis né', in *Je suis né* (Paris: Editions du Seuil, coll. La Librairie du XXe siècle, 1990) pp. 9–14 (p. 10).
18. See my 'Resisting The Whole Picture'.
19. *W ou le souvenir d'enfance*, pp. 97–99.
20. Ibid., p. 107 (my emphasis).
21. Ibid., p. 173 (my emphasis).
22. See *W ou le souvenir d'enfance*, p. 62; on Perec's destruction of his own body of text through his use of annotation, see Sheringham, *Devices*, p. 322.
23. *W ou le souvenir d'enfance*, pp. 45–64.
24. Ibid., p. 62.
25. Dori Laub, 'Bearing Witness or the Vicissitudes of Listening', in Felman and Laub, pp. 57–74 (p. 69).
26. On these issues, see (amongst other essays in the same volume) Alain Finkielkraut, 'From the Novelistic to Memory', in *Auschwitz and After: Race, Culture, and 'the Jewish Question' in France*, ed. by Lawrence D. Kritzman (New York: Routledge, 1995), pp. 83–97.
27. *W ou le souvenir d'enfance*, p. 63.
28. Ibid., p. 64.
29. See Lejeune, *Mémoire*, p. 167.
30. *W ou le souvenir d'enfance*, p. 18.
31. I use 'Winckler' to refer to the protagonist, whilst Winckler refers to the missing boy.
32. *W ou le souvenir d'enfance*, p. 220.
33. See Bellos, *Life*, pp. 224–31, 371–72, 619–35 for treatments of Gaspard as a protagonist in *Le Condottiere*, and *La Vie mode d'emploi*; and what Bellos calls the 'Winckler cycle'. The recurrence of the protagonist does not preoccupy Bellos, however. On Gaspard Winckler's reappearances

and association with the autobiographical, see Anna Maria Battaglia, 'Georges Perec: "L'Indicible vers quoi tend désespérément le désir d'écrire"', in *L'effetto autobiografico: scritture e letture del soggetto nella letteratura europea*, ed. by Edda Melon (Turin: Tirrenia, 1990), pp. 183–201 (p. 187).

34. Perec, 'Lettre à Maurice Nadeau', in *Je suis né*, pp. 51–66 (p. 65). On Perec's unfinished autobiographical projects, see Lejeune, *Mémoire*.
35. Doubrovsky, p. 128.
36. Perec, 'Le Rêve et le texte', in *Je suis né*, pp. 75–79 (p. 76).
37. For this conception of autobiography, see Pascal; May, p. 154; and Gusdorf, p. 122.
38. Sheringham, *Devices*, pp. 6–8.
39. See Lejeune, *Mémoire*, p. 75; and Claude Burgelin, *Georges Perec* (Paris: Editions du Seuil, coll. Les Contemporains, 1988), p. 31.
40. 'Le Rêve', p. 75.
41. Perec, 'Les Gnocchis de l'automne, où réponse à quelques questions me concernant', in *Je suis né*, pp. 67–74 (p. 68). Like Sarraute, Perec is convinced that writers need to find another means of representing reality (including the reality of the self), but he is dismissive of the thought of the *nouveaux romanciers* on the subject. See Claude Burgelin and Georges Pérec [*sic*], 'Le Nouveau Roman et le refus du réel', *Partisans*, 3 (February 1962), 108–18, and Stella Béhar, *Georges Perec: écrire pour ne pas dire* (New York: Peter Lang, 1995), pp. 1–6.
42. Perec, 'Engagement ou crise du langage?', *Partisans*, 7 (Nov–Dec 1962), p. 123, cited in Béhar, p. 4.
43. *La Boutique obscure, prière d'insérer.*
44. Perec, 'Le Travail de la mémoire', in *Je suis né*, pp. 81–93 (p. 81).
45. *W ou le souvenir d'enfance*, p. 222.
46. Ibid., p. 85.
47. Ibid., p. 105–06; fragment XIV (pp. 101–06) describes the organizational system in further detail.
48. Perec acknowledges that the use of systems which constrain writing causes him to tread a fine and dangerous line between constriction and creativity. See Béhar, p. 110.
49. Nineteen episodes of W were published in the review between 16 October 1969 and 1 August 1970.
50. See Perec, 'Tentative d'inventaire des aliments liquides et solides que j'ai ingurgités au cours de l'année 1974', in *L'Infra-ordinaire* (Paris: Editions du Seuil, coll. La Librairie du XXe siècle, 1989), pp. 113–30. *Lieux* and other unfinished autobiographical projects are described or excerpted in 'Lettre à Maurice Nadeau'; *Penser/Classer* (Paris: Hachette, 1985), pp. 25–29; and *Espèces d'espaces* (1974), 2nd edn (Paris: Galilée, 2000), pp. 41–51, 91–110. See also Lejeune, *Mémoire*, pp. 145–209 and Bellos, *Life*, pp. 417–21.
51. As the pages of *Je me souviens* are not numbered, references to memories noted therein refer to the number of the memory.
52. *W ou le souvenir d'enfance*, p. 17.
53. Perec employs a play on words here that exploits the fact that the name for the eighth letter of the alphabet in French has the same sound when pronounced as the word for axe, *hache*. This homophone allows his formulation 'l'histoire avec sa grande hache' at once to refer to official history, history with a capital H, and also to history as being bloody — history with its great axe.
54. *W ou le souvenir d'enfance*, pp. 203–06.
55. *Espèces d'espaces*, p. 164 (emphasis Perec's).
56. See *Espèces d'espaces*, pp. 59–66.
57. cf. Barthes, *Mythologies* (Paris: Editions du Seuil, 1957); Michel de Certeau, *L'Invention du quotidien*, I: *Arts de faire*, ed. by Luce Giard (Paris: Gallimard, coll. folio, 1990).
58. *Espèces d'espaces, prière d'insérer.*
59. *Je me souviens, prière d'insérer* on back cover.
60. *Je me souviens*, memory no. 144.
61. On the use OuLiPo make of these two types of memory, see Peter Consenstein, 'Memory and Oulipian Constraints', *Postmodern Culture*, 6.1 (September 1995) <http://www.infomotions.com/serials/pmc/pmc-v6n1-consenstein-memory.txt> [accessed 31 July 2006].

62. *Je me souviens*, memory no. 333.
63. *Je me souviens*, memory no. 331.
64. *Je me souviens, prière d'insérer* on back cover.
65. See also Lawrence D. Kritzman, 'Introduction: In the Shadows of Auschwitz: Culture, Memories, and Self-Reflection', in Kritzman (ed.), pp. 1–11.
66. *W ou le souvenir d'enfance*, p. 88. Perec reached the age of 37 on 7.3.73, a key date in the composition of the book. On '37' as a numerical signature, see Bellos, 'The "Third Dimension" of Georges Perec's *W ou le souvenir d'enfance*', *French Studies Bulletin*, 70 (1999), 1–3, (p. 3, n. 7).
67. 'Le Travail', p. 91.
68. Sheringham, *Devices*, pp. 137–46.
69. 'Le Rêve', p. 76; see also *La Boutique obscure, prière d'insérer.*
70. *W ou le souvenir d'enfance*, p. 146.
71. This generation gap is acknowledged by actor Sami Frey, who performed *Je me souviens* on stage in the original 1988 and later 2003 production. See Brigitte Salino, 'Sami Frey se souvient, encore une fois', *Le Monde*, 23 September 2003, p. 23.
72. *Je me souviens, prière d'insérer* on back cover.
73. 'Le Travail', p. 83.
74. Ibid.
75. *Je me souviens, prière d'insérer* on back cover.
76. See Lejeune, *Mémoire*, pp. 247–50 for the success of this endeavour: OuLiPo published their own version, and a selection of writers' responses were published in *Le Figaro, Libération* and *Globe*. However, for Lejeune, repeating Perec's exact project is not the most desirable response: 'Mieux vaut [...] écrire autre chose, qu'on ait soi-même autant envie d'écrire que Perec les *Je me souviens...*' [It would be better to write something else, something which one has as much desire to write as Perec did his '*I Remember*'s]. See Lejeune, *Mémoire*, p. 250.
77. *Je me souviens*, p. 147.
78. Robert Bober (dir.), *Récits d'Ellis Island* (1980); Perec features in the film conducting interviews, and is credited with writing it. See also the project in book form: Georges Perec and Robert Bober, *Récits d'Ellis Island: histoires d'errance et d'espoir* (1980), 2nd edn (Paris: P.O.L, 1994).
79. Perec, 'Ellis Island: description d'un projet', in *Je suis né*, pp. 95–103 (p. 100).
80. Susan Rubin Suleiman describes her own autobiographical reading desire for Holocaust writing in 'War Memories: On Autobiographical Reading', in Kritzman (ed.), pp. 47–62.
81. 'Ellis Island', pp. 100–01.
82. On Perec's relationship to Jews and Jewishness, see Marcel Bénabou, 'Perec et la judéité', *Cahiers Georges Perec*, 1 (1984), pp. 15–30.
83. On forgetting, see Bellos, *Life*, pp. 68–71. See also pp. 552–53 for his argument that the phantom letter episode is not quite what it seems: that Perec dissembles on his knowledge of Hebrew, or lack thereof.
84. 'Ellis Island', p. 99.
85. See Finkielkraut.
86. An example of such a protective attitude is shown in a personal attack on David Bellos by a former curator of the Fonds Georges Perec, who disputes the ethics of Bellos's handling of artefacts. See Hans Hartje, 'Georges Perec: des relais pour écrire', *Rivista di letterature moderne e comparate*, n.s. 51 (1998), 57–68 (pp. 59–60).
87. Robert Misrahi, '*W*, un roman réflexif', *Arc*, 76 (1979), 81–86.
88. Misrahi, p. 81.
89. See *La Boutique obscure*, dream no. 16.
90. See Bénabou, 'Perec et la judéité', and Bellos, p. 523.
91. 'Ellis Island', p. 98. The emphasis is mine: in this piece Perec intimates through *parler à côté* that detained at Ellis Island were those found guilty of no crime; people detained on the strength of their political views, presumed to be antagonistic to the US government.
92. 'Ellis Island', p. 95.
93. Lejeune, *Pacte*, p. 23.

CHAPTER 4

❖

Genet Inside and Out
Autobiography, Marginality and Empowerment

Jean Genet's autobiographical writing tends to be left out of studies focussing on self-conscious, postmodern French autobiography.[1] In one sense, this is not surprising. Genet started to write his autobiographical narratives during periods of imprisonment in 1942 and 1943.[2] Thus his venture into the autobiographical considerably pre-dates the self-reflexive turn in French literature and thought behind the appearance of the *nouveau roman*, and the ascendancy of structuralist and poststructuralist theories: the movements often (at least implicitly) credited with sparking the apparently subversive, self-conscious approaches to writing the self that I discussed in my first chapter. Yet, as Jacques Derrida recognizes, Genet's autobiography is deconstructive *avant la lettre*: if autobiography is postmodern whenever it deconstructs its way out of the generic envelope of autobiography, and destabilizes positivist conceptions of selfhood, then Genet's autobiographical writing deserves to be called postmodern.[3] In his *Notre-Dame-des-Fleurs*, *Miracle de la rose* and *Journal du voleur*, Genet simultaneously invokes the genre of autobiography, yet distances himself from it. In these works he also articulates, much as Sarraute does, a particular conception of selfhood whose qualities are such that it defies being seized in writing. In his treatment of the genre of autobiography, and his conceptualization of the self, Genet shares considerable similarities with Sarraute, or Perec. This is despite the fact that Genet writes without reference to discourses surrounding autobiography (particularly psychoanalytic theories of the self) which both Sarraute and Perec acknowledge as a prominent part of their intellectual landscape.

Despite writing in advance of the deconstructive turn, it is arguably Genet, out of all the writers featuring in this volume, who works most energetically in his self-writing to challenge the presumption that autobiography leads the reader back to the writer's self, and gives the sum of the person who wrote it; it is he who does most to contest the notion that by reading the autobiographical output of an individual, one can read and ingest, not only a text, but a person.

Where Genet would seem to part company from the writers studied so far is in what drives his apparent subversions of autobiography. In Genet, declarations of the self's ineffability do not stem from an apparently honest concern to highlight deficiencies in the autobiographer's self-knowledge: deficiencies that, seemingly coincidentally, then have the side-effect of making it impossible for the reader to acquire possession of what (according to their narratives) eludes autobiographers themselves: a secure grasp of the author's self. Unlike writers such as Doubrovsky, Genet does not draw attention to the slipperiness of the self (and the consequent difficulty of representing or understanding it) for the sake of acknowledging an aspect of what he perceives to be the truth of the self, even before it comes to writing (or writing comes to it). Bearing witness to his own lack of autonomy over his self, foregrounding his inability to determine what it is: this is not Genet's goal. Indeed, his goal is quite the reverse. In *Journal du voleur* especially, it is made explicit that a self is being *fashioned*, not chronicled, and so the affirmation of the inaccessibility of this self to its reader takes on a performative quality. The self is *made* slippery, not found to be so. That is to say, in a process reminiscent of the operation of Lejeune's autobiographical pact (only in reverse), assertions of the self's slipperiness *bring about* the state of ineffability which is claimed to be the property of the Genetian self. (At least, this is the aim; we shall see that the result is in practice often quite different.) Thus, for Genet, asserting the self to be unknowable is far from being an admission of a lack of understanding or self-mastery, as it is for Perec and (ostensibly) Sarraute. For this writer, such declarations, instead of testifying to a lack of sovereignty over the self, or a poor grasp of what the self is, in fact *enact* that sovereignty. They do this by shaping the self and determining its identity — an identity marked by its unknowableness. Similarly, the failure to produce a more conventional autobiography is a deliberate choice: not, as it is for Perec, a foregone conclusion rendered inevitable by the presence of insurmountable obstacles.

It will be argued here that Genet's resistance to autobiography, and, in particular, to the traditional approach to reading it, stems from an insight into the imprisoning properties of autobiography. In my first two chapters, I suggested that the genre of autobiography performs the function of an intangible regulatory matrix; that it acts as a framework of 'unstated laws' which constricts the autobiographical self, allowing the other who inhabits or embodies that framework — in this case the reader — to determine what the self should be. Autobiography thus re-subjects the autobiographer in writing to the sort of restrictive framework which thinkers such as Lacan, Foucault and Althusser claim that we are all invisibly subjected to in life.

In life, Genet, of course, was known for his defiance of the law: a resistance which we shall see extending to the laws of the genre of autobiography and its consumers.[4] We shall find Genet peculiarly alert to autobiography's subjectifying effect on the self; and, like Sarraute, it is an effect he is determined to resist. His means, however, are rather different from hers, and involve using his marginalized position as a criminal and a homosexual as a lever in a bid to keep his readership at an enforced distance. Being seen not to write autobiography, not to deliver its fruits, is crucial to Genet's resistance to subjectification. This is the light in which we should read Genet's very pronounced insistence that his readers are not provided with the authoritative insight necessary to allow them to know and to consume his self — a process which involves disempowering it and bringing about its subjectification.

Genet's work therefore challenges the notion that what leads to the undermining of the genre of autobiography is a heightened awareness, against the backdrop of late-twentieth-century French thought, of epistemological uncertainties which are held inevitably to dog the individual's attempt to know, and to write, him- or herself. His autobiographical writings alert us to the possibility that autobiographers present their task as impossible, their selves as unseizable for strategic purposes. In Genet's case it is clear that the strategy involves pitting the author against a reader in an atmosphere of conflict. What is perhaps less evident is the particular degree of threat posed to the author by those readers who, being engaged in identity politics with the aim of valorizing queer identities, would seem to be the most sympathetic to his cause.

Amongst the writers studied in this book, it is Genet who most vehemently dissociates himself from a model of autobiography which involves seeing both the text and the self as consumable commodities. Paradoxically, however, it is also Genet whose self is the most consumed. To judge by critical reception, Genet's self is the one that readers have been most ready to assume that they know and have the measure of as a result of their textual encounter with the author. My purpose here is to explore how it is that an author so determined to remain outside the law, to escape being shackled by autobiography, nonetheless gets caught in its trap.

If autobiography is a trap for Genet, it is the risk of being identified, or even identified with, that makes it one. Genet's prison writings reveal an insight, borne of the experience of incarceration, into the connection between having knowledge over another and having power over them. Since Genet's goal is ultimately to resist being subject to any other's power, demonstrations of his resilience to that power are required. Part of this resilient stance on issues of knowledge and disclosure is to defy the other's desire and demand for knowledge about his self. It is as an act of defiance against this other, and autobiography itself, that we need to understand what otherwise appears a rather curious decision by Genet to write autobiographically.

Autobiography, Knowledge, Power

Although they cultivate an ambiguous relation to autobiography, both *Miracle de la rose* and *Journal du voleur* abide by the terms of Lejeune's autobiographical pact (being first-person narratives where the narrator-protagonist is named as Jean Genet), and both ostensibly take this narrator's life as their focus.[5] In *Notre-Dame-des-Fleurs*, the challenge to the genre is more immediately apparent. Here, the narrator (who is once again named with the same name as the author), focusses not on his own life, but chiefly on the life of a transvestite protagonist called Divine, the creation of his fantasy.

In the light of his criminality, the fact that Genet wrote autobiographically at all is noteworthy. This is a genre whose founding works, as was noted in Chapter 1, are both entitled '*Confessions*': autobiography has been recognized as the product of a deeply rooted confessional mentality in the Western world, a mentality in which it is embedded, and, which, as I shall argue here, it sustains. Since the confessional mentality is expressed most strongly in religious and criminal discourses, the publication of a '*Journal du voleur*' [Thief's Journal] may not appear surprising. However, the referentiality traditionally expected of autobiography applies to criminal autobiographers as much as any others, requiring them, if they are to obey the laws of the genre, to draw attention to their existence, and also to give an honest account of themselves and their doings: activities which seem sure to attract the attention of the 'long arm of the law' and work against the interests of the lawbreaker.

Genet minimizes the risk attached to referentiality by ensuring that his primary emphasis in his self-writing is not on providing information to the reader about his past. Genet insists in *Miracle de la rose*, for example, that his work is first and foremost a crafted literary object: 'Voilà donc le ton que je prendrai pour parler de Mettray, d'Harcamone et de la Centrale. Rien ne m'empêchera, ni l'attention aiguë ni le désir d'être exact, d'écrire des mots qui chantent' [This, then, is the tone that I shall adopt to speak about Mettray, Harcamone and the Central [Prison]. Nothing will prevent me, neither acute attention nor the desire to be precise, from writing words which sing].[6] This prioritization of the style of the narration over what is narrated continues to operate in *Journal du voleur*:

> De cette période je parle avec émotion et je la magnifie, mais si des mots prestigieux, chargés, veux-je dire, [...] de prestige plus que de sens, se proposent à moi, cela signifie peut-être que la misère qu'ils expriment et qui fut la mienne est elle aussi source de merveille. Je veux réhabiliter cette époque en l'écrivant avec les noms des choses les plus nobles.[7]
>
> [About this period I speak with emotion and I magnify it, but if prestigious words — loaded, I mean to say, more with prestige than with meaning — suggest themselves to me, it signifies perhaps that the wretchedness which they express and which was mine is itself also a source of wonder. I want to rehabilitate this era by writing it with the names of the most noble things.]

Here, Genet reveals the true agenda operating in *Journal du voleur*, one equally present in *Notre-Dame-des-Fleurs* and *Miracle de la rose*. As Genet makes clear in a direct narratorial address to the reader early in *Journal du voleur*, the pursuit of literariness in his self-writing, reflects a concern, not to transmit knowledge through his writing, but rather, to exercise power:

> Ce journal que j'écris n'est pas qu'un délassement littéraire. A mesure que j'y progresse, ordonnant ce que ma vie passée me propose, à mesure que je m'obstine dans la rigueur de la composition [...] je me sens m'affermir dans la volonté d'utiliser, à des fins de vertus, mes misères d'autrefois. J'en éprouve le pouvoir.[8]
>
> [This journal that I write is not simply a literary recreation. As I make progress in it, ordering what my past life suggests to me, as I stubbornly keep to the rigour of its composition, I feel myself strengthen in the desire to use, for virtuous ends, my former wretchednesses. I feel the power of them.]

What Genet's narrators in *Miracle de la rose* and *Journal du voleur* each seek is the narratorial self-empowerment which would result from successfully achieving their aim to transform a wretched, sordid past life into a beautiful literary object. However, there is also a conspicuous concern that these literary projects should not satisfy the curiosity of the reader, and so occasionally their narrators vaunt the extent of their mastery by openly withholding information. In *Miracle de la rose* the narrator insists: 'je n'ai pas la prétention de vous mettre au fait de tous les mystères (et les dévoiler) qui sommeillaient dans la Colonie [de Mettray]' [I do not claim to inform you about all the mysteries (and uncover them) which were sleeping in the colony [of Mettray]].[9] This same narrator also makes clear that the passive boy called Jean Genet in this text offers no interpretative key to the present-day Genet outside the text, emphasizing what he says is the flesh-and-blood author's active, rather than passive, sexual role.[10]

Autobiography is a worthwhile exercise for Genet insofar as it allows the author to display mastery: mastery over the form his self-representations and self-writings take; mastery over language; and finally, mastery over those who read it. Crucially, this demonstration of the autobiographer's sovereignty involves betraying — although not destroying — the autobiographical contract that he invokes in all three works studied here. From an author who describes betrayal as one of the 'trois vertus' [three virtues] alongside criminality and homosexuality, such a move is hardly astonishing.[11] What is unexpected in Genet's autobiographical writing is not so much the efforts made to emphasize the outlaw status of Genet's narrators: efforts resulting in the transgression of another law, the law of genre. Rather, what is startling is the strength of insight that Genet has into the links between autobiographical narration, knowledge, and the subjectification of the self. It is this lucidity which make that transgression so vital for him.

In many respects, insights from Genet's prison writing anticipate Foucault's work on subjectification, *Surveiller et punir*.[12] Here, Foucault links the realms of the law, knowledge and power to reveal the existence of an apparatus used by various social institutions to ensure the compliant subjection of their charges to a more or less intangible regulatory framework, one reminiscent of the Lacanian Other that we encountered in Chapter 2. Foucault details how the evolution of the judicial institutions from the eighteenth to the twentieth centuries sees the establishment of a prison system which aims, not only to punish convicted criminals by restricting their liberty, but also to force lawbreakers to recognize and accept the legitimacy of both the laws, and the institutions of society which uphold and promote them. The purpose of forcing this recognition is to bring about the subjection of inmates, and to do this, these institutions develop an array of subjectifying techniques that force lawbreakers into a position of compliant subjection. Thus, the prison regime evolves to emphasize discipline, through the imposition of routines, and surveillance. The inmate is placed under constant watch: the result of this surveillance is that all he does is known, and each instance of disobedience can be punished. As the prisoner ends up becoming a known quantity to his jailers, the need for supervision diminishes, until the prisoner has so completely internalized prison discipline that he polices his own actions to the point of compliance with the regime. The goal is to create: 'le sujet obéissant, l'individu, assujetti à des habitudes, des règles, des ordres, une autorité qui s'exerce continûment autour de lui et sur lui, et qu'il doit laisser fonctionner automatiquement en lui' [the obedient subject, the individual subjected to habits, rules, orders, an authority that is exercised continually around him and upon him, and which he must allow to function automatically in him].[13]

Foucault devotes a lengthy treatment to the model carceral regime operating in the agricultural colony for juvenile delinquents at Mettray, the institution where a young Genet was incarcerated, and which is described by the narrator as his home in *Miracle de la rose*.[14] Descriptions given by Foucault and Genet dovetail on many points, despite the fact that Foucault describes the penitentiary colony as it was on its opening in 1840, whereas Genet was remanded there in 1926.[15] Genet reports that everyday life is run according to a strict timetable that dictates what specific activities should be performed, and precisely when:

> Lever à six heures. [...] On s'habillait. Cinq minutes au lavabo. Au réfectoire, nous buvions un bouillon, et on partait pour l'atelier. Travail jusqu'à midi. On revenait au réfectoire jusqu'à une heure et demie. A l'atelier encore. A six heures, à la soupe. A sept heures, au dortoir.[16]
>
> [Rise at six o'clock. We would dress. Five minutes at the wash-basin. At the refectory, we would drink a gruel, and then leave for the workshop. Work until midday. We would go back to the refectory until half past one. To the workshop again. At six o'clock, to soup. At seven o'clock to the dormitory.]

This description is echoed in the later account of how prisoners' bodies are subject to externally-imposed discipline in *Surveiller et punir*:

> Le point d'application de la peine, [...] c'est le corps, c'est le temps, ce sont les gestes et les activités de tous les jours; [...] [q]uant aux instruments utilisés, ce [...] sont [...] des formes de coercition, des schémas de contrainte appliqués et répétés. Des exercices [...]: horaires, emplois du temps, mouvements obligatoires, activités régulières, méditation solitaire, travail en commun, silence, application, respect, bonnes habitudes.[17]
>
> [The point of application of the penalty is [...] the body, time, everyday gestures and activities; [...] [a]s for the instruments used, these are forms of coercion, schemata of constraint, applied and repeated. Exercises [...]: time-tables, compulsory movements, regular activities, solitary meditation, work in common, silence, application, respect, good habits.][18]

If Genet is interested in the same features of prison life as Foucault, it is because, as the very enterprise of writing a memoir about Mettray proves, he shares Foucault's insight that an inmate's self is transformed by his prison experiences: 'la prison est en moi-même, composée des cellules de mes tissus' [the prison is in myself, made up of the cells of my tissues].[19] Although Genet prefers to emphasize that *he* incorporates *the prison*, reduces *it* to being a part of *him*, the polyvalency of the word 'cellule' [cell] means that he simultaneously suggests that carceral discipline may have claimed another victory: that he is made up of the fabric of the prison, *its* cells. This linguistic ambiguity points up a tension in Genet's writing: although his autobiographical narratives may be designed to create a situation in which the narrator has self-mastery, despite being subject to the control of the prison, the features pinpointed by Genet and Foucault which are used in prisons to facilitate control are sufficiently efficient that the risk of being subsumed to the prison structure is ever present. The implication is that Genet may not, after all, be entirely impervious to being recuperated by controlling systems. Judith Butler argues that Foucault misses out an important aspect from his account of the disciplinary mechanism that produces compliant subjects: the subject's 'passionate attachment' to its own subjectification.[20] She contends that individuals desire their own subjection, making it very difficult for them to break free of their status as subjects, and the reason for that desire is that, by being subjectified, the individual is also culturally intelligible to others. The question is, how far does Genet ultimately escape that desire to be culturally intelligible to others which subjectification brings?

Genet's narrators show resistance to the regime governing their prison existences by thwarting its goals. For example, the narrator of *Miracle de la rose* recognizes that the police–prison system tries to expose its inmates to good moral examples, but he denies its efficacy: 'il existe les surveillants, les avocats, les flics, mais ils sont là pour donner plus de signification à notre honte (et à sa splendeur) en lui opposant leur vie aimable et digne' [Supervisors, lawyers, and cops do exist, but they are there to give greater meaning to our shame (and its splendour) by offering their decent and dignified lives as a contrast].[21] In response to the moral pressure exerted by the regime, Genet's prison writing tends to celebrate precisely the behaviour which most challenges the disciplinary system promulgated in judicial and penal institutions. An instance of this occurs in *Miracle de la rose*, where the narrator chronicles how prisoners are supplied with general issue clothing, the wear and care of which fits into the technique of subjectification. Genet's narrator, 'Genet', reports that the inmates adapt their clothing — adding, for example, extra pockets — according to their own private semiotic code, in order to express their personality, sometimes even a particular sexual role. This small-scale disobedience testifies to the widespread illicit sexual acts occurring in Mettray, and the flourishing homosexual subculture, which constitute expressions of defiance of the disciplinary code.

All acts that are, to the eyes of the institutionalized, abject, disgusting, sub-human are glorified, and Genet's narrator strongly identifies himself with them: '[m]'inhumaniser est ma tendance profonde' [dehumanizing myself is my profound tendency], states the 'Genet' who narrates *Notre-Dame-des-Fleurs*.[22] Being called a monster, no longer being recognized as a part of human society, represents the ultimate sanction of the disciplinary system and the sign of its failure. At its extreme point, the perpetrator of such behaviour is not individualized, but *dehumanized* — that is, placed outside the realm over which society claims jurisdiction. This is the position achieved by the murderers Pilorge, the dedicatee of *Notre-Dame-des-Fleurs*, and Harcamone, Genet's inspiration in *Miracle de la rose*. Genet's goal is to arrive at this liberated position of the *hors-la-loi*, the one truly outside the law; and his autobiographical writing is a tool to be deployed, both to achieve this position, and to *show* it being achieved.

In Genet's case, writing is a practice that in itself constitutes an act of rebellion. In part, the ability of his act of writing to inflame the powers that be becomes clear at the point where Genet's manuscripts are confiscated by his jailers: his response to re-write the missing material is characteristically defiant.[23] Genet's jailers seem to share with Kristeva a sense that creative writing has a subversive potential. In her *Révolution du langage poétique*, Kristeva credits creative writing with the ability to undermine logocentric modes of thought, and by extension the institutions that depend on them; for Cixous, this is exactly what Genet's writing achieves. She considers that his work voices 'une féminité foisonnante, maternelle' [an abundant, maternal femininity] which undermines hegemonic masculine, patriarchal discourse.[24] Yet the choice of genre has a crucial importance here. Genet may vaunt his immunity to the institutions of subjectification, and his autobiographical writing seems to allow the author to demonstrate his self's immunity to the interventions of the reformative system. However, here a trap presents itself, since autobiography may also permit the categorization and classification of the Genetian self under a system which transforms knowledge of someone into power over them.

For Foucault, autobiography is directly implicated in the operation of intangible subjectifying frameworks.[25] He argues that, as subjectified beings, we possess a blind spot that obscures the fact that the act of telling (particularly about sexual matters) is a collusion with a mechanism designed to exercise constraint on the individual:

> L'obligation de l'aveu nous est maintenant renvoyée à partir de tant de points différents, elle nous est désormais si profondément incorporée que nous ne la percevons plus comme l'effet d'un pouvoir qui nous contraint; il nous semble au contraire que la vérité, au plus secret de nous-même, ne 'demande' qu'à se faire jour [...].[26]
>
> [The obligation to confess is now relayed through so many different points, is so deeply ingrained in us, that we no longer perceive it as the effect of a power that constrains us; on the contrary, it seems to us that truth, lodged in our most secret nature, 'demands' to surface [...].][27]

That writing the self could be a form of subjectifying that self is borne out by evidence that the disciplinary mechanism operating in the prison draws on the transmission of autobiographical knowledge as part of its strategy. The imposition of discipline is in part achieved in the scopic order: inmates are watched over to see that they do not partake in antisocial behaviour (Foucault cites homosexual acts as a particular example[28]). The disciplinary gaze also involves a visual scrutiny of the subjects which are in the process of being produced: this gaze makes the detainee simultaneously an object of power, and of knowledge.[29] Autobiographers, as we have seen, frequently invoke visual metaphors, describing their works as self-portraits. Thus the uses to which the disciplinary gaze can be put has special implications for this genre. More tellingly still, Foucault reports that biographical information is collected from prisoners: that is to say, *an autobiographical narrative is demanded from them* on entry to the institution. This leads to their individualization in the authority's eyes: detainees are classified according to the knowledge gained about them.[30] All of these processes are implemented to advance the subjectification of inmates. Foucault notes a correlation between the extent of a person's lawbreaking activity, and the extent to which they are individualized by the mechanism of institutional discipline. He remarks that the homosexual — even when not imprisoned — becomes, like the prisoner, a species to be observed, investigated and classified, whereas the heterosexual population does not.[31] Being identified as a homosexual criminal is therefore fraught, for it invites particular scrutiny from the subjectifying authorities. A mark of Genet's defiance is that he claims this identity for himself. Jonathan Dollimore suggests that such defiance can be rewarded with a 'transgressive reinscription' of a dissident identity.[32] Such an identity damages the systems and discourses that label it deviant, rather than simply leading to the recuperation of another specimen who becomes individualized and subjectified. However, Genet's success at this depends on him constructing his homosexual, criminal self as impenetrable to the viewing and reading observers: putting it literally 'beyond their ken'. Only in this way can he *be seen* to resist subjectification, by producing texts which show that the institutions enclosing the narrator fail to operate their mechanisms on him.

Genet's sensitivity to the dissecting gaze directed at prisoners to promote obedience and punish transgressions, and his determination not to succumb to it, is revealed in his own redeployment of it in *Notre-Dame-des-Fleurs*. At one point the narrator departs from his characteristic style to introduce his protagonists in an empirical manner, reminiscent of the anthropometric descriptions obtained following physical examinations of detainees undertaken by institutions.[33] 'Genet' thus casts himself as the scrutinizing force: 'Signalement de Notre-Dame-des-Fleurs: taille 1,71m, poids 71kg, visage ovale, cheveux blonds, yeux bleus, teint mat, dents parfaites, nez rectiligne, membre en érection: longueur 0,24m, circonférence 0,10m' [Description of Our Lady of the Flowers: height 1.71 m, weight 71 kg, oval face, blond hair, blue eyes, dull complexion, perfect teeth, straight nose, penis when erect: length 24 cm, circumference 10 cm].[34] Here Genet subverts medical discourse, by expanding its remit to include amongst the usual 'vital statistics' measurements of a uniquely erotic interest. The narrator's talent makes him capable of turning the tables on his jailers: he becomes no longer principally someone who is subject to the controlling scrutiny of a warden, but someone who, whilst subject to surveillance, can subject others to a controlling and desiring gaze for the purposes of his own secret pleasure. This is emblematized in the narrator's description of his illicit masturbation stimulated by the sight of an unknowing prison warder.[35] The *jouissance*, or thrill, obtained is only heightened by the pleasure that comes from turning the surveillance back on his jailer and imposing a taboo desiring gaze on the 'petite vache' [little squealer].[36]

The signal sent out by this manoeuvre is that the narrator does not meekly allow himself to become an individual that can be known, and over whom power can be exerted. Instead, the narrator is in control, and jealously guards his own position of knowledge. This attitude informs Genet's resistance to an orthodox approach to self-writing, resulting in the difficulties we have seen in ascribing his prose works to the literary genre of autobiography. Just as Genet's intradiegetic self turns the tables on the warder, so too Genet's works defy being exploited as fodder either for the prison warder or for the reader looking to gather as much intimate information as possible about the subjectified individual in order to expand their field of knowledge. Genet gestures towards the type of narrative he will not supply in order to evoke the observation-knowledge-power economy which his outlaw selfhood is staked upon resisting.

This sensitivity to the processes of subjectification calls for us to reassess the significance of how Genet approaches autobiography. Genet offers us a scrambled autobiography: the initial apparent straightforwardness of the memoir of prison experience that *Miracle de la rose* seems to offer is undercut by reverie, as the narrative spirals away from the documentary to pay mystical homage to Harcamone, the distant object of desire and fascination for the narrator.[37] *Journal du voleur*, despite some conformity to the conventional model of autobiography, delays the typical autobiographical opening that details the moment of birth until page 49 of the text. In this way, Genet both invokes the conventions of the genre of autobiography, and reveals a resistance to being bound by them. This is compounded by the narrator's sudden dereliction of his task, as he abandons any appearance of providing the chronological progression associated with conventional autobiography by announcing: 'les chapitres qui suivront (j'ai dit qu'un grand nombre est perdu) je les livre en vrac' [the chapters which follow (I have said that a large number are lost) I deliver up at random].[38] If the autobiographer's fundamental purpose is to tell the reader who the author is, then *Journal du voleur* positions itself as a decidedly reluctant autobiography.

By contrast, *Notre-Dame-des-Fleurs*, the furthest removed from conventional autobiography out of the works by Genet studied here, periodically vaunts its autobiographical credentials. We note that the project of this 'Genet' is to 'refaire à ma guise [...] l'histoire de Divine [...], l'histoire de Notre-Dame-des-Fleurs, et *n'en doutez pas, ma propre histoire*' [to re-create in my own way the story of Divine, the story of Our Lady of the Flowers, and, *don't doubt it, my own story*].[39] Moreover, a correspondence between Genet the narrator and the chief protagonist is established (albeit insecurely) by the narrator's explanation that Divine originates from him: 'de moi je fais Divine' [from myself I create Divine].[40] However, the narrator also locates Divine's origin in her boyhood self, Louis Culafroy: if Divine 'is' the narrator Genet, so must Culafroy be. Genet's identity is thus rendered elusive, being dispersed amongst three characters. The narration of the narrator's fantasy life, rather than the one he lives, is also significant in this regard. Whilst this would seem to separate the work from autobiography, as Perec's *W ou le souvenir d'enfance* shows, fantasy is not to be divorced from autobiography: the characters 'Genet' describes are important figures in his life, albeit that it is the mental life, not the experiential life (necessarily limited in this narrator's case) which is concerned. Moreover, Genet suggests elsewhere that this cultivation of an interior world is an important resistance tactic for those under intense surveillance: 'je ne vis pas un seul instant sur terre qu'en même temps je ne le vive dans mon domaine secret' [I do not live one moment on earth which I do not simultaneously live out in my secret realm].[41] *Notre-Dame-des-Fleurs* is an exercise in self-writing, but one where the narratorial self is liberated from the confinement of the confined Genet, to be projected on to others: shadowy characters neither entirely inside the narrator's fantasy, nor his reality — and always beyond the grasp of the reader.

Genet invokes the genre of autobiography by using its hallmark features in his writing, yet the purpose of this gesture towards autobiography is to highlight how the writer resists the drive to conform to its codes: he will not comply with the economy of categorization which is implicated in the subjectification of the self. Such defiance would not be conveyed by a refusal to engage with the genre at all: autobiography is a suspicious form of literary expression, whose own generic parameters are best challenged, not ignored. Genet's self-writings inhabit an in-between position, neither conforming to the usual definitions of autobiography, nor clearly failing to do so. To the observer-reader they are thus generically unintelligible, beyond the law of genre.

This position *hors-la-loi* [outlaw] is one that Genet seeks also for his selfhood, and his manipulation of genre is an integral part of a more fundamental project to portray a selfhood that is unlike, unfathomable, and incomprehensible to any other: in short, an unintelligible, isolated self.

Abjection and the Isolated Self

Genet's sensitivities to the mechanisms of subjectification see him emphasize his failure to cooperate with the institutions that bring this about, including the institution of autobiography itself. Accordingly, in Genet's case autobiography is used, not to anchor the identity of the self, but to undermine the basis for that anchoring. Genet's excursus into the autobiographical illustrates that, contrary to the assumptions underlying the genre, Genet is not the product of his origins. His self is not a result of how and where he was born, or to whom. In an echo of Sartre's existentialist doctrine, Genet shows that people 'start' being who they are: thus Divine is not born, but simply commences her existence; and Culafroy, who is born, does not die, but simply ceases to be. The narrator of *Journal du voleur* similarly describes a transformation in his being at the age of sixteen, arising from the fact that 'en moi-même je sentais le besoin de devenir ce qu'on m'avait accusé d'être' [in myself I felt the need to become what I had been accused of being].[42]

Genet also pays special attention to how the name, often presented in autobiographies as the anchor of the self, fails in his case to explain who he is. The narrator of *Journal du voleur* informs us that his criminal deeds make it necessary to dissimulate his identity behind false passports and assumed names; yet beyond this pragmatic resistance to confirming his official identity, Genet demonstrates a diminished sense of personal investiture in his own name. This arises, it is implied, from his inability to seek out a truth about himself from it. Whereas most people take it for granted from their earliest age that the surname specifies the other from whom we originate (the father), Genet shows himself as being deprived in this respect:

> Quand j'eus vingt et un ans, j'obtins un acte de naissance. Ma mère s'appelait Gabrielle Genet. Mon père reste inconnu. J'étais venu au monde au 22 de la rue d'Assas.
>
> — Je saurai donc quelques renseignements sur mon origine, me dis-je, et je me rendis rue d'Assas. Le 22 était occupé par la Maternité. On refusa de me renseigner.[43]

> [When I was twenty-one, I obtained my birth certificate. My mother was called Gabrielle Genet. My father remains unknown. I came into the world

> at number 22 Assas Street. 'I shall find out something about my origins then,' I said to myself, and I went to Assas Street. Number 22 was occupied by the maternity hospital. They refused to give me any information.]

Genet compensates for this lack of information by developing an affinity for the broom flowers that bear (almost) the same name as he does: 'Quand je rencontre dans la lande [...] des fleurs de genêt, j'éprouve à leur égard une sympathie profonde' [When in the country I encounter broom flowers, I experience a profound sympathy with them].[44] The claim for a closer sense of kinship with flowers than with progenitors is reinforced by the recurrence of extended floral figures (the broom, the rose, 'Notre-Dame-des-*Fleurs*' [Our Lady of the *Flowers*]) in Genet's work. Having identified himself with the flowers, his true origins become irrelevant to his identity. Genet shows how the epistemological strategies associated with autobiography are incapable of supplying the keys to his identity.

The use value of autobiography for Genet is that it can increase the sense that his self is unknowable. With the objective of preventing his self becoming an object for his reader's knowledge and consumption, his goal is not to write his self. Rather, it is to 'réussir [s]a légende' [succeed in creating his legend]. The purpose of Genet's self-writing is to acquaint the reader with a self — but only insofar as it is a self with which it will prove impossible to become acquainted. This is what ultimately confirms Genet's self as being beyond the grasp of the autobiographical narrative, its reader, and, by extension, the law. This project takes the form of Genet's bid to achieve for himself something that his most exalted characters possess: *sainteté*, or saintliness: an isolated position which involves cultivating an abject identity.[45]

Genet is well known for his frequent inversions of the values of good and evil; that is to say, for embracing the position of the abject, which in its everyday sense signifies that which is 'cast off, rejected; brought low in position, condition or status; in low repute; lacking courage; despicable; self-abasing'.[46] In *Notre-Dame-des-Fleurs*, this capacity to embrace what mainstream society terms repugnant is described as what confers sainthood on Divine (her most precious attribute). Saintliness, then, represents, not a status, but a certain stance: it represents the virtue of embracing what is most foul or *immonde*: 'la sainteté c'est de faire servir la douleur. C'est forcer le diable à être Dieu. C'est obtenir la reconnaissance du mal' [saintliness is making use of pain. It's forcing the Devil to be God. It's obtaining the recognition of evil].[47] According to *Journal du voleur*, this is the attitude which Genet aspires to for his selfhood.

However, Genet's saintly abjection is not a quality of his selfhood which his autobiographical works document: instead, his writing represents the means by which Genet's abject identity can be secured. Accordingly, his self-writings are characterized by a sustained preoccupation with the realm of the abject. In his autobiographical writing Genet vaunts his taste for all that mainstream society calls vile and despicable. This leads to a eulogy to everything that is abject in the dictionary's sense, and a determination to embody whatever society fails to tolerate, in particular criminal and homosexual orientations: 'Je me reconnaissais le lâche, le traître, le voleur, le pédé qu'on voyait en moi' [I recognized in myself the coward, the traitor, the thief, the poof that others saw in me].[48] According to his self-representations, whatever society excludes from itself, Genet worships. Definitive proof of Genet's commitment to nonconformity with society's rules comes in his enduring fascination with men who are sufficiently base and resilient to socialization that they break the ultimate taboo: murder. In *Notre-Dame-des-Fleurs*, Divine is venerated for reaching 'cet état surhumain ou extra-lucide [...] de l'assassin aveugle qui tient le couteau, le fusil, ou la fiole' [this superhuman or hyper-lucid state of the blind assassin who holds the knife, the gun or the poison-vial].[49] Indeed, this work is dedicated to the memory of a dead murderer, Maurice Pilorge: his execution was the penalty for the murder of his male lover, whom he had also robbed prior to the killing. Without this example, Genet affirms in his authorial preface, 'je n'eusse jamais écrit ce livre' [I would never have written this book].[50] Similarly, the deeds of the double murderer Harcamone, memorialized in *Miracle de la rose*, draw 'Genet' to him, with the result that Harcamone functions throughout the text as the veiled and absent phallus, the forever unattainable object of the narrator's desire.

In a gesture of veneration for all forms of the abject, Genet attempts to identify himself with these exemplary, inspirational criminals, whose 'fautes parfois [...] font surgir la poésie' [faults sometimes precipitate poetry].[51] This narratorial glorification of what is abject and vile constitutes an attempt on the part of 'Genet' (or is that Genet?) to exclude himself from society, as one who incomprehensibly adores what his peers abhor. However, this is not the only way in which this author harnesses the abject, with the aim of eluding the forces that would subject him to their law.

It is useful here to consider the abject from another viewpoint. Kristeva theorizes the abject from the perspective of psychoanalysis, positing that the abject is horrifying and disturbing because it is *between positions*: it is 'ni sujet ni objet' [neither subject nor object], but threatens the security of both subjectivity and objectivity as states.[52] For Kristeva, the abject is first encountered when the infant self experiences a need to split itself off from its mother's self and body in order to become its own self, but it cannot posit the mother as an object, for it knows only a conjoined self. A crisis in separation occurs whereby the mother's bodily presence stirs up hatred and yet is not accepted as other, as the object which will be inevitably lost. The abject can thus be understood to oscillate between two forms. It is a troublesome and troubling presence, being what is excluded from the self but not yet made other. Thus to be abject means both to be what is rejected, and what is in-between. Perceiving the abject, the thing which is not subject and not object, as disgusting or taboo is the first step in recognizing boundaries between self and other. However, from within the logic of the abject it is impossible for this recognition to occur, since the abject state is characterized by a perverse response to the law of the symbolic (society's law), which is neither recognized *nor is refused recognition*.

In his resistance to having his text or his self categorized, Genet provides an almost textbook example of the abject disposition Kristeva describes:

> Ce n'est donc pas l'absence de propreté ou de santé qui rend abject, mais ce qui perturbe une identité, un système, un ordre. Ce qui ne respecte pas les limites, les places, les règles. L'entre-deux, l'ambigu, le mixte. Le traître, le menteur, le criminel à bonne conscience.[53]

> [It is thus not lack of cleanliness or health that causes abjection but what disturbs identity, system, order. What does not respect borders, positions, rules. The in-between, the ambiguous, the composite. The traitor, the liar, the criminal with a good conscience.][54]

In particular, Genet's demonstrated inclination to defy and invalidate the economy of knowledge, observation and power which subjectifies him (and to be seen to do so) corresponds with the work of the abject: 'l'*abject*, objet chu, est radicalement un exclu et me tire vers là où le sens s'effondre' [what is *abject*, [...] the jettisoned object, is radically excluded and draws me toward the place where meaning collapses].[55] The abject in Kristeva's thought is the nexus where loss of sense and the excluded are brought together and mutually reinforce each other. The attractiveness of the abject for one such as Genet is connected with its challenge to the epistemological order. Categories themselves are attacked by the abject, making it possible to occupy an isolated position beyond that order's power to conceptualize. This position is that of the *hors-la-loi* or outlaw — but not simply of the outlaw who defies the codes of society: rather, of the one who is outside the law in the sense that their being and conduct is beyond the law's comprehension.

The abject in the Kristevan sense, namely a state marked by an unintelligible indeterminacy, is much exploited by Genet in his autobiographical writings. A key locus for the abject in Genet's work is in his elaboration of the concept of *sainteté* [saintliness], the condition that he tells us he aspires to secure for himself: for Genet, the indeterminate abject is built into the very notion of the saint.[56] As the concept of saintliness develops across Genet's autobiographical works, it becomes clear that what he terms a saint is someone who has become a type of icon, a pure image. *Sainteté*, or saintliness, is the name given to the instant when it becomes apparent that, in the eyes of others, an image substitutes for an individual: an image inadequate to convey the magnitude of their person, and which empties out the identity from the self. In the case of the Genetian saint, there is an acknowledgement that the person is untouchable behind the mask of their image. In poststructuralist terms, *sainteté* results from the ineffaceable mark of the slippage between the signifier and the signified. To recognize this slippage and to cultivate it allows the subject to transcend the coercive strictures of society, as Divine finds: '"[...] Qu'importe *à moi* le souvenir qu'il garde de moi. Je suis une autre. Je serai chaque fois une autre." [...] Ainsi, elle se trouvait toujours prête pour quelque nouvelle infamie, sans ressentir la crainte de l'oppobre' ['What difference does it make *to me* how he remembers me. I am other. Each time I will be other.' Thus, she found herself always ready for some new infamy, without feeling the fear of opprobrium].[57] What Divine articulates, and derives her sense of empowerment from, is the indeterminacy of her identity. As the identity of a saint is predicated on the substitution of this pure image for selfhood, a saint is neither the image, nor not the image. The virtue of the saint is to elude knowledge, and evade categorization. In the Kristevan sense too, then, Genet's saints are abject.

Evading categorization is not only the preserve of the saint, however. Genet's portrayal of the complex gender identifications of the *folles* [queens] in *Notre-Dame-des-Fleurs* reveals their ability to scramble the gender boundaries that institutions recognize. This includes the institution of language: despite the predominant use of feminine pronouns and adjectives, the narrator reminds us that, having 'her' origins in Culafroy, 'Divine est *aussi* un homme' [Divine is *also* a man].[58] Refusing to restrict himself to the established binary gender categories, Genet illustrates a preference once more for a position where what the self *is* exceeds the limit of categories imposed on it. This applies to sexual categories too: Genet's autobiographical writing is peppered with characters such as Notre-Dame-des-Fleurs and Bulkaen (and 'Genet' himself), who resist categorization, fitting neither into the sexual roles of the macho 'dur' [tough guy], nor of the effeminate, passive 'enculé' [bum boy]. The manly Notre-Dame-des-Fleurs has an effeminate name of the type reserved usually for 'folles' [queens], whilst in *Miracle de la rose*, Bulkaen 'avant que d'être un casseur, [...] un "gars régul" — et bien qu'il fût tout cela — il était d'abord "un mec qui s'fait taper dans la lune"' [was, before being a delinquent, a 'regular bloke' — and even though he was all those things — he was first and foremost 'a bloke who takes it up the arse'].[59] Bulkaen's is a difficult and precarious situation, since the tough inmates are characterized by their (sexual) invulnerability. To maintain this ambiguous position is therefore all the more admirable, even inexplicable — and most importantly, abject: 'Bulkaen était un ange pour arriver à se tenir si élégamment en équilibre au-dessus de sa propre abjection' [Bulkaen was an angel to manage to keep his balance so elegantly above his own abjection].[60]

This elegant, rather than dirty, position of abjection is something which Genet cultivates for himself too. Genet glorifies criminals found guilty of the most heinous of crimes, citing them as his muses: muses who, by the very 'virtue' of their crimes, stimulate his creativity. When the narrator of *Miracle de la rose* tells us that Harcamone's crimes 'libérèrent de tels effluves de roses qu'il [Harcamone] en restera parfumé, et son souvenir et le souvenir de son séjour ici, jusqu'aux plus reculés de nos jours' [liberated such a rosy fragrance that he (Harcamone) will keep their perfume, and so will the memory of him and of his stay here, until the most distant of our days], he is suggesting that the form these roses take is that of his own writing.[61] These crimes are the springboard transforming 'Genet' into a writer — something else besides the criminal delinquent the narrator portrays himself as. Becoming known as an author is itself an abject strategy: its effect is to confer on him an over-determined identity as both writer and abject criminal. The occupation of each of these positions prevents him from fully occupying the other. This consequently enables Genet as narrator to hedge his bets where his identity is concerned (much as the author did in life): an important step in Genet's project to remove himself from the surveillance-power economy that would categorize and subjectify him. Sartre locates the essence of Genet's defiance and triumph in his statement that 'je serai le voleur' [I shall be the thief]; the implication of Genet's handling of categorization is that this empowerment *vis-à-vis* the law is achieved at the point where, to distort the quotation, 'je serai *plus que* le voleur' [I shall be *more than* the thief].

This in-between abject, although less prominent in Genet's work than the disgusting abject, has an important role to play in Genet's empowerment: without it, the risk is that Genet will simply be recuperated into the surveillance-knowledge-power economy as a lawbreaker, rather than recognized for being beyond the reach of the law.

For Foucault, however, no one is beyond the reach of the law; even the prisoner who has committed the most heinous crimes is reattached to society by allowing himself to be subject to the judicial system, which will play its part, as one system alongside others, in re-subjectifying him:

> le délinquant n'est pas hors la loi; il est, et même dès le départ, dans la loi, au cœur même de la loi, ou du moins en plein milieu de ces mécanismes qui font passer insensiblement de la discipline à la loi, de la déviation à l'infraction.[62]
>
> [The delinquent is not outside the law; he is, from the very outset, in the law, at the very heart of the law, or at least in the midst of those mechanisms that transfer the individual imperceptibly from discipline to the law, from deviation to offence.][63]

Much is therefore at stake in the project Genet pursues: he exploits — perhaps even perverts — the conventions of autobiography. He produces multiple, conflicting and self-consciously unreliable self-representations in a bid to make his self unintelligible, causing it to exceed categorization, and thus become abject in the Kristevan sense. The difficulty for Genet arises when this second sense of the abject is itself marginalized from his venture. This is what we shall see occurring in the interface between Genet and his readers.

Readers and Identifications

An early indication that harnessing the abject in his autobiographical writing may not have the desired effect of securing for Genet the position of the *hors-la-loi* that he covets comes in Sartre's magisterial existentialist biography of the writer.[64] This reveals how the philosopher has been hoodwinked by Genet's ambiguous relationship to literary genre into applying the information the author supplies about his protagonists to the Genet who exists outside the text.[65] In his discussion of Genet's situation in language, Sartre conflates Divine, as well as the 'Genet' who narrates *Miracle de la rose*, with the real-life Genet, drawing conclusions on this author's own relationship with language. We are told in *Notre-Dame-des Fleurs* that the *argot* of the *durs* [macho men] is reserved exclusively for virile, active men, and that Divine is admonished when she uses it: 'La gonzesse qui fait son dur' [The chick is talking like her man].[66] Sartre declares that as a 'homosexuel passif' [passive homosexual], Genet 'n'a pas le droit d'en user [de l'argot] pour communiquer' [does not have the right to use it [slang] in communication]. He thus identifies the writer with his protagonist.[67]

In this example, Genet's tactic of apparently disseminating his selfhood between various protagonists in his autobiographical writings, making this self more elusive for whoever tries to pin it down, has been so successful in scrambling readings of the Genetian self that Sartre is seemingly unaware of his own error in assuming that Divine's situation maps on to that of the flesh-and-blood Genet. This sets the scene for subsequent critical engagements with Genet and his work.

A burgeoning critical preoccupation with issues of identity and politics, and in the possible intersection of the two, has been instrumental in the revived interest that scholars and critics have shown in Genet since the early 1990s. The biographical and the autobiographical take centre stage here, with recent critics frequently gravitating towards those of Genet's writings which focus on the Palestinians, incarceration, or homosexuality.[68] Earlier discussions in this study have revealed autobiography to be particularly rich terrain for the articulation of identity politics. In the realm of queer theory, insights that sexual identities are inherently political have led to calls to develop a politics of identity around homosexuality.[69] This project has taken two forms: either deconstructing sexual identities (a strand of queer theory often associated with Butler's work), or else reconfiguring existing sexual identities in such a way as to reclaim them.[70] Autobiographical texts play an especially prominent role in this second endeavour, and Genet's autobiography in particular. In what turns out to be a somewhat incongruous move, his autobiographical works have been mobilized by critics as affirmations of queer — more specifically, male homosexual — identities.

At a time when homosexual acts between consenting adult men had only just been decriminalized in the United Kingdom, discussion of homosexuality in Genet's work depicted it as a 'problem', and treated it alongside the other problem of 'evil'.[71] More recently, however, Genet has become a central figure in a gay pantheon. This is due to his frankness about his own sexuality, and to what were in their time unusually open and lengthy treatments of homosexual themes.[72] Homosexuality, far from being a problem, becomes for several critics a point of identification with the author.

We see an example of this in the work of Neil Bartlett, who reveals his attraction to Genet as a writer of a 'dirty book'.[73] He then goes on to posit the existence of a gay trait in writing — 'monotony' — which forms a point of commonality between Bartlett himself and Genet, amongst other authors. Reading, identification, and desire in the literary critic, it is made glaringly apparent, are very closely intermingled. For James Creech, the homosexuality that he as a critic shares with Genet allows for more than just identification: it provides a privileged degree of insight into the author's work, allowing this critic to reach a level of understanding that others cannot reach.[74]

For Leo Bersani, the identification that he makes with Genet on the basis of a common sexual preference is a starting point for a rather grander project. In his *Homos*, Bersani argues that if homosexual identity is to be reconfigured, it is important that this be done from within homosexual desire. As a self-identified gay man, he turns to Genet's portrayal of homosexual sex for an insight into what an emancipatory queer praxis should involve. Two men enjoying anal sex, standing one behind the other, as do Riton and Erik in *Pompes funèbres*, transcend a purely sexual *jouissance* [thrill]: they assert 'the radical homo-ness of their homosexual adventure, emerging from their refusal, or inability, to love anything *other* than themselves — which might be translated politically as their failure to accept a relation with any given social arrangement'.[75] For Bersani, Genet, as a 'gay outlaw', exemplifies the kind of attitude which queer theorists should adopt and which should dictate the direction of queer theory. Vital to Bersani's position is the notion that the distance separating Genet from the community at large can be bridged by 'homos'.

However, just as we saw with Perec, this sort of identification that critics develop with Genet for political ends is problematic.[76] In this case, some critics see in Genet (and those of his literary works with the most developed homosexual themes) the basis for mobilizing what has been described as 'politics of identification', whereby a particular individual makes a deliberate, and political, decision to emphasize their commonality with a certain other individual.[77] This is designed to advance the cause of gay identity politics by rendering dissident sexual identities more visible. When this project is carried through into the domain of the literary, with identifications being made between readers and writers, it encounters particular pitfalls. For example, Butler counsels that we should not look to the writing (and by extension reading) of autobiography as a tool which will contribute to a triumph over homophobic oppression, since a queer individual who writes in the first person is — just like their straight counterparts — susceptible to subjectification to the heterosexist system before and during their writing act.[78]

Another factor which makes such identifications between reader and writer problematic is that they rely on the premise that autobiography supplies the type of authoritative information about the living author necessary to ascertain what his identity is, and to establish an identification with him on the basis of it. Such assumptions, as we have seen, are the very ones which French autobiographers have been most keen to challenge. Indeed, in the case of Genet, this very knowledge of the author is precisely what he is most invested in withholding from his reader: allowing readers to become acquainted with the 'real' Genet through his work is antipathic to his overriding concern in his autobiographical writing to keep his identity slippery, and so resist being a known — and thus subjectified — quantity.

If queer theoretical critics fall prey to reimposing categorization on Genet, it is perhaps because he himself falls back on categorization where others are concerned: principally (and ironically) his readers. Unlike Sarraute and Perec, Genet does not attribute the failure of autobiographical works to wholly convey the self and life of the autobiographer to deficiencies deriving from the nature of autobiography itself, or the nature of selfhood. The authorial disclaimer in Genet's case does not inform the reader, implicitly or otherwise, that 'I cannot write my self/life'. Rather, the message is that '*you* cannot read my self/life'. What Genet's self-writings communicate to his readers is that they will be unable to distil 'the truth' about him from his writing. In part this is because, as we have seen, writing is an instrument used to consolidate his saintliness — the individual's possession of a hidden dimension that will never be fathomed.

However, Genet gives a second reason, which receives greater and more explicit emphasis in his prose, for why his readers can never hope to gain the knowledge that would satisfy their consuming desire, but would also leave Genet subjugated. That is the reader's own presumed shortcomings. Each of Genet's three autobiographical narrators draws attention to these; the overarching argument they make is that the reader will never be able to identify with Genet or his protagonists, for their existences are far removed from what the reader will know or be able to understand. The life of an imprisoned criminal must contrast with that of the reader, who is assumed to be law-abiding, and will in consequence never know 'l'épaisseur, que vous ne pouvez qu'imaginer, des murs de la prison' [the thickness, which you can only imagine, of the prison walls].[79] Nor can the reader understand the criminal's mentality: Genet writes, '[v]ous avez le souci de votre honneur, de votre réputation, vous calculez pour les sauver. Le casseur, dans son métier, ne fait pas ces calculs' [You are concerned with your honour, your reputation, you reckon to preserve them. The burglar, in his job, does not make these calculations].[80] Not being able to know, or even adequately imagine, the world of the prisoner leaves the reader epistemologically disenfranchised next to the jailbird narrator.

The extended depiction of the homosexual milieu in *Notre-Dame-des-Fleurs* also lends Genet an opportunity to refuse commonality of experience with the reader, who is resolutely constructed as heterosexual, and whose 'straightness' goes beyond being attracted exclusively to the opposite sex. Divine and her peers are queer, not only because they are involved in same-sex relationships, but because those relationships themselves are not conducted according to the codes operating in heterosexual society, which would not — it is implied — tolerate between men and women the erotic triangles that Divine lives through with Notre-Dame-des-Fleurs, Mignon and Seck Gorgui: 'Nos ménages, la loi de nos Maisons, ne ressemblent pas à vos Maisons. On s'aime sans amour. Ils n'ont pas le caractère sacramentel. Les tantes sont les grandes immorales' [Our relationships, the law of our establishments, are not the same as your establishments. We love without loving. There is no sacramental quality to them. Queers have no morals].[81] Such interventions are designed to discourage the reader from making identifications with the autobiographical narrator; but ironically, the reader most likely to defer to these pronouncements is the one who has adopted the model of reader relations associated with conventional autobiography — the genre that promotes the possibility of the reader gaining sufficient knowledge of the autobiographer to be able to make identifications with him or her in the first place.

Genet's reader, then, is 'straightened' (in more than one sense) by Genet, in a move which reverses the phenomenon detected by Emma Wilson in her study of how literary texts can queer their readers.[82] Being 'straight', Genet's readers are not permitted to achieve sainthood in the image of Divine, Harcamone or 'Jean Genet', and therefore, on being exposed to the repugnant abject, they may aspire to no more than acclimatizing themselves to the taste of (or indeed for) filth and bodily fluids. Persistent references to 'votre monde' [your world] in *Journal du voleur* and *Miracle de la rose* demarcate clearly a narrative space where the filthy abject is glorified (to the empowerment of excluded, 'ab-jected' subjects such as Divine and Harcamone), and resolutely separate it from the realm of the reader, for whom this glorification — and consequently the empowerment that derives from it — is impossible. Furthering this process of acclimatization to which the reader is subjected, passages in *Notre-Dame-des-Fleurs* describe the narrator's masturbation, whilst the same effect is produced in *Miracle de la rose* by the central emphasis on all forms of the disgusting abject:

> je n'ai voulu par ce livre que montrer l'expérience menée de ma libération d'un état de pénible torpeur, de vie honteuse et basse, occupée par la prostitution, la mendicité et soumise aux prestiges, subjuguée par le charme du monde criminel.[83]

> [My only desire in this book was to show the experience I have had in being liberated from a state of awful torpor, from a base and shameful life, taken up with prostitution and begging, and submitting to the seductions, being subjugated by the charm, of the world of the criminal.]

Descriptions of the abject existence Genet leads in Mettray involve frequent mentions of bodily excreta, such as the smell of farts, excrement stains on clothing and drops of semen on Bulkaen's penis in the morning. This creates a textual space organized around the male body. The creation of this dirty space, or to put it another way, the soiling of this textual space, enacts the defilement of the thoroughly respectable bourgeois reader at whom the narrative is aimed. In the words of Colin Davis: 'Genet offers a [...] partnership built on shifting sands of pretence, indifference and betrayal; his unedifying texts demonstrate that non-encounters and sham dialogues may be just as characteristic of the experience of reading as the encounter of alliance.'[84] The reader who seeks to elevate and empower himself or herself educationally or socially by gaining knowledge of the works of the literary canon will attain such elevation only at the price of being trawled through the territory of the repugnant abject — bodily odours, semen, excrement — as well as criminality, betrayal and homosexuality — in the course of reading Genet's autobiographical works.[85]

This defilement of the reader would seem to be intended as a gesture of Genet's mastery. His readiness to provoke the reader's revulsion at an abjection this reader cannot (in Genet's view) possibly embrace confirms the author's freedom from the constraints and taboos society imposes. This interpretation is supported by Genet's reference in *Pompes funèbres* to '[l]a poésie ou l'art d'utiliser les restes. D'utiliser la merde et de vous la faire bouffer' [poetry or the art of using up waste. Of using shit and making you eat it].[86] Genet must be able to violate and betray his readers to prove that he is free from their control, influence, and moral codes: to show that he is genuinely outside the law. Yet Genet's manoeuvre risks indicating the opposite: apparent betrayal can itself anchor the 'traitor' into the system from which he wishes to free himself. Paradoxically, his strategy actually undermines the sense of isolation it ought to reinforce, since the particular treatment of the reader provides some basis for identification of the reader with the narrator, despite the myriad textual signals that convey that such an identification is not possible.

If Genet refuses himself to be categorized (as this is the first step to being subjectified, subjugated to the laws governing society), he does not ultimately refuse the principle of categorization, for his texts indicate his willingness to impose categories on and use them against those whom he is anxious to identify as being other to himself. That is to say, Genet does not, in the end, maintain the potentially empowering strategy of abjection that involves cultivating indeterminacy.

Genet's reimposition of categories against readers in his autobiographical works potentially undermines the project to harness one quality of the abject — its blindness to distinctions between things — for the purpose of securing the position of Genet's self as *hors-la-loi*: both outside and beyond the reach of the law. This danger surfaces in the sexual sphere too, where the in-between abject ultimately loses out to the decipherable. This can be seen in the treatment Genet metes out to his homosexual characters, in a manoeuvre that gives us further cause to reconsider the basis for queer theorists' identifications with Genet. In his eagerness to valorize forms of sexual behaviour which his readership will perceive as vile and abject, Genet is paradoxically led once again to reapply the binary sexual categories of the heterosexual hegemony, which ultimately proves to undo his attempts to empower the taking up of a position of abjection. The superiority of such abject characters as Divine and Harcamone comes at the price of marginalizing those whose position is less clear.

Genet's narrators may insist on the superiority of *durs* [macho men] such as Harcamone, Villeroy and Divers, but the price for elevating the status of these characters is that the status of the passive partner in homosexual sex is diminished, causing the denigration within the marginalized community of those who share the sexual identity of the intradiegetic Genet, which is marked by the 'besoin que j'avais de faire jouir les marles' [the need I had to give the tough guys their pleasure].[87] Although Genet's sanctification of Divine seems to provide a mechanism of undoing this marginalization, this reiterates a binary model of homosexuality based on a heterosexual model of desire, according to which sexual desire is desire for the opposite. Two different paths to redemption are laid out by Genet, but the redemption of homosexuals depends on their being clearly identified as either a *macho* [macho man] or a *folle* [queen] and performing the corresponding sexual role. There is no redemption possible of the abject queer who holds a genuinely abject, in-between position, such as Bulkaen, or Notre-Dame-des-Fleurs.

Divine's passivity and camp femininity are amongst the attributes that allow her to reach the most abject depths, leading to her sanctification. This is not a pathway open to Notre-Dame-des-Fleurs. He retains an effeminate nickname despite his macho virility, but this tough guy aspect blocks the possibility of his reaching total, repugnant abjection and thus sainthood. However, the element of camp within him, expressed in his name, troubles his status as a macho object of desire, so that even once incarcerated and confirmed in his abject criminality, he cannot receive the adulation of an Harcamone. Notre-Dame-des-Fleurs's inferiority in this respect is indicated by the narrator's very brief account of Notre-Dame-des-Fleurs's execution, which contrasts with the presentation of Harcamone's death in *Miracle de la rose*. As a murderer, Harcamone wields the ultimate power of the phallus: he is a demigod who exerts real force over others. As such, his death creates reverberations, whereas in the case of Notre-Dame-des-Fleurs, 'une nuit de printemps, on dressa la machine dans la cour de la prison. A l'aube, elle était prête à couper. Notre-Dame-des-Fleurs eut la tête coupée par un vrai couteau. Et rien ne se passa' [one night in springtime, they erected the guillotine in the prison courtyard. At dawn, it was ready to slice. Our Lady of the Flowers had his head cut off by a real blade. And nothing happened].[88]

Our impression that Genet cannot sustain a culturally unintelligible position that involves embracing the in-between abject is ultimately confirmed by instances where Genet wavers in his stance. In all three texts Genet's narrator portrays himself as wishing to escape from the situation of the abject outlaw, back into 'votre monde' [your world], from which he ultimately does not wish to be excluded. The narrators of both *Miracle de la rose* and *Journal du voleur* describe giving up prostitution 'dont l'abjection m'apparaît à mesure que m'attire la gloire du vol' [the abjection of which becomes apparent to me commensurately with the glory which attracts me to theft].[89] In addition, the narrator of *Journal du voleur* tells us that he *himself* could never kill someone, because murder 'irrémédiablement, me retrancherait de votre monde' [irrevocably would cut me off from your world].[90]

What causes Genet to fail in his bid to set himself beyond the law is the fact that ultimately Genet cannot (unlike the admired Bulkaen) maintain the in-between abject position of his intradiegetic selves. Genet is determined to establish a relation with his readership. This is what lies behind such double-edged pronouncements to his readers as the direct address made by his narrator in *Notre-Dame-des-Fleurs*:

> Il faut qu'à tout prix, je [...] me confie d'une façon plus directe. Ce livre, j'ai voulu le faire des éléments transposés, sublimés, de ma vie de condamné, je crains qu'il ne dise rien de mes hantises. Encore que je m'efforce à un style décharné, montrant l'os, je voudrais vous adresser, du fond de ma prison, un livre chargé de fleurs, de jupons neigeux, de rubans bleus. Aucun autre passe-temps n'est meilleur.[91]
>
> [At all costs I must share my confidences in a more direct fashion. I wanted to make this book out of sublimated, transposed elements of my prisoner's life; I fear that it will say nothing about what obsesses me. Even whilst I do my best to employ a lean style, showing the bone, I should like to address to you, from the depths of my prison, a book laden with flowers, snow-white petticoats, blue ribbons. No other pastime is better.]

The ambiguity of the Genetian narrator's position is made clearer in *Journal du voleur*. Despite appearing to express his distance from his readership by the way he exerts control over them, 'Genet' demonstrates in a lyrical passage contorted with contradictions that he needs and desires the reader to desire him, and that the will to bring this about underlies all else:

> A la gravité des moyens que j'exige pour vous écarter de moi, mesurez la tendresse que je vous porte. Jugez à quel point je vous aime par ces barricades que j'élève dans ma vie et dans mon œuvre [...] afin que votre haleine (je suis corruptible à l'extrême), ne me puisse pourrir.[92]
>
> [By the gravity of the means which I require in order to distance you from me, measure the tenderness which I bring you. Judge how much I love you by these barricades which I erect in my life and in my work so that your breath (I am corruptible in the extreme) might not spoil me.]

Notwithstanding the many narrative dodges Genet's narrators make in order to elude being grasped by the readership, their manoeuvrings reveal ultimately an affinity with, and desire for, proximity to the other, whose laws and systems have previously been rejected. This passionate attachment to having some kind of a relation with the other is the basis of Genet's eventual subjection to the governing system he tries to evade: the fault lies in his failure to tolerate a situation in which he has no relation to others, where the outlaw identity he is so concerned to cultivate goes unrecognized. Genet's recuperation comes at the point where his first-person narrators define the Genetian self as other to his readers, by means of the vile abject.

This precipitates a change in the way they can perceive him: from being something which is neither one thing nor the other, to *being* an other — an other that readers can consume: an other whom they can incorporate into their system, by identifying with him.

Although he does not ultimately sustain it, Genet exhibits a wavering attitude to the other who contemplates him which is, for Kristeva, typically abject. What Kristeva tells us about the in-between abject is that it vacillates in its in-betweenness; that it is impossible for it to maintain in perpetuity an equal distance between the two entities to which the abject being does not want to belong, or not belong. In abjection, a violent rejection follows on from a passionate attachment, and the impulses of attachment and rejection remain in flux. Although Genet is unable to sustain this disposition, he arguably comes closer to doing so than do some of his readers.

If the reader were to accept that Genet fits into neither one category, nor another, then Genet would successfully have challenged the binary logic that drives categorization; the same logic that is the motor behind his subjectification. What we have observed, however, is that critical readers of Genet's autobiographical writings tend not to be willing to leave Genet's position undecided, culturally unintelligible. Instead they need to make him intelligible in order to identify with him (or against him) as they read. The in-between abject that Genet attempts to claim for his own self-empowerment is unpalatable to his readers, including the queer theorists who see the means to gay empowerment in Genet's use of the disgusting abject. To their community-minded sensibilities, it is preferable to see Genet taking up a definite position. Instead, *he does not* — which, as Creech points out, is the best 'lieu sûr', or safe haven, for him. Genet therefore lives up to the charge of cowardice brought against him by Christopher Lane, for whom Genet is 'the coward [who] stymies his personal identifications, without damaging society's overarching demands'.[93] However, the mature gay pride of the queer theorist, whilst able to cope manfully with being trawled through the dirt by Genet, cannot cope with the idea of his cowardice.

The fact that readers of Genet's autobiography are unwilling to concede that the author may remain unintelligible is, I argue, an effect of the literary genre to which Genet's texts belong — or rather, from which they do not do enough to isolate themselves securely. Genet's self-writing, resistant as it is to giving away knowledge and power, reveals that the generic system of autobiography relies on transactions of knowledge, which ultimately represent transactions of power. These result from the autobiographical subject placing himself as an object to be viewed, studied and finally known by the reader. His primary insight into the work of power in autobiography is that, as a writer, to allow the reader to obtain knowledge of the autobiographer is to contribute to one's own subjectification, because allowing the reader that knowledge involves the subject being culturally intelligible, capable of being classified as a known quantity by reading or viewing others. *This* is the situation that comes about when autobiography lives up to conventional expectations. This vision of autobiography as a mode of writing that makes the subject transparent, intelligible, is surprisingly often unquestioned by Genet critics. The responses of a number of critical readers from various schools of thought converge on this point: all assume that Genet's autobiographical texts will furnish enough information to provide the basis for resolute identifications or disidentifications with not just the narrator, but the flesh-and-blood person — or 'homo' — behind his writings. It is this resounding critical response that confirms that, just as with his selfhood, Genet does not manage to secure a position beyond the law (the law of genre) for *Notre-Dame-des-Fleurs*, *Miracle de la rose* and *Journal du voleur*.

Readers' identifications with the author of an autobiography, as we have seen, may be the expression of a consuming desire for that author which translates into a consuming approach to both his work and his person. Such identifications may be the first step towards a potentially appropriative projection of qualities on to the autobiographical self that transforms the autobiographer's identity into something he no longer recognizes, and over which he has lost control — a particularly unhappy scenario for Genet, for whom control over the self is all. This highly developed reluctance to fulfil the traditional expectations readers have of autobiography creates difficulties for all readers, irrespective of their sexual identity or politics. This has implications for the *positive* identifications which are made with the author (I am like him and he is like me) as much as the negative ones (I am not like him and he is not like me). In consequence, it invites us to rethink the relationship between autobiography and identity politics.

Notes to Chapter 4

1. For example, it receives very little attention from Lecarme and Lecarme-Tabone, and none from Laouyen. Sheringham does, however, discuss Genet's work: see his *Devices*, pp. 146–48; 210–14.
2. See Edmund White, *Genet* (London: Chatto and Windus, 1993), pp. xiii–xxxv
3. See Jacques Derrida, *Glas* (Paris: Galilée, 1974).
4. For an account of Genet's criminal career, see White; and also Harry E. Stewart and Rob Roy McGregor, *Jean Genet: A Biography of Deceit 1910–1951* (New York: Peter Lang, 1989).
5. In the following discussion I shall differentiate between references to Genet the author and those to his narrators of the same name by styling such narrators 'Genet'.
6. *Miracle de la rose*, p. 26.
7. *Journal du voleur*, p. 65.
8. Ibid., p. 69.
9. *Miracle de la rose*, pp. 304–05; see also similar sentiments in *Journal du voleur*, p. 112, n. 1.
10. *Miracle de la rose*, p. 191.
11. *Journal du voleur*, p. 167.
12. Michel Foucault, *Surveiller et punir: naissance de la prison* (Paris: Gallimard, coll. tel, 1975); trans. by Alan Sheridan as *Discipline and Punish: The Birth of the Prison* (London: Allen Lane, 1977).
13. Foucault, *Surveiller*, p. 152; *Discipline and Punish*, pp. 128–29.
14. See Foucault, *Surveiller*, pp. 343–49, cf. *Miracle de la rose*, *passim*. In his introduction to Stephen Barber's critical biography of Genet, White reports that Foucault, who had already become acquainted with Genet, was in 'regular contact' with him at the time of writing *Surveiller et punir*, although it is not clear what degree of influence this friendship had on Foucault's work. See Stephen Barber, *Jean Genet* (London: Reaktion Books, 2004), p. 8.
15. Information given by White, *Genet*, p. xv.
16. *Miracle de la rose*, p. 22.
17. Foucault, *Surveiller*, p. 152.

18. Foucault, *Discipline*, p. 128.
19. *Miracle de la rose*, p. 43.
20. See Judith Butler, *The Psychic Life of Power: Theories in Subjection* (Stanford, CA: Stanford University Press, 1997), p. 7 and *passim*.
21. *Miracle de la rose*, p. 233.
22. *Notre-Dame-des-Fleurs*, p. 34.
23. See Genet's own account of writing clandestinely in *Miracle de la rose*, p. 55 and White's account in *Genet*, p. 270.
24. See Cixous, 'Sorties', in Catherine Clément and Hélène Cixous, *La Jeune née* (Paris: Union Générale d'Editions, coll. 10/18, 1975), pp. 115–246 (p. 154). On the subversive potential 'feminine' writing has, see Cixous, 'Le Rire de la méduse', *Arc*, 61 (1975), 39–54.
25. To my knowledge, the links between Foucauldian subjectification and conventional autobiography have been largely left unexplored. However, see Alex Hughes, *Heterographies: Sexual Difference in French Autobiography* (Oxford: Berg, 1999), pp. 105–19, for a discussion of how Hervé Guibert's *autofiction* resists the Foucauldian panopticon gaze. See also my 'Autobiography, The Dangers of Knowledge and Genet's Suspect Reader', *French Studies*, 59 (2005), 189–202.
26. Foucault, *Histoire de la sexualité*, 1: *La Volonté de savoir* (Paris: Gallimard, coll. tel, 1976), p. 80.
27. Foucault, *The History of Sexuality*, 1: *An Introduction*, trans. by Robert Hurley (Harmondsworth: Penguin, 1990), p. 60.
28. Foucault, *Surveiller*, p. 203. Except where otherwise indicated, the following discussion of prison discipline is based on *Surveiller et punir*.
29. Ibid., p. 225.
30. Foucault, *Surveiller*, p. 292.
31. Foucault, *Surveiller*, p. 226; see also his *Histoire*, p. 43.
32. Jonathan Dollimore, *Sexual Dissidence: Augustine to Wilde, Freud to Foucault* (Oxford: Clarendon Press, 1991), pp. 279–325.
33. See Foucault, *Surveiller*, pp. 218–25.
34. *Notre-Dame-des-Fleurs*, p. 12.
35. *Notre-Dame-des-Fleurs*, pp. 189–90.
36. Ibid., p. 190.
37. The setting of Fontevrault as a prison in which 'Genet' is incarcerated is also a construction of fiction, rather than a representation of fact, cf. White, *Genet*, p. 92; and Barber, pp. 39–42.
38. *Journal du voleur*, p. 233.
39. *Notre-Dame-des-Fleurs*, p. 12 (emphasis mine).
40. *Notre-Dame-des-Fleurs*, p. 193. White concludes that the extent to which Genet himself may have lived like Divine is uncertain, cf. his *Genet*, p. 241.
41. *Miracle de la rose*, p. 45.
42. *Journal du voleur*, p. 198; cf. Culafroy's explanation of the path he has taken in *Notre-Dame-des-Fleurs*, p. 152.
43. *Journal du voleur*, p. 48.
44. *Journal du voleur*, p. 48.
45. David Houston Jones, in his *The Body Abject: Self and Text in Jean Genet and Samuel Beckett* (Bern: Peter Lang, 2000), provides a reading of the abject in Genet's *œuvre*. His focus is particularly on waste matter and the Christian dimension of abjection, rather than autobiographical identity, which is my concern here.
46. This is a motif of Genet's theatre as much as it is of the prose works I explore here. See the classic discussions of Genet's inversion of good and evil in Sartre, *Saint Genet: comédien et martyr*, published as *Œuvres complètes de Jean Genet*, 1 (Paris: Gallimard, 1952), pp. 134–83, 223–34; and in Georges Bataille, *La Littérature et le mal: Emily Brontë — Baudelaire — Michelet — Blake — Sade — Proust — Kafka — Genet* (Paris: Gallimard, 1957), pp. 203–19; the definition of 'abject' is quoted from the *Shorter Oxford English Dictionary*.
47. *Journal du voleur*, p. 232 (see also p. 244).
48. *Journal du voleur*, p. 198.
49. *Notre-Dame-des-Fleurs*, p. 20.

50. *Notre-Dame-des-Fleurs, prière d'insérer.*
51. *Miracle de la rose*, p. 59.
52. Kristeva, *Pouvoirs de l'horreur: essai sur l'abjection* (Paris: Editions du Seuil, coll. Points, 1980), p. 9; trans. by Leon S. Roudiez as *Powers of Horror: An Essay on Abjection* (New York: Columbia University Press, 1982), p. 1.
53. Kristeva, *Pouvoirs*, p. 12.
54. Kristeva, *Powers of Horror*, p. 4.
55. Kristeva, *Pouvoirs*, p. 9; *Powers*, p. 2.
56. *Journal du voleur*, pp. 232–45
57. *Notre-Dame-des-Fleurs*, pp. 224–25.
58. *Notre-Dame-des-Fleurs*, p. 157. On gender identifications in Genet's work, see Pascale Gaitet, 'The Politics of Camp in Jean Genet's *Our Lady of the Flowers*', in *Jean Genet: Littérature et Politique (Literature and Politics)*, ed. by Patrice Bougon, special edn of *Esprit créateur*, 35.1 (Spring 1995), pp. 40–49; and her *Queens and Revolutionaries: New Readings of Jean Genet* (Newark: University of Delaware Press; London: Associated University Presses, 2003).
59. *Miracle de la rose*, p. 168.
60. Ibid.
61. *Miracle de la rose*, p. 59.
62. Foucault, *Surveiller*, p. 352.
63. Foucault, *Discipline*, p. 301.
64. See Sartre, *Saint Genet*.
65. Identifying Sartre's slip, Derrida remarks that this is a common phenomenon amongst Genet's readers. See Derrida, *Glas*, p. 243. Where Genet critics frequently agree is in finding that Genet's work is strewn with many snares for the reader, citing examples of where their precursors have become entrapped. For examples, see especially: Bataille, pp. 220–22, 235; Philip Thody, 'Sartre and White: Biographers of a Contrary Child', in *Flowers and Revolution: A Collection of Writings on Jean Genet*, ed. by Barbara Read (London: Middlesex University Press, 1997), pp. 25–32; Robert Harvey, 'Genet's Open Enemies: Sartre and Derrida', in *Genet: In the Language of the Enemy*, ed. by Scott Durham, special edn of *Yale French Studies*, 91 (1997), pp. 103–16; Ian H. Magedera, '*Seing* Genet, Citation and Mourning; a propos *Glas* by Jacques Derrida', *Paragraph*, 21 (1998), 28–44; Elizabeth Stephens, 'Disseminating Phallic Masculinity: Seminal Fluidity in Genet's Fiction', in *Genet*, ed. by Mairéad Hanrahan, special edn of *Paragraph*, 27.2 (July 2004), pp. 85–97; and Richard Webb and Suzanne Webb, *Jean Genet and his Critics: An Annotated Bibliography 1943–1980* (London: Scarecrow Press, 1982).
66. *Notre-Dame-des-Fleurs*, p. 42.
67. Sartre, *Saint Genet*, p. 322. cf. my above observation on how Genet takes pains to stipulate in his autobiographical writings that as a man he assumes an active sexual role.
68. See, for example, Clare Finburgh, 'Jean Genet and the Poetics of Palestinian Politics: Statecraft as Stagecraft in "Quatre heures à Chatila"', *French Studies*, 56 (2002), 495–509; Pierre Laforgue, *'Notre-Dame-des-Fleurs' ou la symphonie carcérale* (Toulouse: Presses Universitaires du Mirail, 2002); Frieda Ekotto, *L'Ecriture carcérale et le discours juridique chez Jean Genet* (Paris: L'Harmattan, 2001); Roland A. Champagne, 'Jean Genet in the Delinquent Colony of Mettray: The Development of an Ethical Rite of Passage', *French Forum*, 26.3 (Fall 2001), 71–90. On Genet and homosexuality, see my 'Friend or Foe? Misidentification and Genet's Queer Reception', in *Soi-disant: Life-Writing in French*, ed. by Juliana de Nooy, Joe Hardwick and Barbara E. Hanna (Newark: University of Delaware Press, 2005), pp. 26–40; Stephens, '"Je suis un mensonge qui dit toujours la vérité": Genet's Queer Subjectivities', in de Nooy, Hardwick and Hanna (eds), pp. 41–52; and also her 'Disseminating'.
69. For a useful account of the evolutions in the identity politics of sexual minorities, see Steven Seidman, 'Identity and Politics in a "Postmodern" Gay Culture: Some Historical and Conceptual Notes', in *Fear of a Queer Planet: Queer Politics and Social Theory*, ed. by Michael Warner (Minneapolis: University of Minnesota Press, 1993), pp. 105–42.
70. The classic example of the first tendency is Butler, *Gender Trouble: Feminism and the Subversion of Identity* (New York: Routledge, 1990); the second tendency in queer theory, as exemplified by Leo Bersani, *Homos* (Cambridge, MA: Harvard University Press, 1995), will concern us

particularly in this chapter. For an overview of queer theory, see Donald E. Hall, *Queer Theories* (Basingstoke: Palgrave Macmillan, 2003).

71. For the reading of homosexuality as a 'problem', see Thody, *Jean Genet: A Study of his Works and Plays* (London: Hamish Hamilton, 1968), pp. 25–54.
72. For Genet as a figure in a gay pantheon, see Dollimore, along with the following studies of gay and lesbian writing, which both accord Genet a prominent position: Christopher Robinson, *Scandal in the Ink: Male and Female Homosexuality in Twentieth-Century French Literature* (London: Cassell, 1995); and Paul Robinson, *Gay Lives: Homosexual Autobiography from John Addington Symonds to Paul Monette* (Chicago: University of Chicago Press, 1999).
73. See Neil Bartlett, 'The Uses of Monotony: Repetition in the Language of Oscar Wilde, Jean Genet, Edmund White and Juan Goytisolo', in Read (ed.), pp. 113–27 (p. 120).
74. James Creech, 'Outing Jean Genet', in Durham (ed.), pp. 117–40.
75. Bersani, p. 171.
76. A tendency amongst Genet scholars generally to 'domesticate the otherness of Genet's texts by finding in them echoes of their own values' is noted by Colin Davis, *Ethical Issues in Twentieth-Century French Fiction: Killing the Other* (Basingstoke: Macmillan, 2000), pp. 156–57.
77. On the politics of identification, see Butler, *Bodies that Matter: On the Discursive Limits of 'Sex'* (London: Routledge, 1993), pp. 223–30; and Diana Fuss, *Identification Papers* (New York: Routledge, 1995). For observations on identifications made by queer theoretical critics with Genet, see Davis, p. 157.
78. On gay autobiographical writing in particular, see Butler, *Bodies*, pp. 122–24. On subjectification, see also her *Psychic Life*.
79. *Notre-Dame-des-Fleurs*, p. 15.
80. *Miracle de la rose*, p. 38.
81. *Notre-Dame-des-Fleurs*, pp. 59–60.
82. See Emma Wilson, *Sexuality and the Reading Encounter: Identity and Desire in Proust, Duras, Tournier and Cixous* (Oxford: Clarendon Press, 1996).
83. *Miracle de la rose*, p. 39.
84. Davis, p. 155.
85. On the treatment of the reader, see Sartre, *Saint Genet*, pp. 463–510; and Davis, 'Genet's *Journal du voleur* and the Ethics of Reading', *French Studies*, 48 (1994), 50–62.
86. Genet, *Pompes funèbres* (Paris: Gallimard, coll. L'Imaginaire, 1953), p. 190.
87. *Miracle de la rose*, p. 191.
88. *Notre-Dame-des-Fleurs*, p. 222.
89. *Miracle de la rose*, p. 148.
90. *Journal du voleur*, p. 120.
91. *Notre-Dame-des-Fleurs*, p. 131.
92. *Journal du voleur*, p. 235.
93. Christopher Lane, 'The Voided Role: On Genet', *MLN*, 112 (1997), 876–908 (p. 899).

CHAPTER 5

Hélène Cixous
Autobiography, the Ethics of Knowledge and Strategies of Self-Writing

Questions of identity, politics, the politics of identity and the identifications readers make with authors surface once more in latter works by Cixous.[1] A comparatively recent evolution in Cixous's writing career has been her turn, in a clutch of texts written in the 1990s, towards a more public exploration of her life in Algeria prior to her definitive emigration to France.[2] This treatment of the Algerian past enables an exploration of the significant effect that Cixous's hybrid, multifaceted ethnicity has on a personal identity which proves to have been indelibly marked by her experience of growing up in colonial Algeria as a non-Algerian, but also non-French, Jew.[3] For readers well acquainted with Cixous's *œuvre*, this autobiographical turn marks a significant thematic departure, as well as a reconciliation with a genre from which Cixous had previously kept her distance.[4] In literary and academic circles, Cixous's identity as a writer had previously been bound up with her academic and literary explorations of questions of gender: in particular the gender of writing, and the possibility of writing in the feminine gender, using an *écriture féminine* [feminine mode of writing].[5]

In her *Hélène Cixous: photos de racines* (hereafter abbreviated to *Photos de racines*), *Les Rêveries de la femme sauvage: scènes primitives* (hereafter *Les Rêveries de la femme sauvage*) and *Le Jour où je n'étais pas là*, this gendered identity takes a back seat as Cixous places questions of knowledge, lack of knowledge and faulty knowledge of the Cixousian self at the heart of her autobiographical endeavours. Whilst Cixous's complicated ethnic identity and her relationship to it is a particular object of this ignorance or mis-knowledge, the identity she has acquired as a feminist is implicated too. The adventure of writing the self thus brings in its wake adventures in knowing the self for both writer and reader. Cixous's preoccupation with knowledge in this group of texts operates on two levels. Most straightforwardly, Cixous uses her autobiographical writings since 1990 to correct some of the failures of knowledge directed at her person, adding to and challenging the knowledge which her audience has of her; and also, ultimately, the knowledge she has of herself.

More abstractly, however, *Photos de racines* sustains the challenge that Cixous's distinctive experimental, poetic prose has long directed at phallogocentric notions of epistemology. In this genre-defying text she interrogates the epistemological possibilities that different modes of autobiographical discourse open up or close down. Cixous inquires into *how* we can know our own or another self. This interrogation of the basis for our knowledge of the self leads to a reflection on conventional ways of writing the self. Unsurprisingly in an author known for breaking out of the paradigms governing creative and academic writing, the genre of autobiography is a specific target of Cixous's critique in *Photos de racines*. The basis for this critique lies in Cixous's concept of self–other relations: as Gusdorf states, autobiography as a genre is predicated on the concept that the self has an individuality, a distinctness which ultimately separates it from others (although naturally it maintains relations with them that will be crucial in shaping what kind of individual it is).[6] Yet a long-standing theme in Cixous's *œuvre* is that the boundaries between self and other are far more pervious.[7] We have learned from Sarraute that such an insight will inevitably have implications for the author's relationship to the genre of autobiography; so it proves with Cixous. In *Photos de racines* and subsequent self-writings, Cixous pursues her interest in the boundaries of selfhood beyond its ramifications for autobiography as a genre: she draws on her own biography to explore where the borders between self and other lie, and what possibilities there are for their relation to one another. In particular, Cixous investigates the possibility (and the implications for self-writing) of a relation with the other based on fusion. In pursuing this idea, Cixous remains on familiar ground for readers well acquainted with her work: a vision of a relation between selves based on merging, giving and generosity (and marked as 'feminine'), a relation corresponding to what Cixous calls 'love', was posited as long ago as her 1975 essay 'Sorties'.[8]

The critique of autobiography in *Photos de racines* is, quite literally, only part of the story. In her two later Algerian-themed autobiographical works, Cixous resorts to very different strategies of writing her self. The voyage into Algeria becomes a voyage into the knowledge Cixous has of herself, and which readers do not have. As Cixous's exploration of interactions between her self and others deepens, some more unexpected perspectives emerge which cause us to reassess many of our impressions about the author.

In these later works Cixous's interrogation of the basis for our knowledge of our own or another self gradually extends into an investigation into the ethical issues subtending our search for such knowledge. Here we find Cixous travelling onto territory similar to that covered by Sarraute as she considers what one self is entitled to demand of another. These reflections on interpersonal relations lead to an unsettling of the ways we have of reading and knowing Cixous's self: in particular, her insights call into question prevailing ideas about how Cixous herself relates to others, including her readers, and how they can relate to her. Whereas for many readers Cixous herself has been associated with a paradigm of self–other relations characterized by openness, intimacy, even amalgamation between self and other, the portrayal of contact between self and other in the author's more recent self-writings challenges the way we have come to know her, revealing to us a self irreconcilably estranged from others and from herself; a self, moreover, whose estrangement is to be respected by others, not rectified. Out of this unbridgeable estrangement, both *Les Rêveries de la femme sauvage* and *Le Jour où je n'étais pas là* pursue a meditation on knowledge that extends beyond the initial narratorial preoccupation with knowing the self better, or helping others to know it better. In these self-writings Cixous interrogates the ethics of knowledge itself. This is a move which will lead to an apparent redefinition of her own ethic of 'love', which has provided the ideal behind her vision of selfhood, as well as a renegotiation of the relationship she prefers to have with the reader. This is a journey in writing the self that will be seen to have profound implications for the self that Cixous writes, as well as the way that this self is written and related to by others. Cixous's writing of the self becomes a writing of self-estrangement: a development which has important consequences for Cixous's relationship with the genre of autobiography, leading her autobiographical practice to take an unexpected turn back towards a more traditional incarnation of autobiography. Where our journey into Cixous's self-writing starts, however, is with the more familiar image of her as someone departing from autobiographical norms.

Hors la loi du genre? Cixous, Autobiography, Deconstruction

Whilst it is not an assessment that the writer herself has latterly endorsed, in the eyes of many, Cixous remains known primarily as a feminist, and as a theorist. Although she has long maintained a prodigious output of fictional writing, plays and essays, perhaps her best known work, and the one which has arguably done the most to seal her reputation and secure this enduring association with the feminist movement, is her polemical essay of 1975, 'Le Rire de la méduse'.[9]

In this work, concerns with the realm of autobiographical expression are already present. Cixous argues that women, unlike men, are unable to infuse their writing with their own subjectivity: the particularly feminine subjectivity that marks them as women. For Cixous, the masculine, logocentric values which shape language and discourse exclude specifically feminine modes of thought and expression from writing. (This is obviously a particularly serious state of affairs in autobiography, whose *raison d'être* is to be a privileged site for the expression of subjectivity.) She calls for this exclusion of the womanly from all written discourse to be remedied: 'que la femme s'écrive: que la femme écrive de la femme et fasse venir les femmes à l'écriture' [Woman must write her self: must write about women and bring women to writing].[10] The lyrical, metaphorical and connotative use Cixous makes of language in 'Le Rire de la méduse' illustrates what form this more authentically feminine writing, this writing 'à l'encre blanche' [in white ink], will take.[11] This call to arms marks the birth of Cixous's legendary *écriture féminine* [feminine writing], and at the heart of it is the objective of making a place in writing for specifically feminine autobiographical expression.

It is little wonder, then, that Cixous's work has been widely taken up by feminist critics. It has proved especially influential for feminist autobiography scholars, who, as we have seen in Chapter 1, seek a form of autobiography more hospitable to women. In this essay, Cixous is alert to the way that writing, because it is always writing in the masculine, has historically alienated women from their womanly identities (and in particular from their bodies). Her aim is to use a specifically feminine self-writing to reverse that alienation and bring about a change in the relationship women have to their own identities. With her 'Le Rire de la méduse', Cixous inspires feminist critics studying autobiography by offering them an answer to a problem we first encountered in Chapter 1: the question of *how* women should go about writing their selves in such a way as to avoid the 'cultural ventriloquism' that occurs when a female autobiographer is forced by genre constraints to perform 'a gesture of impersonation' and 'speak like a man'.[12]

It is in this way that Cixous comes to be associated with a practice of autobiography which is at once transgressive and emancipatory for women. In a follow-up to her monograph on the poetics of women's autobiography, Sidonie Smith takes up in detail this inquiry into how the female self should be written.[13] Analogously to certain queer theorists commentating on Genet, Smith is interested in the ways that women's self-writing might advance the feminist cause. She sees in Cixous a champion of a new feminist autobiography, citing the author as not only as the inspiration for her project to identify a form of feminine self-writing that will prove empowering for women, but also as a practitioner of it. This new mode of autobiographical expression is what Smith dubs 'the autobiographical manifesto'. Central to it is the renegotiation of the fraught relation women have with the genre of autobiography, so as to allow the experience of alienation that comes with writing the self to be transformed into one of liberation: the liberation of a female subjectivity freed from, amongst other things, the arbitrary constraints imposed by the genre of autobiography. Smith envisages that this liberation will allow for a form of self-writing to emerge which can be more avowedly political in its emphasis and emancipate women in the realm of writing and beyond. She takes Cixous's 'Le Rire de la méduse' as an exemplary instance of self-writing which harnesses the personal to political ends, advancing the cause of women, and locates in Cixous's approach in this essay to writing womanhood the guiding principles for a feminist autobiographical manifesto.

What, then, are this manifesto's guiding principles? One imperative for the autobiographical manifesto, in Smith's view, is to revise the importance which conventional autobiography lays on the self as an individual: in the context of an emancipatory feminist project, Smith suggests that the specificity of the individual may be less important than the similarity of that individual to others. One writing individual may come to function as a spokeswoman for several, providing a means of working against a culture which has enforced or promoted muteness on the part of many women. A second way in which Smith's feminist mode of autobiographical writing departs from conventional autobiography is to downplay the importance of a writer's personal history as a formative element in the constitution of the writing self. An 'autobiographical manifesto' will not be restricted to the past life of a woman: it will refuse a mimetic approach that concentrates on representation, and look instead to her future. The goal of such a work is therefore not to give an objective, truthful account of an existing woman's life. Rather, it paints a portrait of the author herself which also speaks for women, or indeed any other marginalized group or groups in society to which the author belongs. This portrait will, by its example, enjoin women to resist the constrictions society imposes on them, and enable them in working towards developing an autonomous selfhood that can defy the social expectations which become attached to women.

For Smith, what the female-authored autobiographical texts which have the goal of promoting female emancipation should *not* do is to mimic the discourse of what she calls 'the ideological "I"': that is, the hegemonic subject who will be assumed to be behind any autobiography.[14] Whilst she acknowledges a potential to destabilize an ideological discourse by infiltrating it, ultimately, Smith argues that attempts to write in such a way as to gain the advantages that this discourse confers — the advantages of 'authority, legitimacy, readability' — are illegitimate in writings that have the avowed goal to empower women as autobiographical authors.[15]

Smith sees it as important that the autobiographical manifesto makes a bold challenge to an ideology that divides legitimate subjects, whose life-writing is admitted to the canon, from illegitimate subjects, whose self-expressions are repressed. Thus it should expose the systems that promote a certain ideology of the subject, which is detrimental to those selves who are colonized, enslaved, dominated by that hegemonic subject. Beyond this, the function of the autobiographical manifesto is to 'make manifest', to show the 'perspective[s] on identity and experience' of those marginalized by traditional autobiographical discourse.[16] To do this an appropriate language and register to describe such experiences needs to be found, and here is where the Cixousian notion of *écriture féminine* makes an important contribution.

A necessary consequence of this politically motivated reformulation of the autobiographical project is the collapse of autobiography, as the term is commonly understood. Smith sees this as what 'Le Rire de la méduse' sets out to do. Referring to the essay by its English title, she writes: 'Cixous's provocative "Laugh" is certainly a manifesto. The language that establishes its tenor is the language of revolution — future-oriented, explosive, subversive. Its expressed gesture is toward both the breaking up of the old and the positing of the new.'[17] In Smith's reading, Cixous produces in 'Le Rire de la méduse' a radical, feminist form of self-writing which takes the demolition of established genres such as autobiography as just the first of its political aims.

Smith's concept of the autobiographical manifesto, inspired in part by 'Le Rire de la méduse', is instructive to us as readers of Cixous's more autobiographical texts on two levels. Firstly, it suggests how the genre of autobiography might have its configuration altered in such a way as to affirm female experience and subjectivity, rather than negate or ignore them. Equally significantly, it reveals the values and goals which Cixous is perceived in some feminist quarters to bring to her writings of the self: Smith's reading of Cixous is emblematic of a strong tendency in the reception of the author, whereby she is situated first and foremost as a writer with a feminist agenda.[18] This is not a position that the author herself finds altogether comfortable, as we shall see. In the previous two chapters of this study we noted a tendency amongst certain commentators to resort to what Davis has described as an 'appropriative understanding which domesticates its object in order to shore up the powers of the [reading] subject'; this is the moment to ask if a similar phenomenon surrounds Cixous.[19] The increased prominence of personal testimony in Cixous's writing through the 1990s and into the new millennium allows us the opportunity to assess how far the priorities sometimes perceived to be behind Cixous's self-writing match up to the priorities in evidence in her more recent autobiographical texts. How far is the vision of Cixous as a militant autobiographer, attacking the genre as part of an ultimately feminist campaign, borne out by the project she pursues subsequently in her self-writing? Is it justifiable to see in Cixous the author of a feminist autobiographical manifesto, or is this another example of an appropriative reading which threatens to consume the autobiographical self and transform it into something which the author cannot recognize?

For those well acquainted with Cixous's writings, the notion that Cixous sets herself up as an antagonist to the genre of autobiography is far from implausible: the key distinguishing features of Cixous's writings have been their experimental qualities; indeed any successful *écriture féminine* presupposes a willingness to step outside the conventions and rules governing writing and thought.[20] Moreover, as Mairéad Hanrahan has noted, Cixous seems to harbour suspicions of conventional autobiography.[21] This is already evident in her treatment of the genre in her 1983 work *Le Livre de Promethea.*[22] This work is subtitled a 'fiction', and certainly it does not fit a traditional description of autobiography as a first-person account of the author's life. Neither does it initiate a Lejeunian autobiographical pact, as there is a separation between the narrator and the two protagonists, H and Promethea — albeit an insecure one, since H is depicted as writing a book about her affair with Promethea, who is the principal focus of Cixous's narrative.[23] The narrator reinforces the dissociation of the text from the genre of autobiography with a forceful affirmation:

> L'autobiographie n'existe pas. Mais tant de gens croient que cela existe. Alors je déclare ici solennellement: l'autobiographie n'est qu'un genre littéraire. Ce n'est pas un genre vivant. C'est un genre jaloux, décepteur, — je le déteste. Quand je dis 'Je', ce n'est jamais le sujet d'une autobiographie, mon je est libre.[24]
>
> [Autobiography does not exist. But so many people believe that it exists. So I declare here solemnly: autobiography is only a literary genre. It is not a living genre (or genus). It is a jealous, deceitful genre/genus — I hate it.[25] When I say 'I', it is never the subject of an autobiography, my 'I' is free.]

This attack on autobiography, although ostensibly setting out to assert that there *is* no autobiography in *Le Livre de Promethea*, suggests that *if* there is no autobiography here, it is because it is undesirable that it should exist, for it has despicable qualities. The narrator's assault on autobiography seems less reliable as a statement on whether autobiography exists or not than it is as a statement of the narrator's investment in it not existing.[26] The affirmation that the autobiographical 'I' is never the *subject* of an autobiography, but is free, reveals that Cixous's narrator sees being 'subject' as synonymous with being constrained: this raises the intriguing possibility that she detects in the genre subjectifying properties such as those we were concerned with in the previous chapter, and that this may motivate her reluctance to be seen as participating in an autobiography.

The denial of autobiography in *Le Livre de Promethea* slides into something that begins to look more like a deconstruction of autobiography. In a statement that undercuts previous assertions of the genre's non-existence and unsettles the generic status of the work still further, the narrator appears to admit that the text being written remains non-autobiographical more through a deliberate ploy on the part of the narrator than anything else, hinting that the narratorial techniques which distance the narrative from the genre of autobiography are a mere fig leaf to cover a would-be autobiographical narrative: 'Pour l'instant je ne peux me dispenser de H. Je n'ai pas encore le courage mental de n'être que Je. Je ne redoute rien autant que l'autobiographie' [For the moment I cannot dispense with H. I do not yet have the mental courage to be only I. I fear nothing as much as autobiography].[27]

It seems that something more than a straightforwardly playful deconstruction of the opposition between autobiography and non-autobiography takes place here. The failure to situate the work generically has an important effect in shaping readers' responses to the text: it prevents readers from assuming that through the narrative they have acquired knowledge of events or situations relating Cixous's own life; it also allows *Le Livre de Promethea* to maintain a state of generic uncertainty. Lejeune tells us that this does not occur if a given generic identity is claimed for the text and another refuted: he asserts that as part of the operation of genre, readers always read against the grain of the genre which is claimed for the text they are reading.[28] Thus, narratorial assertions that a given work does *not* fit a particular genre only tie the work more closely into that genre as readers seek out evidence in the text to the contrary. Deconstruction appears more effective than denial as a tactic to distance a particular narrative from the genre of autobiography.

As for the reason why it should be important to establish this distance, we note that in her commentary on the ploy of using a third-person narration that passes through H, *Le Livre de Promethea*'s narrator admits to a *fear of autobiography*. We do not learn what the awful consequences of writing autobiography might be. Perhaps the quality of the affair itself might be damaged by being recorded in an autobiography? Or does the narrator fear the repercussions that might ensue as a result of what her autobiography would be narrating, namely a lesbian love affair? Although we can only speculate about *why* autobiography is fearful to the narrator, what is beyond speculation is this association of fear with autobiography. The disclosure that autobiography is a highly intimidating enterprise suggests that a narratorial denial that it exists, or that the text being narrated is an autobiography, might be a convenient means for the would-be autobiographer to maintain her otherwise vulnerable equilibrium. The intimation is that the suspicion toward autobiography expressed in Cixous's *Le Livre de Promethea* is rooted in anxiety toward the genre, rather than a political revolt against it. This intimation must be registered as we consider the relationship Cixous establishes with the genre of autobiography in her subsequent self-writings.

Photos de racines takes *Le Livre de Promethea*'s engagement with the genre of autobiography — and also the distancing manoeuvres employed towards it — much further. Indeed, *Photos de racines* might be conceptualized as precisely the kind of feminist autobiographical manifesto which Smith considers that Cixous is drawn to produce.[29] We need only look at the form taken by the work, subtitled 'essai' [essay], to see where the idea that it offers a radical challenge to the genre of autobiography might originate. In terms of form, *Photos de racines* is the most experimental of the works I explore in this study, its very structure offering an implicit challenge to autobiography. The volume runs to some 215 pages and comprises five sections, the majority of which are devoid of conventional autobiographical narrative. By far the longest section is the first, entitled 'Entre Tiens' ['Inter Views'], comprising a dialogue between Cixous and the volume's co-author, Mireille Calle-Gruber. Another section incorporates the text of two papers given by Derrida and Cixous, each of which establishes the pair as intellectual interlocutors; a third section contains two essays on Cixous's writing by Calle-Gruber. The very presence of these contributors reveals that, as is signalled by the title chosen for the English translation (*Hélène Cixous, Rootprints: Memory and Life Writing*), the ambit of *Photos de racines* extends far wider than the life, or even the person, of the author: those things to which autobiography conventionally confines itself.[30] This volume is resolutely not about only Cixous. In a gesture which aligns the work with Smith's vision of an autobiographer who 'speak[s] as one of a group', other selves form a community around Cixous in this text, and play a crucial role in creating the text itself.[31]

A further unconventional feature of *Photos de racines* is its use of images. As the work's title suggests, it includes a photographic element: this is contained in the relatively short fourth section entitled 'Albums et légendes', which is devoted to a selection of photographs and Cixous's commentaries on them.[32] Incorporating images into the only part of the volume to deliver anything approaching a conventional autobiographical narrative, *Photos de racines* inevitably recalls the text I discussed in Chapter 1, Barthes's *Roland Barthes*. Thus in *Photos de racines* we find an instance of another unconventional departure in contemporary autobiography, which it is beyond the scope of this book to treat fully: the recourse to images in life-writing.[33] Yet despite the idiosyncrasies of presentation, 'Albums et légendes', through its exploration of Cixous's geographical and familial origins and childhood, contains at least a grain of the conventional autobiographical endeavour — that is to say, it does impart some knowledge to readers about Cixous's origins — and it is this section of *Photos de racines* that has chiefly occupied the few critics who have given their attention to the work.[34] However, here as elsewhere, suspicion is heaped on the genre of autobiography: an epigraph to the section refutes the possibility that autobiography can be distinguished from other genres by the author's intention to give a dependably truthful account of him- or herself, warning: '*Toutes les biographies comme toutes les autobiographies comme tous les récits racontent une histoire à la place d'une autre histoire*' [All biographies like all autobiographies like all narratives tell one story in place of another story].[35] In its lucidity on the blind spots of traditional autobiography, this disclaimer reinforces the message that Cixous's enterprise here differs significantly from that associated with traditional autobiography. Simultaneously, however, it also aligns *Photos de racines* with a whole class of writings of the self: self-writings distinguished by self-conscious attempts to mark their distance from autobiography — numerous examples of which we have already encountered in this study. Furthermore, in a revealing display of doublethink, this disclaimer also acknowledges that the text before us, *even if not autobiography*, will nevertheless withhold certain stories, just as autobiography does — thus prompting readers to wonder how this work really is different from a more traditional autobiography.

In problematizing its own generic status, the 'Albums et légendes' chapter picks up a thread present from the outset of *Photos de racines*. Explicitly as well as implicitly, this work devotes considerable attention to questions of genre, the genre of autobiography especially, and it makes strenuous efforts to mark its distance from it. This is done predominately through deconstruction, although denial features too: already in the opening section of *Photos de racines*, the text echoes *Le Livre de Promethea* by incorporating an explicit repudiation of the label 'autobiography' as a descriptor for this text: 'Il ne peut y avoir écriture autobiographique parce que ledit "pacte autobiographique" qui codifie le genre est inopérant' [There cannot be autobiographical writing here because the 'autobiographical pact' which codifies the genre is inoperative], states Calle-Gruber, whose very presence as co-author obstructs this autobiographical pact.[36] This is one instance of considerable energy being expended in establishing the text's status as the kind of 'not-autobiography' I discussed in Chapter 1.[37] What this suggests is a significant investment on the part of those who expend it in the notion that *Photos de racines* could never be an autobiography, and in the allied notion that Cixous is 'hors la loi du genre' [a 'genre outlaw']: someone who does not obey the rules (any) genre imposes on authors.[38]

It is useful to recall at this point, however, that 'la loi du genre' [the law of genre], according to Derrida, is this: that although genres have rules (laws) which demarcate one genre from another, the law of genre is that genre always has contamination at its core: there is always a borderline around any genre which belongs to it, and yet is not contained within it.[39] One of the many implications of this idea is that genres themselves do not obey their own rules: they are outlaws to themselves. This would mean that the 'genre outlaw' who refuses to conform to generic codifications is ultimately not outside genre at all. This difficulty in definitively leaving a given genre behind is demonstrated within *Photos de racines*. In a mark of the vacillation which is characteristic of the ambiguous stance taken towards autobiography and the autobiographical in this text, we find that a persistent desire to indulge in writing autobiography is being acknowledged in the very same move as it is dismissed. This occurs where Cixous introduces some brief recollections of her childhood in Oran with the preface that: 'Et puis, je pourrais raconter des histoires... ce serait une sorte d'autobiographie (rires)' [And then, I could tell stories... it would be a sort of autobiography (*laughs*)].[40] As a result of its sustained reference to autobiography, it is difficult to see *Photos de racines* as establishing itself in the relationship of alterity with autobiography which Smith seems to demand of the autobiographical manifesto. Indeed, it is precisely by trying to establish its alterity from the genre that *Photos de racines* comes closer to it.

Where *Photos de racines* corresponds more closely to Smith's vision of a manifesto that breaks out of established autobiographical paradigms is in its treatment of Cixous's biography. The 'Entre Tiens' section successfully subverts a central aspect of the project commonly associated with autobiography: the recovery of the history of the writing self. The very title of this work — in full, *Hélène Cixous: photos de racines* — implies that this volume will explore the 'racines' [roots] of Cixous, thus capitalizing upon one of the main premises on which autobiography is conventionally founded: namely, the importance of understanding an individual's past and origins in order to reach an understanding of their present-day self. In 'Entre Tiens' this expectation begins to be powerfully undercut.

Over the course of the 120-page interview granted to Calle-Gruber by Cixous, the dialogue passes over almost entirely any biographical information pertaining to Cixous: the questions and responses concern Cixous's writing self, mostly examining the qualities of her textuality and her experience of writing. Significantly, when discussing time, Cixous refutes the primacy of chronology, stating that in writing her goal is 'd'être présent au présent...' [being present to the present], and that 'L'écriture [...] ne me permet pas de reprendre du passé' [Writing [...] does not allow me to take back the past].[41] The emphasis on the present moment rather than the past in the interview would seem to reflect this sentiment. However, there are indications that there may be something else besides a purely intellectual conviction behind the absence of the past in Cixous's discussions with Calle-Gruber. At one point, Cixous makes brief reference to her experience of living through Algeria's bloody war of independence: she cites 'la mort, [...] les mas-sacres [*sic*], [...] la trahison, [...] la barberie' [death, [...] massacres, [...] betrayal, [...] barbarity],[42] her recollections being self-consciously juxtaposed with a 'fenêtre' [window], which states:

> *Ne pas retourner*:
> Je ne retourne pas à Oran.
> N'aime pas revenir?
> Aime garder embaumé embau-
> mant *Souvenirs d'épices*. Rue
> Manégat. Nom à odeur
> d'épices.[43]

[To not return: / *I will not return to Oran. / Do not like coming back? / Like to keep embalmed embalming* / Memories of spices. *Manégat Street. / Name with odour of spices.*][44]

The periodically appearing 'windows' in 'Entre Tiens' contain, we are informed in a prefatory note, text from beyond the text: material from Cixous's notebooks. The presence in *Photos de racines* of this particular 'window' strongly suggests that the autobiographical endeavour to reconnect with the past is shrouded in a certain awkwardness for Cixous. Until now, the basis for the critique that the genre of autobiography is subjected to in *Photos de racines* has seemed to lie in politically or ideologically motivated objections to some of its aspects, but there is an indication that the objections contributing to this critique may be rooted in something more personal. The implication of the notebook entry is that if the territory of the past, like that of autobiography, is ground on to which Cixous does not venture, this may be because something in the encounter is unwelcome. The appearance of this window in *Photos de racines* points to a split response on the question of how to relate to the past; a question that is brought to centre stage in *Les Rêveries de la femme sauvage* and *Le Jour où je n'étais pas là*: should one attempt to recapture the past, to interrogate it? Or should one leave it totally undisturbed?

In the later 'Albums et légendes', the reader is offered something of the kind of expository treatment of the author's personal history which earlier sections of the work had problematized, but this is limited to a brief and not altogether willing voyage into Cixous's genealogy and geographical origins. This section takes what we now recognize as a characteristically ambivalent position towards the autobiographical enterprise. It includes some traditional autobiographical fare: reminiscences alongside photographs of some significant people and places in Cixous's family history (reinforcing the text's emphasis on a plurality of selves, rather than the autobiographical self). Yet 'Albums et légendes', with its delayed return to origins, is no Holy Grail: readers are warned not to expect this historical coda to a predominantly literary-theoretical text to supply the key to the Cixousian self. Cixous emphasizes her distance from her 'Racines. Miennes? Mes si étrangères racines' [Roots. Mine? My so strange (or foreign) roots], thus discouraging readers from grounding their image of the authorial self in the information they have nonetheless been allowed to glean from this excursus.[45] Emphasizing that her family roots are 'étrangères' not merely in the sense of foreign, but also in the second sense of the word, strange and unfamiliar, Cixous highlights the irrelevance to her present self of the visual material from the family photo-album she is about to present to us, and the apparent ethical desirability of leaving it alone:

> Vieil album dépenaillé. Respecter le dépenaillement. Le dépenaillement est le secret: portrait de la mémoire de la famille. Album, mémoire, cimetière, abandonnés. On avance, en semant derrière soi les pierres de deuil. Album d'abandon. Fidèle à l'abandon. Respecter l'abandon. [...] Album en ruines à respecter. C'est la mémoire même. Lieu sur lequel je ne reviens pas.[46]
>
> [Old tattered album. Respect the tatteredness. The tatteredness is the secret: portrait of the family memory. Album, memory, cemetery, abandoned. One goes forward, sowing the stones of grief behind oneself. Album of abandonment. Faithful to the abandonment. Respect the abandonment. [...] Album in ruins to be respected. It is memory itself. A place I do not return to.][47]

Cixous's gesture of opening her family photo-album to her readers becomes a gesture tinged in duplicity: a move ostensibly drawing readers into closer intimacy, a deeper understanding of the person of the author is one that supplies *some* knowledge about her, but *frustrates* their desire for precise detail. The first illustration to be presented is of 'le sol originaire, le pays natal de mon écriture' [the originary earth, the native country of my writing]:[48] on the facing page is a map of Europe and North Africa, unannotated and impersonal.[49] Only sketchy accounts of Cixous's family history are given, but we do discover from the later text that, owing to individual migrations and changes to national borders, Cixous's various family members have, over the generations, called numerous lands home, and have, between them, held a dazzling list of nationalities.[50] On the subject of Cixous's own national identity, the narrative stops short of providing clarity, ending in the statement: 'j'ai adopté une nationalité imaginaire qui est la nationalité littéraire' [I adopted an imaginary nationality which is the nationality of literature].[51] This remark is explained by the difficulty Cixous reports in laying claim, due to her ethnicity and birthplace, to French nationality: as she has written elsewhere: 'affirmer "je suis française" est un mensonge ou une fiction. De l'autre [côté] dire "je ne suis pas française" est un manquement à la politesse' [to assert 'I am French' is a lie or a fiction. On the other hand, to say 'I am not French' is impolite].[52]

To evoke the lands of one's ancestors is familiar ground for an autobiography to cover. Yet in 'Albums et légendes', the opportunity to revisit familiar ground is used to unsettle the reader who anticipates the decisive factual account that an autobiography might seem to promise, with the narrative stressing instead the bewildering plurality of cultural influences shaping the person of the author.

With its marginalization of autobiographical narrative, its emphasis on the present moment of writing, and its presentation of Cixous as a part of an intellectual community rather than as an individual, *Photos de racines* conforms in a number of respects to Smith's vision of a feminist autobiographical manifesto. However, Cixous is not so much engaged in 'the breaking up of the old' genre of autobiography as a deconstructive critique of some of the conventional approaches to autobiographical writing and preoccupations of the autobiographical narrative. Yet whilst *Photos de racines* interrogates and challenges facets of autobiography, deconstruction emerges as an inadequate strategy to distance the text securely from autobiography. *Photos de racines* may present much else to the reader besides biographical information, itself delivered in an idiosyncratic and non-totalizing way, but it does not altogether leave traditional autobiography behind: Cixous's own roots, her past and the genre of autobiography itself each retain a presence in this work; the conventionally autobiographical aspiration of imparting knowledge to the reader about Cixous's self is not, as evidenced by the genealogy and chronology of Cixous's life which the text supplies, wholly abandoned.

This leaves the question of how far Cixous's engagement with autobiography here is a feminist engagement. *Photos de racines* could be considered feminist in its critique of epistemological desire, which it never straightforwardly accommodates but tends to thwart. However, it is unclear what motivates Cixous's arresting approach to self-writing in this text: whether it is indeed a feminist project that Cixous pursues, or whether the unease about participating in a mode of self-writing which privileges the transfer of knowledge of the self from self to other could be rooted in something more personal than political.

Where an ethic that might be called feminist is perhaps most in evidence is in Cixous's exposition in *Photos de racines* of her vision of the connection between self and other, although even in this regard we shall see that Cixous's relationship with feminism is far from straightforward; and as Cixous redefines the basis for this connection, we shall find that the relationship with the feminist reading other becomes increasingly difficult to accommodate.

Self and Other: Fusion or Distance?

The participation of Cixous's academic interlocutors in *Photos de racines* implicitly provides some indication of the importance the other has in Cixous's self-realization. In 'Albums et légendes', the introduction of the diverse family figures who are the source of Cixous's hybrid ethnic identity provides the occasion for a more explicit exposition of Cixous's vision of how the self relates to the other. In this section of *Photos de racines*, we encounter a Cixousian self whose contours are fluid: in giving an account of her grandparents, Cixous, referring to her grandmother by the name she has in their German-speaking household, remarks that 'Omi [...] est un peu m, o, i' [Omi [...] is a bit *me*].[53] This declaration is more than an indicator of a particularly close emotional bond or identification with a close relative: it signals a capacity to combine with other selves. Reflecting the porous boundaries of Europe through which her family members have passed, the Cixousian self is portrayed as porous too: able to incorporate, and be incorporated by, the other; indeed, several others.

In this way, the richness of Cixous's ethnic heritage is presented as invigorating, for it is this which allows her to fuse many 'racines' [roots] together: Cixous may be in part her grandmother, but she is equally able to embody other family members of a different provenance. Hanrahan discusses how Cixous uses the poetic device of prosopopoeia in 'Albums et légendes' to merge her subject position with that of her dead grandfather, Michael Klein.[54] At his graveside her tears flow 'Parce que je suis mort. Je suis si mort. Parce que je suis devenu cette pierre de bois levée qui répète mon nom et ma date de mort' [Because I am dead. I am so dead. Because I have become this raised wooden stone that repeats my name and my date of death].[55] This is a fleeting connection, however: almost as quickly as it is made it is disavowed: 'Suis-je issue de cet homme qui s'en va? Moi-même je n'y crois pas. Ou plutôt: j'y incrois' [Am I born of this man who goes off? I myself do not believe it. Or rather: I unbelieve it].[56] Michael Klein is left behind as the narrative focusses on another fusion: the merger Cixous describes herself as having experienced with her brother to become 'Hélène-et-Pierre'.[57] 'Albums et légendes' offers more than an account of Cixous's blood relations. What it offers is an account of relations *tout court*: relations between the Cixousian self and its familial others, relations who, at this point, find themselves not to be separated by time or place; indeed, not separate at all.

Cixous's depiction of conjoined selves is not, in itself, necessarily a gesture of feminist intent, as becomes apparent when we remind ourselves that the exuberant metamorphosis of the Cixousian self into others and back again has echoes of the concept of the intersubjective self elaborated by the decidedly non-feminist Sarraute. What has been positioned as feminist is the ethic behind that depiction.

The portrayal of a self which fuses with others in 'Albums et légendes' corresponds to an important Cixousian concept that presides over all her work: the notion of 'love'.[58] In Cixous's usage, 'love' refers to a particular sort of generous, giving disposition which governs the interaction between self and other as they encounter each other. Whilst 'love' refers to a mode of relations with the other, it also implies a particular vision of selfhood. For Cixous, part of being open and generous to the other involves opening the self to the other; allowing that other to merge with the self, rather than being an antagonist to it, to the point that the self is no longer conceivable as a singular, discrete entity. The self comes into being, then, with and through the other.[59] This is an insight which informs the treatment of self and other in the 'Albums et légendes' chapter, but it is in 'Entre Tiens' where we see it enacted.[60]

The unorthodox typographical rendering of this chapter's title gives an indication of its distance from the conventional 'interview' (hence the preference here for the term 'dialogue'). An 'interview' lays emphasis on, and confers authority on, the interviewee, typically restricting the interviewer to a limited and subordinate role as someone who solicits, directs and clarifies the interviewee's utterances. 'Entre Tiens' offers something rather different. Fittingly, this is announced, through a deployment of *écriture féminine*, in the very rendering of its title. The typographical presentation of the compound word 'entretiens' [interviews] highlights its rich semantics. A significantly extended space is used to split the word into its two constituent parts; thus the reader alert to polyvalency in language will discern connotations that evoke the Cixousian ethic of love: as well as meaning 'between', 'entre' in French is an imperative verb, meaning 'enter'. The word 'tiens' also has an imperative function, meaning 'hold', but it also evokes the possessive pronoun '[le] tien': 'yours'. A vision of being beckoned in, held, given something is thus conjured up, chasing away the less 'loving' dynamic of a more conventional interview. This atmosphere of cosy intimacy is carried through to the dialogue itself: periodically, the transcription records the eruption of Cixous's '(rires)' [laughing]. Calle-Gruber is not only a scholar of Cixous's work, but her colleague and collaborator. Her contribution here is very significant: for the reader hoping to discover Cixous's self through *Photos de racines*, Calle-Gruber in a quite concrete sense is the one through whom that self is able to come into being. On occasions Cixous responds evasively to what is put to her: she asserts, for example, that 'je ne lis jamais mes livres' [I never read my books], and so has forgotten what they contain and cannot consequently comment on their content.[61] It is Calle-Gruber who then speaks for the author, stepping in to explain Cixous's remark; frequently it is she who elucidates aspects of Cixous's thought and practice which the writer herself does not.[62] If, for Cixous, the self is a fusion of the self and the other that it encounters, then Calle-Gruber's participation in this dialogue indicates that Cixous's reader too can be one of these others who contributes to the making of the Cixousian self.[63]

On this evidence, *Photos de racines* seems to offer a markedly different vision of reader relations to the hierarchical model based on the notion of the author as authority which is associated especially with traditional autobiography. In the first place, the inference from the collaboration between Cixous and Calle-Gruber is that in their brand of self-writing, the relationship between the self who writes and the other who reads is not hierarchical nor authoritarian. Moreover, the reader of *Photos de racines* is not gifted with intimate, fulsome knowledge of Cixous's self. This is unsurprising, for such a gift, the chance to receive and consume information about the autobiographer, is what texts that obey the traditional autobiographical blueprint for reader relations award as the reader's prize for being a passive bystander. Such a stance is alien to the Cixousian vision of reader relations as we find it performed in 'Entre Tiens'.[64] Instead of an active writer who supplies readily digestible personal information to a passive reader who receives it, instead of the self being consumed by the other, there is fusion, and an intimate encounter between self and reader marked by the presence of what Cixous terms 'love'.

From this standpoint, it is possible to see in *Photos de racines* a feminist contribution to the poetics of autobiography. By its example, *Photos de racines* may be seen as addressing the issue of the hierarchical power relations between writer and reader which are in-built in autobiography, an issue often occluded in feminist autobiography criticism. It appears to present an alternative model of reader relations for the genre, which involves the autobiographical self descending from a position of authority and mastery to a position of equality with the reader, with each regarding the other as a companion, not an object to be possessed or controlled.

However, whilst this reading of *Photos de racines* is commensurate with some of the aspirations voiced in the text itself — the idea of undoing hierarchies is directly discussed — and with the way Cixous has often been read by critics, it is also a reading which overlooks certain aspects of this work.[65] Co-existing with what might be called its non-phallogocentric or feminine qualities are elements which reveal tensions in Cixous's relationship with her reading other, and which call into question interpretations of Cixousian reader relations as entirely harmonious.[66]

The discernible frictions between writing and reading selves in *Photos de racines* prefigure tensions that become more manifest in the later *Les Rêveries de la femme sauvage* and *Le Jour où je n'étais pas là*, and they concern the issue of knowledge. This time, rather than broader epistemological questions, it is the question of the knowledge that the reader can lay claim to of Cixous's self that is at issue. As with other authors, anxieties surface over proximity and the presence of a consuming dynamic in encounters between self and other.

The relation of intimate fusion that we observe Cixous creating with her reader in *Photos de racines*, replicating the fusions we witnessed between the Cixousian self and her ancestors, is only one of the stories *Photos de racines* tells. Cixous's readers are not always perceived as allies who facilitate the expression of the self. When they stray from this role, a joyous fusion is far from how the encounter with them is perceived. This is apparent from early on in 'Entre Tiens', where Cixous asserts her project to be a poetic, rather than theoretical one. Hierarchizing the poetic over the theoretical via a metaphorical comparison between a creature that flies (the poetic) and the emergency toolkit that keeps a car on the road (theory), she views theoretical approaches to texts as limited: 'Je suis donc inquiète quand je vois certaines tendances de lectures: elles prennent la roue de secours pour l'oiseau' [So I am worried when I see certain tendencies in reading: they take the spare wheel for the bird].[67] Calle-Gruber's response makes clear that Cixous is targeting her own readers here; moreover, Calle-Gruber's reference to 'une situation nord-américaine' [a North-American situation] reveals that Cixous has a particular constituency in mind: an Anglo-American feminist readership 'qui, sous le nom de "théorie féministe", s'est limitée, excluant tes livres de fiction, à quelques essais ou articles: *Le rire de la méduse*, *Sorties*, les interventions de *La jeune née*' [which, under the name of 'feminist theory', has excluded your books of fiction, limiting itself to a few essays or articles: 'The Laugh of the Medusa', 'Sorties', your participation in *The Newly Born Woman*].[68]

Calle-Gruber goes on to attack such readers in strong terms. For her, their selective reading amounts to a mutilation of the author: 'Procéder à cette amputation est injuste envers ton travail qui est pluriel; débordement' [To carry out this amputation is unjust to your work which is plural; overflowing].[69] For Calle-Gruber, Cixous's readers represent a liability:

> Le risque, avec une écriture attentive aux subtilités, c'est que la paresse, la surdité, ou la surprise fassent qu'on n'entende qu'une voix; qu'on s'arrête à un aspect. Que la lecture réduise et réifie parce que c'est plus facile.[70]
>
> [The risk, with writing that is attentive to subtleties, is that laziness, deafness, or surprise should lead people to hear only one voice, to stop at a single aspect. That the reading should reduce and reify because this is easier.][71]

Cixous's response to these remarks is to place her more militantly feminist writings in context. As she has done elsewhere, she describes them as more a product of circumstances than deliberate gestures of radical-feminism: 'Ma vocation, il faut le dire, n'est pas politique' [My vocation, I must say, is not political].[72]

This is a revealing exchange between Cixous and Calle-Gruber. It reveals that, from a Cixousian standpoint, readings such as Smith's which would harness her self-writing for a feminist project are consuming readings: reductive interpretations which misappropriate the work with which they engage. The fact that, in a text apparently driven by Cixousian 'love', we find space devoted to a surprisingly forceful treatment of a particular constituency of Cixous readers suggests that being 'misread' or 'mis-known' in this way is perceived by Cixous and her co-author as objectionable, and highly undesirable. It also exposes a considerable authorial investment in remedying the situation. More revealingly, the treatment of the reader in this first chapter of *Photos de racines* indicates also that, even in a text apparently far removed from the genre of autobiography, and the 'masculine' economy which governs it, there is still a play of power relations between self and other in operation, and that readers once more find themselves in the thick of it.

The deconstructive self-reflexiveness that overarches both sections of *Photos de racines* to which Cixous contributes can be seen as an instrumental strategy in defying the consuming reader. The undermining of conventional structures of autobiography provides a way to take back control of the transaction of knowledge: limiting the reader's knowledge of the author, but more particularly, questioning their *appetite* for knowledge. Management of the reader's response is achieved in other ways besides. *Photos de racines* does much to 'correct' the readings it marks out as undesirable. Much is done, for example, to lift Cixous out of the feminist context she is often placed in, not least through the focus in 'Albums et légendes' on her hybrid Algerian-Jewish background. In the light of its subversion of the conventional project of autobiography to supply information about the author's individual life and personal development, it is ironic to find that the response in *Photos de racines* to the misreadings of the reader inclined towards Cixous's theoretical output involves something quite at home in traditional autobiography:

supplying readers with additional knowledge to provide a more rounded image of the author and her concerns. 'Entre Tiens' includes commentary on many of Cixous's fictional texts; there is also much exposition of how Cixous conceives her own work. This is offered by both Cixous and Calle-Gruber, whose evident intimacy with the author's writings as well as her person enables her to function as a model reader and exemplum to other readers. Indeed, Calle-Gruber plays the role which Wilson argues that Cixous requires of her readers: the role of the specular other who provides the author with a mirror image of herself.[73]

Yet even an exchange with an exemplary reader with whom Cixous enjoys a 'loving' relation of interchange and fusion can prove the source of awkwardness. Unexpectedly, Calle-Gruber's interventions reveal the intimate reader's participation to be occasionally somewhat problematic, and, once again, the difficulty which arises has its roots in the theme of knowledge. Whilst the readers of Cixous who are criticized in 'Entre Tiens' are those who lack adequate knowledge and understanding of the author, in Calle-Gruber's case the rare difficulty she as a reader sporadically poses to Cixous is that she possesses too much of these commodities. It is frequently Calle-Gruber who elucidates Cixous's ideas in the dialogue between them (an exposition carried over into her own lengthy essay on Cixous later in the volume), but there is some evidence that this may not be an entirely comfortable situation for Cixous. For example, at the point where Calle-Gruber explains Cixous's concept of bisexuality via a commentary of one of her novels, Cixous gives the reply, 'Je ne vois pas ce que je pourrais dire de mieux (rires). Reste seulement à faire écho' [I do not see how I could say it better [*laughs*]. There remains only to respond by echoing this].[74] Evidently, there is no repudiation here of the kind we have seen directed at other readers, as Cixous's intervention and the transcription of her laughter confirms. There is no suggestion of an erroneous reading: quite the reverse. Yet there is in Cixous's reply the suggestion of a need not merely to provide an echo, but to take some distance from what Calle-Gruber has said. We note that her immediate response to the subject of bisexuality is one of disavowal:

> Le mot 'bisexuel' n'appartient pas, je crois, à mon univers d'écriture, mais, il est en provenance d'une langue d'époque. [...] Si ce terme-là, qui est tellement daté donc tellement désuet, avait fait apparition dans le champ de l'écriture, je m'en serais moquée je l'aurais joué [...]. Mais quand même, s'il en a été question c'est bien que, à l'époque — car c'est vraiment du passé: pour moi du moins — j'avais affaire à des manifestations, des effets d'opposition sexuelle très violents.[75]

> [The word 'bisexual' does not belong to my universe of writing, I believe, but it comes from the language of the time. [...] If this term, which is so dated thus so obsolete, had appeared in the field of writing, I would have made fun of it I would have played with it [...]. But nonetheless, if it came up, it is indeed that at the time — because it is really the past, for me at least — I had to deal with very violent manifestations and effects of sexual opposition.][76]

Cixous's emphasis on the irrelevance of this concern to her current preoccupations not only reinforces her distance from the feminist movement, but also has the effect of relativizing Calle-Gruber's explanation of the value of this aspect of her thought. If there is a merit for certain readers in acquiring more knowledge of aspects of the author's work and thought, there are some areas where greater knowledge is not worth seeking out. However, this text also shows us that the fault is not solely with the reader if an awkward desire for knowledge of the Cixousian self arises: the fault lies in the ethic that has been at the centre of the self-writing project pursued in *Photos de racines*. Cixous herself observes that a desire for knowledge is fuelled by 'love': 'Il n'y a qu'en amour qu'on veut connaître l'origine, la généalogie de quelqu'un' [It is only in love that we want to know the origin, the genealogy of someone].[77] Accordingly, Cixous comes to reformulate this ethic of 'love' in a process whose beginnings we see in *Photos de racines* and which carries on into her later self-writings. In the new version of the ethic of 'love', the emphasis is not on fusion between self and other, but distance:

> Mais il y a aussi l'incompréhension positive. C'est peut-être ce que nous découvrons en amour; ou en amitié-amour: le fait que l'autre est tellement autre. Est tellement pas-moi. Le fait qu'on puisse se dire tout le temps: là justement, je ne suis pas comme toi.[78]
>
> [But there is also a *positive incomprehension*. It is perhaps what we discover in love; or in friendship-love: the fact that we can say to each other all the time: here, I am not like you.][79]

In the ethic of love as it begins to appear in *Photos de racines*, we see an incorporation of something of Cixous's concept of fidelity, which stresses the need not to 'murder the other', as Susan Sellers puts it, but to give it space.[80] This gives rise to the ideal of 'Aimer ne pas comprendre. Aimer: ne pas comprendre' [Loving not knowing. Loving: not knowing]; an injunction which will lead Cixous to a quite different approach to autobiographical writing in *Les Rêveries de la femme sauvage* and *Le Jour où je n'étais pas là* compared to what we have seen in *Photos de racines*.[81]

In the two latter works, the ethic of fusion between self and other that is so crucial to the way that Cixous writes the self in *Photos de racines* is lost. The loss of this feminine, even feminist, ethic results from Cixous being confronted with a new and unexpected quality of the self as she attempts to explore her roots further in these two more recent works. Far from showing the self's aptitude to fuse with others, these journeys into Cixous's past reveal how the self harbours an other within itself with which it cannot be fused. The Cixousian self that appears in *Les Rêveries de la femme sauvage* and *Le Jour où je n'étais pas là* is one marked by estrangement: an estrangement from the other without, but also the other within. This leads to a radical evolution in how Cixous writes her self, as an emphasis on an intimate openness in transactions with the other is supplanted by a new ethic of estrangement, and distance. Suggesting that Cixous's vision of an inherently multiple, hybrid self which represents the capacity to harmoniously fuse with others is itself a mis-knowledge of her self, Cixous's new departure in writing the self estranged consequently calls for a renegotiation of relations with the other, including the other who reads. This reading other is no longer invited to join *with* the author, but is instead asked to embrace the ethic of 'aimer ne pas comprendre': staying at a respectful distance. Promoting this new ethic will, ironically in an author so renowned for her literary experimentation, entail leaving behind the 'autobiographical manifesto' of *Photos de racines* and will lead Cixous back to a much more traditional approach to writing the self.

Cixous's Mis-known Self: Writing (Self-)Estrangement

With the publication in 2000 of *Les Rêveries de la femme sauvage* and *Le Jour où je n'étais pas là*, the extent to which Cixous's concerns have evolved since her feminist activism in the 1970s, and the direction they have taken, is further emphasized. *Les Rêveries de la femme sauvage* recounts the narrator's childhood in Algeria and reveals her relationship to the country, whilst in *Le Jour où je n'étais pas là*, Cixous's narrative tells the story of how her first child, who was born with Down's Syndrome, died in infancy. In these texts, Cixous gives the impression of being now reconciled with autobiography as a genre. The most striking evidence of this is that, in a *volte face* by comparison to *Photos de racines*, these two narratives do both conform to the conventional expectations of autobiography, each having a first-person narrator named as Hélène who leads the reader through a mostly linear narrative of her past life. Unlike *Le Livre de Promethea*, or *Photos de racines*, there is no metanarrative commentary which undermines the association between author, narrator and protagonist. However, the access to knowledge of the Cixousian self which the reader gains comes at a price: *Les Rêveries de la femme sauvage* and *Le Jour où je n'étais pas là* approach autobiography only to revisit the theme of the lack of knowledge circulating about the autobiographical self. This is a self who is not known by others, and who also cannot know herself because a lack of knowledge estranges her from her own geographical and personal situation. If the writing self is unable to know itself, *Les Rêveries de la femme sauvage* and *Le Jour où je n'étais pas là* suggest that outsiders' attempts to know who she is are doomed to failure. In a revelation that sheds new light on attempts made in *Photos de racines* to divert the reader away from seeking privileged knowledge about the Cixousian self, these two works also reveal that when outsiders act upon false knowledge of Cixous, this heightens her sense of self-estrangement, inability to know herself and vulnerability to the other.

Cixous's primal confrontation with unknowing others who damage her sense of self occurs in her homeland: although Algeria may be the country of her birth, the narrator's concern in much of *Les Rêveries de la femme sauvage* is to show how she was 'never to arrive' in Algeria, and feel at home there. She explains: 'Tout le temps où je vivais en Algérie je rêvais d'arriver un jour en Algérie, j'aurais fait n'importe quoi pour y arriver [...] je ne me suis jamais trouvée en Algérie' [All the time when I lived in Algeria I dreamed of arriving one day in Algeria, I would have done anything to get there; I never found myself in Algeria].[82] Her estrangement from the country arises because Cixous is always perceived by others as an outsider: she tells us that she was always thought of as French by her schoolmates — the only exception apparently being the parents of her friend Françoise, who considered her Jewish first and foremost (and consequently refused to allow her to enter their house). Yet she (and her brother) did not identify as French, resented being known to others for what they were not, and felt the misknowledge (what Lacan calls *méconnaissance*) directed against them prevented them from achieving their desire to get to know their country. They were:

> fous et malades du besoin de l'Algérie, de la réalité intérieure de ce pays qui était notre pays natal et pas du tout nôtre, de la chair, de l'habitat, de l'arabité de l'arabitude, du trésor plein de trésors auquel nous n'avions pas accès.[83]
>
> [mad and sick with need for Algeria, for the interior reality of this country which was our country of birth and not at all ours, for the flesh, for the habitat, for the Arabness of the Arabness, for the treasure full of treasures to which we did not have access.]

Exacerbating the sense of estrangement from Algerians, there is the wound of being estranged from her own family members by this predicament of not belonging. The narrator's unhappiness at not fitting in in Algeria is intensified by her mother's apparent equanimity about her relationship, as an exile, towards her adopted country: she is apparently unconcerned about belonging in Algeria, yet, ironically, although she (unlike Hélène herself) makes no effort to integrate, her profession as midwife facilitates her integration, placing her: 'Au sein même de la fertilité de cette Algérie, dont nous, et surtout moi, nous rêvions depuis que je marchais d'atteindre un jour le corps, les bras, les seins, les mains' [at the very breast of the fertility of this Algeria that we, and especially I, dreamt of since I started walking of one day making it to her body, her breasts, her hands].[84]

The level of intimacy Hélène's mother attains with the country drives a wedge between her and her children, afflicted by a particular sort of 'mal de pays' [homesickness]: the narrator recounts that her mother's ease in the face of her children's dis-ease convinces them that she cannot empathize with their pain. The resultant estrangement from their own mother rather undermines the narratives of harmonious fusions between the Cixousian self and family members that we encounter in *Photos de racines*. As much as the damage that outsiders inflict when they construct Hélène as other against her will hurts, it is when she is experienced as other to her own family that she mourns most. Her father's death during her childhood visits a terrible trauma on Cixous, one very frequently revisited (as her more ardent readers know) in her fictional writing, starting with *Dedans*.[85] However, a hitherto unknown dimension of this pain is revealed in *Les Rêveries de la femme sauvage*: the fact that she is also grieving for her intimacy with her brother. Although their intimate connection is chronicled in the 'Albums et légendes' section of *Photos de racines*, the narrator of *Les Rêveries de la femme sauvage* states that she had already lost it prior to this bereavement: 'j'étais déjà coupé de mon frère, notre vie intérieure coupée en deux vies extérieures et coupée de moi-même' [I was already cut off from my brother, our interior life cut into two exterior lives and cut off from myself].[86] It is indeed possible to interpret *Les Rêveries de la femme sauvage* as being a response not so much to Algerians who mistakenly saw in her a French colonizer, but rather as a response to the charge made by her brother: '— Tu n'as pas connu l'Algérie' ['You didn't know Algeria'].[87] He alleges that whereas, as a child, he liked to explore his homeland on the bicycle they were jointly given as a present, she preferred to stay in and read books, and therefore did not come to know Algeria.

However, the narrative of *Les Rêveries de la femme sauvage* demonstrates that what the brother believes is his superior knowledge is actually *méconnaissance* [misknowledge]: despite her brother's accusation that she never knew Algeria, the narrator asserts she *does* know the country she cannot call her own. If anything, her pain comes from knowing the country *too* well: well enough to know how everything is organized around corrupt practices, how those in power have contempt for the Algerian population, and how it is more comfortable not to know these things: 'Je saute je vois tout. Touvoir seule sans mon frère est une épouvante. Les gens ont des appareils pour ne pas entendre' [I jump I see everything. Allseeing alone without my brother is a horror. People have aids in order not to hear].[88] It is this uncomfortable clairvoyance that Cixous tells us is responsible for her decision to go to France, to escape 'malgérie' [Malgeria], the place where, due to others' hurtful failure to know her, or to allow her to know them, she is estranged from herself. Yet this course of action itself creates a situation in which Cixous is further estranged from her own life and family, and this is the preoccupation of *Le Jour où je n'étais pas là*.

In this text too, the painful question of knowledge is at the core of the autobiographical self's estrangement. We are told that Hélène goes to France leaving her infant son, born with Down's Syndrome, in the care of her mother. Her son dies, and *Le Jour où je n'étais pas là* tells the story of the narrator's quest to be told by her family, decades later, the story of what happened: a story in which she should, as Georges' mother, have played a part — but she did not. As in *Les Rêveries de la femme sauvage*, knowledge is the source of discord in *Le Jour où je n'étais pas là* also. Here again there is another who believes he knows the narrating self: once more it is the brother who knows what she does not know, having been present at the hospital where her son died; here again, the resultant sense of being estranged, from her brother as from the event that she should have witnessed, is painful.

Significantly, Cixous's narrator concludes that just as others should not have expectations of knowing her self, neither should she: to assist her mourning process she attempts to ascertain from her mother and brother precisely what the events were leading up to her son's death, and concludes that the endeavour is unethical, for although it was her son who died, the memories she tries to delve into are not hers, and 'on ne reprend pas l'enfant qu'on a donné' [one does not take back the child one has given away].[89] The attempt to commit her child's death to writing forces a painful revelation on Cixous's narrator, who realizes that the harmonious fusions with family members described in *Photos de racines* are fanciful, and were ruptured by her decision to quit her role as mother to her handicapped son. Her mother, Georges' surrogate mother, 'm'en veut' [resents me], and the brother Cixous describes as a part of her in *Photos de racines* is portrayed as having borne a grudge against his sister for having abandoned her child: ' — Tu as refusé cet enfant pleut mon frère sévère aux yeux durement clairs, c'est ce que je pensais dit-il' ['You rejected that child' my brother weeps stern with hard bright eyes, 'that's what I thought' he said].[90] The narrator's rude realization in *Le Jour où je n'étais pas là* of her estrangement from her own life, and from those family members with whom she claims such close connection in *Photos de racines*, leaves a mark on the form taken by the text. Like *Les Rêveries de la femme sauvage*, *Le Jour où je n'étais pas là* employs the traditionally autobiographical first person, but whereas in *Les Rêveries de la femme sauvage* the first person pronoun is predominantly 'nous', emphasizing the bond between Cixous and her brother, in *Le Jour où je n'étais pas là* the narrating 'I' assumes the prominent position traditionally accorded it in autobiography as a result of its perceived isolation from its familial others.

The narrator's estrangement, and her uncomfortable insights into its causes, are the melancholic motors behind the production of these two texts. *Les Rêveries de la femme sauvage* suggests that the experience of estrangement from others and from one's own self generates creative forces. When describing the genesis of the work, the narrator of *Les Rêveries de la femme sauvage* uses the vocabulary of demonic possession to explain how the text was produced: 'j'avais noté les premières lignes que le Venant me dictait' [I had noted the first lines which the Apparition dictated to me].[91] The device of the possessed narrator also figures this new-found self-estrangement in *Le Jour où je n'étais pas là*. Cixous presents herself as being forced to write by another, an external force imposing its ghostly presence on the writer, ensuring 'le Livre' [the book] will be written: 'il y avait un livre qui était venu s'ajouter à la confusion, si je voulais dormir il m'éveillait, le livre lui ne dort jamais' [there was a book which had come to add to the confusion, if I wanted to sleep it kept me awake, the book never sleeps].[92] The authorial recourse to an uncanny spectre, sleepless like the lost infant, provides a means of accomplishing two tasks. The uncanny force behind these texts both familiarizes what is unfamiliar for the narrator, whilst also conveying to the reader the presence of an unencounterable otherness that will definitively forestall our aspiration of getting to know the author through her writings, even when they seem at their most confessional. This frustration of the reader's imputed desire for intimacy with the narrator is confirmed by a discrepancy in names: the attentive reader of Cixous's work notices that Calle-Gruber's chronology of Cixous's life in *Photos de racines* names her dead child as Stéphane; in *Le Jour où je n'étais pas là*, he is called Georges (the name of her dead father).

A consequent effect is that, as readers, we cannot feel that our participation as readers of *autobiography* is desired by Cixous: *Le Jour où je n'étais pas là* is described as a book delivered by destiny, not the author: 'Le destin c'est que nous finissons par faire ce que nous ne voulions *surtout-pas-faire*' [Our destiny is that we end up doing what we want *above-all-not-to-do*].[93] Again, this coincides with the account given by the narrator of *Les Rêveries de la femme sauvage*, where the reader is told that the book has come into being in spite of her: 'Je n'ai jamais voulu écrire sur l'Algérie ce pays natal inconnu [...] l'idée d'écrire ne m'est même jamais venue' [I never wanted to write on Algeria this unknown land of my birth, the idea to write never even came to me]; this changes when the narrator starts to 'hear' the sound of her childhood dog Fips barking, prompting the words that begin this text.[94] The descriptions of the narrator's writing double and the auditory manifestation of her childhood dog seem deliberately to call to mind Freud's concept of the uncanny: that which is 'nothing new or alien, but something which is familiar and old-established in the mind and which has become alienated from it only through the process of repression'.[95] The emergence of the uncanny confirms a condition of self-estrangement: the uncanny is reintegrated into the subject, but not with the ease of a part of the self fitting back into place. The uncanny remains clothed in alterity for the self, even as it is reintegrated; henceforth the past, and the self in the past, assume an excessive character, seeming to resist belonging entirely to the writing (or indeed any other) self.

The reader who accepts the notion of a self that is mobile because it is internally estranged (not because it is plural, as in *Photos de racines*) will abandon the aim of gaining a complete knowledge of the autobiographical subject. This is a level of intimate knowledge which, for Cixous, it is unethical to aspire to; and when others presume knowledge, as *Photos de racines* shows, this causes the author disquiet and incurs her exasperation. Cixous's somewhat duplicitous handling of the potentially encroaching outsider in *Photos de racines*, who is both enticed and repudiated, is mirrored in the relationship her narrators in *Les Rêveries de la femme sauvage* and *Le Jour où je n'étais pas là* have with the uncanny 'Venant' [Apparition], which is not her but yet is of her. The device provides a means of spiriting the writing self out of the text: this distances Cixous's self from the reader of the text, but for Cixous herself, it means that the element of the autobiographical project concerning the search for the self need not be abandoned. In *Les Rêveries de la femme sauvage* and *Le Jour où je n'étais pas là*, the text resulting from Cixous's uncanny encounter with herself serves to re-root the author, reconnecting her with the estranged parts of her life, as the narrator of *Les Rêveries de la femme sauvage* admits: the purpose of the narrative is to assuage her sense of melancholy solitude, and in this it succeeds: 'Mais maintenant plus j'en parle et plus j'y reviens [...] plus je me sens chez moi au Clos-Salembier maintenant et rétrospectivement' [But now the more I talk about it and the more I go back there the more I feel at home in Clos-Salembier now and in retrospect].[96]

Les Rêveries de la femme sauvage and *Le Jour où je n'étais pas là* are confessional works written to correct the unknowing assumptions made about Cixous by those who consider they know her, but are ignorant of her complicated ethnic heritage, difficult relation to Algeria and tragic experience of motherhood. These false impressions reflect back an inaccurate image to the author, whose recent autobiographical narratives reveal the extent to which she has been disturbed by not recognizing herself in the estranged visions of herself harboured by others. Although the radical format and joyously unconventional nature of *Photos de racines* implies that it is through generic innovation that such unhealthy readerly expectations should be corrected, this strategy is supplanted by a far more conventional approach in *Les Rêveries de la femme sauvage* and *Le Jour où je n'étais pas là*: texts which, whilst maintaining some characteristics of Cixousian *écriture féminine* — neologisms, taking on the voice of the other and idiosyncratic use of pronouns — are nevertheless recognizably autobiographical in a way that *Photos de racines* is not. Paradoxically, the damaging potential for self-writing to create a reading encounter that the reader risks perceiving as complete and enlightening, when it is only partially so, are best rectified by instigating an autobiographical encounter closer to the traditional generic norms previously rejected by Cixous's narrators.[97] The use of this tactic in *Les Rêveries de la femme sauvage* and *Le Jour où je n'étais pas là* does not, however, produce texts that aid and abet the consuming reader. They problematize the desire for knowledge of the autobiographical self, question the ethics of this desire to gain knowledge, and in the process give back knowledge of the self to the self. As a result, the reader who has previously encountered in Cixous an exponent of genre-defying poetic writing and a 'loving' concept of self–other relations finds herself in the same situation as the one inclined to appropriate Cixous as a feminist writer. Both find themselves positioned as consuming Cixous's self, and are repudiated, not 'loved'.

Notes to Chapter 5

1. Emma Wilson has located concerns with identity politics in some of Cixous's works published prior to 1990, although in these cases it is sexual identity which is at stake, rather than ethnic, national or political identity, which are the aspects of Cixous's identity that most preoccupy me here. See Wilson, 'Hélène Cixous: An Erotics of the Feminine', in *French Erotic Fiction: Women's Desiring Writing, 1880–1990*, ed. by Alex Hughes and Kate Ince (Oxford: Berg, 1996), pp. 121–45.
2. *Les Rêveries de la femme sauvage: scènes primitives* is the work which concentrates most squarely on these experiences, although they are also an important aspect of the narrative in *Le Jour où je n'étais pas là*. See also Cixous's 'Pieds nus', in *Une enfance algérienne*, ed. by Leïla Sebbar (Paris: Gallimard, 1997), pp. 53–63. As yet, critical engagements with the Algerian turn in Cixous's writing are still few, but see Jennifer Yee, 'The Colonial Outsider: "Malgérie" in Hélène Cixous' Novel *Les Rêveries de la femme sauvage*', *Tulsa Studies in Women's Literature*, 20 (2001), 189–200; Nick Harrison, 'Learning from Experience: Hélène Cixous's "Pieds nus"', *Paragraph*, 27 (2004), 21–32; and my 'Writing Self-Estrangement: Possessive Knowledge and Loss in Cixous's Recent Autobiographical Work', in *Hybrid Voices, Hybrid Texts: Women's Writing at the Turn of the Millennium*, ed. by Gill Rye, special edn of *Dalhousie French Studies*, 68 (Fall 2004), pp. 69–77.
3. For the author's own account of her ethnic identity and Algeria's place in it, see Cixous, 'Mon Algériance', *Les Inrockuptibles*, 20 August 1997, pp. 70–74; trans. by Eric Prenowitz and published in English as 'My Algeriance, in Other Words: To Depart Not to Arrive from Algeria', in *Stigmata: Escaping Texts* (London: Routledge, 1998), pp. 153–72. On Cixous's writing of her Jewish identity, see Christa Stevens, 'Judéités, à lire dans l'œuvre d'Hélène Cixous', *International Journal of Francophone Studies*, 7 (2004), 81–93.
4. This is not to suggest that Algeria had never hitherto featured in her work: Cixous's Algerian connection is acknowledged — albeit much more briefly — in her work as far back as her seminal essay 'Sorties'. See Cixous, 'Sorties', pp. 130–33. On Cixous's ambivalent relation to autobiography in her writing, see Mairéad Hanrahan, 'Of Altobiography', in *Revisiting the Scene of Writing: New Readings of Cixous*, ed. by Julia Dobson and Gill Rye, special edn of *Paragraph*, 23.3 (November 2000), pp. 282–95.
5. Valuable accounts of Cixous's notion of *écriture féminine* and of her feminist engagement early in her career can be found in Verena Andermatt Conley, *Hélène Cixous* (Hemel Hempstead: Harvester Wheatsheaf, 1992) and Morag Schiach, *Hélène Cixous: A Politics of Writing* (London: Routledge, 1991). See also the incisive presentation in Abigail Bray, *Hélène Cixous: Writing and Sexual Difference* (Basingstoke: Palgrave Macmillan, 2004).
6. See my discussion of autobiography as a genre in Chapter 1.
7. This is a widely recurring motif of Cixous's fictional and other writings. An early articulation of her concept of the self's porosity to the other, presented here as a 'feminine' quality, can be found in 'Sorties', pp. 161–63.
8. Cixous writes on the concept of 'love' and the feminine disposition for giving in 'Sorties', pp. 143–44; 161–63; see also the account given of the importance of this disposition to Cixous in Susan Sellers, *Hélène Cixous: Authorship, Autobiography and Love* (Cambridge: Polity Publishers, 1996), especially pp. 8–11; 63–73.
9. Hereafter, 'Rire'. This essay is published in English as 'The Laugh of the Medusa', trans. by K. and P. Cohen, in *The Routledge Language and Cultural Theory Reader*, ed. by Lucy Burke, Tony Crowley and Alan Girvan (London: Routledge, 2000), pp. 161–66 (repr. from *New French Feminisms: An Anthology*, ed. by Elaine Marks and Isabel Courtivron (Brighton: Harvester Wheatsheaf, 1981), pp. 245–51). The English version will hereafter be referred to as 'Laugh'.

10. 'Rire', p. 39; 'Laugh', p. 161.
11. 'Rire', p. 44; 'Laugh', p. 166.
12. Smith, *Poetics*, p. 57.
13. See Smith, 'The Autobiographical Manifesto: Ideas, Temporalities, Politics', in Neuman (ed.), pp. 186–212.
14. Smith, 'Manifesto', p. 190.
15. Smith, 'Manifesto', p. 187.
16. Smith, 'Manifesto', p. 191.
17. Smith, 'Manifesto', p. 195.
18. The relationship between Cixous and feminism, and feminist scholars, persists in being problematic. Feminist scholars have been critical of what they have perceived as unhelpfully essentialist or Utopian tendencies in her work: see, for example, Toril Moi, *Sexual/Textual Politics* (1985), 2nd edn (London: Routledge, 2002), pp. 100–25. Meanwhile, scholars following Cixous's approach to reading texts criticize Anglo-American feminists for failing to be sensitive to the subtlety of an *œuvre* that celebrates a Derridean 'différance', a multiplicity and deferral of meaning which is antagonistic to much of scholarly discourse (including feminist discourse), where the goal is to pin down meaning. For this perspective, see Peggy Kamuf, 'To Give Place: Semi-Approaches to Hélène Cixous', in *Another Look, Another Woman: Retranslations of French Feminism*, ed. by Lynne Huffer, special edn of *Yale French Studies*, 87 (1995), pp. 68–89; and Mary Lydon, 'Re-Translating no Re-Reading no, rather: Rejoycing (with) Hélène Cixous', in Huffer (ed.), pp. 90–102. On Cixous's difficult relationship with feminism, see the account given by Bray; and, for a Cixousian view, that of Ian Blyth with Susan Sellers, *Hélène Cixous: Live Theory* (New York: Continuum, 2004).
19. Davis, *Killing the Other*, p. 12.
20. Experimental qualities can be discerned in the vast majority of Cixous's prose writings (leaving aside her theatrical work, which falls outside the remit of this study). These are particularly pronounced in her fictions of the 1970s and early 1980s, such as *Neutre* (Paris: Grasset, 1972), as well as in more discursive pieces such as *Vivre l'orange* (Paris: Editions des femmes, 1979). Ampler treatments of Cixous's experiments in writing can be found in Martine Motard-Noar, *Les Fictions d'Hélène Cixous: une autre langue de femme* (Lexington: French Forum, 1991); Conley; and Blyth with Sellers.
21. See Hanrahan, 'Of Altobiography'.
22. Cixous, *Le Livre de Promethea* (Paris: Gallimard, coll. Blanche, 1983).
23. On genre in *Le Livre de Promethea*, see Hanrahan, 'Cixous's *Le Livre de Promethea*: A Diary in an Other Form', *French Studies*, 55 (2001), 195–206.
24. *Promethea*, p. 27.
25. Cixous seems to be playing here on the dual meaning of 'genre' in French: as well as 'genre', it also means 'genus' — the biological classification at the next level of breadth after 'species'.
26. This interpretation of Cixous's narratorial technique as a tactic to prevent *Le Livre de Promethea* from being assimilated into the genre of autobiography is also the one made by Sellers, *Authorship*, p. 56.
27. *Promethea*, p. 27.
28. See Lejeune, *Pacte*, p. 26.
29. Whilst her reading does not discuss the work as an 'autobiographical manifesto', an argument for reading *Photos de racines* as a feminist autobiography has been made by Mary E. Schipa, 'Hélène Cixous: sur la piste d'une autobiographie féministe', *Romance Review*, 5.1 (Spring 1995), 29–37. This is not a thesis shared by Hanrahan: see her remarks in 'Of Altobiography', p. 289, n. 15.
30. Hélène Cixous and Mireille Calle-Gruber, *Hélène Cixous, Rootprints: Memory and Life Writing*, trans. by Eric Prenowitz (London: Routledge, 1997); hereafter, *Rootprints*.
31. Smith, 'Manifesto', p. 193.
32. *Photos de racines*, pp. 177–208.
33. To explore this phenomenon further would take me into very different territory from my discussion here. The incorporation of photographs into autobiographical texts implies a quite other relationship between author and reader to that which I explore here: the reader is no longer a reader or consumer simply of words, able to create their own images to fill out their

understanding, but is supplied with images (not necessarily originating in the author) to read, or consume, instead. Besides the works with a photographic element that I discuss in this study, *Photos de racines* and *Roland Barthes*, see also Marie NDiaye, *Autoportrait en vert* ([Paris?]: Mercure de France, 2005); and Annie Ernaux and Marc Marie, *L'Usage de la photo* (Paris: Gallimard, 2005) for examples where photography is used in life-writing.

34. The only studies to date with a focus on *Photos de racines* of which I am aware are those by Schipa; Hanrahan, 'Of Altobiography'; and my own 'Writing Self-Estrangement'.
35. *Photos de racines*, p. 179, emphasis in original text; *Rootprints*, p. 178.
36. *Photos de racines*, p. 95; *Rootprints*, p. 86.
37. Hanrahan, in her 'Of Altobiography', remarks on Cixous's 'resolute refusal [...] of the genre of autobiography itself', despite an 'all-pervasive [...] autobiographical dimension' in her work (p. 283).
38. *Photos de racines*, p. 149; *Rootprints*, p. 149.
39. Derrida, 'La Loi du genre', in *Parages* (Paris: Galilée, 1986), pp. 249–87 (first publ. in *Glyph*, 7 (1980), 176–201).
40. *Photos de racines*, p. 104; *Rootprints*, p. 95.
41. *Photos de racines*, p. 106; *Rootprints*, p. 97.
42. *Photos de racines*, p. 105; *Rootprints*, pp. 96–97.
43. *Photos de racines*, p. 105. Emphasis is the authors'.
44. *Rootprints*, p. 96. Emphasis is the authors'.
45. *Photos de racines*, p. 181; *Rootprints*, p. 179 (translation modified).
46. *Photos de racines*, p. 181.
47. *Rootprints*, p. 179.
48. *Photos de racines*, p. 183; *Rootprints*, p. 181.
49. *Photos de racines*, p. 182; *Rootprints*, p. 180.
50. *Photos de racines*, pp. 183–207.
51. *Photos de racines*, p. 207; *Rootprints*, p. 204 (translation modified).
52. 'Mon Algériance', p. 72.
53. *Photos de racines*, p. 185; *Rootprints*, p. 183 (translation modified).
54. See Hanrahan, 'Of Altobiography', pp. 284–86. Hanrahan's article performs a reading of *Photos de racines*, making the 'Albums et légendes' section its focus in preference to the other parts of the work; a move which could be taken as an index of a more general phenomenon: the reader's desire for autobiography, a desire so strong that it leads to the fetishization of the text. As will become clear, I do not share Hanrahan's confidence that all traces of authoritarian reader relations are excised from *Photos de racines*.
55. *Photos de racines*, p. 188; *Rootprints*, p. 186.
56. *Photos de racines*, p. 189; *Rootprints*, p. 188.
57. *Photos de racines*, p. 203.
58. The notion of 'love' is itself a feminist notion, in that the giving which lies behind 'love' counters what is posited in 'Sorties' as a 'masculine' concern with 'having'; with property and possession. On Cixous's concept of 'love', see especially Sellers, *Authorship*. The work pre-dates the resurgence of the autobiographical in Cixous's work and, despite the title, does not treat 'autobiography' at any length.
59. This understanding of the self's dependency on the other to bring it into being is articulated in the course of the discussion between Cixous and Calle-Gruber. See *Photos de racines*, pp. 22–23.
60. Note, however, that Cixous's conviction that she is able to speak 'through' others or in their place as a result of this fusion has been the subject of an ethical critique. See Sarah Cooper, 'The Ethics of Rewriting the Loss of Exile in *Manne aux Mandelstams aux Mandelas*', in Dobson and Rye (eds), pp. 311–23.
61. *Photos de racines*, p. 106; *Rootprints*, p. 97.
62. This is exemplified where Calle-Gruber remarks (in an intervention edited out of the English translation of *Photos de racines*) that 'j'aimerais préciser ce que tu [Cixous] entends par "l'humain" constitutif de ton écriture de fiction' [I would like to specify what you [Cixous] mean by 'the human' which constitutes your fictional writing], *Photos de racines*, p. 34.

63. Cixous has written widely about writing as a particularly privileged place for the loving encounter. See, for example, her 'What Is It O'Clock? Or the Door (We Never Enter)', in *Stigmata*, pp. 57–83. Here she avers: 'When I write I ask for your hand; with your hand I'll go too far and I won't be afraid anymore of not coming back. Without my knowing it, it is already *love*. Love is giving one's hand' (p. 74).
64. For a discussion of the reception of Cixous and reader relations in her work, see Gill Rye 'Agony or Ecstasy? Reading Cixous's Recent Fiction', in Dobson and Rye (eds), pp. 296–310.
65. See *Photos de racines*, pp. 24–26; of the many readings of Cixous which emphasize the principles of generosity and non-hierarchical relations in her work, see, for example, Blyth with Sellers; and Lydon.
66. In the context of Cixous's fictional writing, Wilson has drawn attention to a controlling aspect to Cixousian reader relations that follows from her tendency to position the reader as a specular other. See especially Wilson, *Sexuality*, pp. 120–27.
67. *Photos de racines*, p. 14; *Rootprints*, p. 4.
68. *Photos de racines*, p. 14; *Rootprints*, p. 4.
69. Ibid.
70. *Photos de racines*, p. 14.
71. *Rootprints*, p. 4.
72. *Photos de racines*, p. 15; *Rootprints*, p. 6. Prior to the publication of *Photos de racines*, Cixous had previously made similar points about her feminist activities. See, for example, her 'De la scène de l'Inconscient à la scène de l'Histoire: chemin d'une écriture', in *Hélène Cixous: chemins d'une écriture*, ed. by Françoise van Rossum-Guyon and Myriam Díaz-Diocaretz (Paris: Presses Universitaires de Vincennes; Amsterdam: Rodopi, 1990), pp. 15–34 (pp. 27–28).
73. See Wilson, *Sexuality*, pp. 96–129.
74. *Photos de racines*, p. 59; *Rootprints*, p. 50.
75. *Photos de racines*, pp. 59–60.
76. *Rootprints*, pp. 50–51 (translation modified).
77. *Photos de racines*, p. 62; *Rootprints*, p. 54.
78. *Photos de racines*, p. 26.
79. *Rootprints*, p. 16
80. See Sellers, *Authorship*, p. 12.
81. *Photos de racines*, p. 27; *Rootprints*, p. 17.
82. *Les Rêveries de la femme sauvage*, p. 9.
83. *Les Rêveries de la femme sauvage*, p. 57.
84. *Les Rêveries de la femme sauvage*, p. 55.
85. Cixous, *Dedans* (Paris: Grasset, 1969).
86. *Les Rêveries de la femme sauvage*, p. 142.
87. *Les Rêveries de la femme sauvage*, p. 19.
88. *Les Rêveries de la femme sauvage*, p. 144.
89. *Le Jour où je n'étais pas là*, p. 190.
90. *Le Jour où je n'étais pas là*, p. 95.
91. *Les Rêveries de la femme sauvage*, p. 10.
92. *Le Jour où je n'étais pas là*, p. 150.
93. *Le Jour où je n'étais pas là*, p. 31.
94. *Les Rêveries de la femme sauvage*, p. 167.
95. Freud, 'The Uncanny' (1919), in *The Standard Edition*, XVII (1955), 217–52, p. 241. We may assume a deliberate use of the Freudian Uncanny by Cixous, who has written on it in her 'Fiction and its Phantoms: A Reading of Freud's *Das Unheimliche* (The "Uncanny")', trans. by Robert. Dennomé, *New Literary History*, 7 (1976), 525–48.
96. *Les Rêveries de la femme sauvage*, p. 166.
97. On the structural resemblance between *Le Jour où je n'étais pas là* and canonical autobiographical texts, including Rousseau's *Confessions*, see Hanrahan, 'Of Three-Legged Writing: Cixous's *Le Jour où je n'étais pas là*', *French Forum*, 28.2 (Spring 2003), 99–113.

CONCLUSION

Genet makes his autobiography a dirty space. In this book, we have also seen autobiography figured as a feminine space, a memorializing space, a space for the expression of marginalized identities, but most often, as an impossible space. To take the authors I have studied here at their word, and at their words, autobiography is the space where we have not been in the course of this book. Yet autobiography has been here all along: this book has been haunted by autobiography from the outset. The authors whose selves we have failed to fully encounter in the course of this book have needed the space of autobiography to exist, much as they may declare they do not inhabit it. The question that has haunted this book is the question of why that should be.

Autobiography in its traditional sense may imply a full first-person account of an individual's life and selfhood, imbued with authority by dint of the fact that the writer behind the narration is also the subject-matter which the narrative takes as its object. We understand that the intellectual climate in which literary autobiographers have worked in the post-war period is one that does not embrace certainty; the spirit of the era has instead been to interrogate what previous generations may have taken as certainties, and to interrogate the concept of certainty itself. Yet the novel has been able to live through the *nouveau roman* [new novel] movement which called established novelistic parameters into question. It has been able to survive assaults on such notions as the omniscience of the third-person narrator and of narrative objectivity, in the process absorbing new practices and approaches without losing its identity as (albeit reconfigured) novel. Why is it, then, that autobiography does not evolve whilst retaining its identity as autobiography? Why must it be slain and replaced by new genres of autobiographical writing?

The authors I study here take great pains to indicate to their readers that the texts they are reading do not belong to the class of narratives called autobiography, and that they take their distance from it. Frequently, direct address to the readership (which we find in Cixous and Genet) is used to inform them explicitly that this is the case. Other means to communicate this distance include dramatic departures from a conventional linear narrative structure (such as those effected by Perec), and radical reconceptions (for example Sarraute's) of what any autobiography has at its core: selfhood. Could it be that such energy is expended to prove this not-belonging to autobiography precisely because in some way these works do? What is posited as the conventional model of autobiography implies a certain relationship between the autobiography's narrator and the reader: the narrator is understood to be the voice of the flesh-and-blood autobiographer who lives outside the text. He or she takes up a position of authority over his or her readership, directing their encounter with the self in the text, and also (because the narrator is assumed to speak as and for the extra-textual author) the self outside it. The effect of the narrator exerting this authority is that the audience is left no room to dispute the narrator's account, and readers are positioned as passive recipients of his or her self-representation.

The often strikingly visible 'departures' from autobiography which are taken by works of self-writing I have studied here are presented as a sign that the aspirations of traditional autobiography are abandoned: the autobiographical narrator no longer expects to supply a full account of him- or herself to a passive audience that will unthinkingly ingest the narrative delivered to them whole, and consider that they have acquired through their ingestion a solid grasp of the autobiographer's person as it exists or existed in life. Indeed, the ethics, as well as the possibility, of this mode of receiving the autobiographical text are a subject of close scrutiny by the autobiographical writers I have studied here. The ethics of the transactions occurring between reader and writer in the space of autobiography (transactions ultimately in the control of the reader) are probed by these authors in their texts. The result is that autobiography is frequently found to be an unethical space. However, our eventual conclusions may lead us to other reasons for this evaluation of autobiography as an unethical space than those proposed by Sarraute, Perec, Genet and Cixous in the course of their self-writings.

The works explored through the course of this book highlight many reasons why the reader should not take a traditional, passive approach to reading autobiographical texts, but adopt a more active, critical one instead. They emphasize the opacity of language and the distortions of representation; the fallibility of memory and the obscure workings of the unconscious as factors which inhibit the production of a faithful image of the author in the medium of text. Sarraute, Perec, Genet and Cixous use their self-writings to interrogate the latent assumptions underpinning the unspoken consensus of what an autobiography is: these assumptions include the idea that autobiographers will have arrived at the genre because they have momentous events to chronicle; because they can bear witness to something which touches a whole population; because there is something noteworthy in the selfhood or experience which they record whose importance transcends the individual to address a wider, perhaps marginalized, community. In addition, these authors often use their writings of the self to question that self's parameters. They question the extent to which the solitary individual who inhabits one body is ever truly solitary, or can ever be confined to one being. Sarraute and Cixous posit the idea that the self is not a single entity to be considered in isolation, but the product of the coming together of several selves: these may be selves of earlier generations who have given it life and with whom it has coexisted; selves it encounters in the present, whose interactions with it contribute to making it the self that it is (although, significantly, we have seen too a reluctance to pursue the implications of this point in respect of the relation between the autobiographer's self and the reader's). Meanwhile, Perec and Genet portray their respective selfhoods as being dispersed between multiple selves, but irrecoverably so: these selves cannot be brought together with or by any other. For them, selfhood is fractured, and denies being known (a position Cixous too comes close to in her most recent autobiographical works). The authors who have occupied our attention seem to use their autobiographical texts to *inquire into*, rather than set out, the self and its experience. This seems to reflect their recognition of the instability and uncertainty of the self they write — a recognition not associated (rightly or wrongly) with conventional autobiography. Having been relieved of the tyranny of the authoritative narrator who states what the self is, rather than inquire into what it may or may not be, we might assume that our position as readers would change too. Without the author as authority (or rather the narrator, as his or her deputy), readers may anticipate that they will be given the freedom to create their own sense of who the autobiographical self is from the text before them. To invite readers to assume an active responsibility for the readings they arrive at would seem to follow naturally from the abandonment of a traditional model of autobiography, and along with it the abandonment of a concept of an unassailable, authoritative narrating self whose pronouncements may not be questioned by the reader, only devoured.

Yet our experience of reading the autobiographical writings of Sarraute, Perec, Genet and Cixous does not correspond to this vision of a new reading experience which the exit from the space of autobiography should bring. For all that the autobiographical narrators we encounter emphasize the insufficiency and lack of authority of their textual self-portraits, and their lack of correspondence to the self outside the text, they retain the old habit of directing the reading of their audience; indeed I have argued that one of the ways they do so is precisely through these declarations of insufficiency. These declarations, along with other narratorial interventions, have the function of conveying to the reader how indigestible the self-representation they meet in the text is; how it is not for their consumption and, even if consumed, will not give them possession of the autobiographer's self. Modern autobiographers do not wish to be associated with the genre of autobiography, but whilst discarding some of the trappings of conventional autobiography they do not, in the end, relinquish them all.

How might we explain this curious positioning with relation to the genre of autobiography? In my view, the answer lies in so-called conventional autobiography itself. I have shown that Lejeune's model of the autobiographical pact embeds within it the idea that autobiography is the site of a play of power relations between the reader and writer of autobiography. Each depends on the other's participation to seal the autobiographical contract, and each one attempts to protect him- or herself from the other's ruses that would threaten the contract, by anticipating them and by responding to them in such a way as to neutralize their effect. Lejeune's model of autobiography lays bare that the autobiographical self depends on the reading other for its self-realization; it exposes that the space of autobiography is a space of conflict between writer and reader which the reader, always coming last to the text, is in a position to win.

In Sarraute and Genet especially, we see an awareness of the operation of intangible systems which govern the self by subordinating it, or causing it to subordinate itself, to the demands of the other that represents society at large. We see too in these authors an awareness of the role discourse — including autobiographical discourse — plays in upholding those systems. Autobiographers,

I argue, have an awareness that autobiography functions as a framework that, like Lacan's symbolic order or Foucault's panopticon disciplinary mechanism, beholds them to the other: embodied here in the other who reads. Thus autobiography threatens autobiographers with a loss of sovereignty over the self, and with the real risk of having it consumed, swallowed up by a larger mechanism, which will irrevocably transform it into something other than what it posits itself as being.

I read autobiography as a site of triangular relations, whereby the writing self, the reading other, and the genre have the potential to be mutually constitutive of each other in the space of the text. In the course of being realized, the identity of each of these three elements is susceptible to being influenced by the operations of the other two. This is what characterizes autobiography. If the autobiographical self finds itself being consumed, misappropriated, distorted by the reader, it is because the identity that autobiography has as a genre is such that it enables this to take place. It is for this reason, I argue, that autobiographers must position themselves out of reach of the genre of autobiography. The genre of autobiography empowers the reader, not merely to consume the autobiographer's self, but to confer its selfhood on it — that is, to be the ultimate arbiter of its identity. In a bid to assert their mastery over their reader and over the mechanisms of the genre, autobiographers attempt to take advantage of the fact that, in the triangular relations between writing self, genre and reading other, the autobiographer's is not the only identity susceptible to being influenced by the operations of the other elements.

We have seen that the way the autobiographer relates to the reader is marked by more or less openly expressed fear, anxiety and suspicion. These reactions are generated by the prospect of the reader mis-knowing the author, perhaps because it is beyond the author, or beyond language, to convey who the autobiographer's self is, or alternatively because the reader will be unwilling to encounter in the text anyone but the specular other that they were hoping to meet. Underlying all these anxieties is somewhere the realization that when writing the self and its life, the autobiographer surrenders control of the self and submits it to the reader to form, create and consume with their own understanding. The recourse to new strategies of writing the self reflects perhaps less the impossibility of writing the self in the traditional way, but more the resistance to having it read and consumed in the way that the inherent instability of autobiography as a genre makes possible. Thus the new self-writing which distinguishes itself from the genre of autobiography does not represent a democratization of autobiography; nor does it constitute an abandonment of traditional patterns of reader relations in autobiography, whereby the author positions him- or herself as an authority directing the reader's understanding of himself. Despite their ostentatious and very self-conscious gestures which assert their distance from autobiography, these texts do not succeed in straying very far from the traditional dynamics of the genre. The autobiographer's investment, to which their writings bear witness, in being seen not to write autobiography stems precisely from a desire not to surrender authority to the reader to determine who the autobiographical self will be.

The narrators of these texts 'confess' only to that loss of sovereignty over the self which is designed to prevent an autobiographical pact from being concluded, from stopping autobiography from taking place in these texts. But, as with the interrogation of the ethics of consuming autobiography, there is a strategic purpose behind this manoeuvre. This is a proclamation of a loss of sovereignty which ultimately seeks to mitigate that very loss by seeking to prevent the consumption, appropriation or transformation of the self that the reader has the power to bring about.

BIBLIOGRAPHY

❖

ABELOVE, HENRY, MICHÈLE AINA BARALE and DAVID M. HALPERIN (eds), *The Lesbian and Gay Studies Reader* (New York: Routledge, 1993)

ADORNO, THEODOR W. and MAX HORKHEIMER, *Dialectic of Enlightenment* (London: Verso, 1997)

AÏSSAOUI, DRISS, 'Présentation', in *Diversité culturelle et désir d'autobiographie dans l'espace francophone,* ed. by Driss Aïssaoui, special edn of *Dalhousie French Studies*, 70 (Spring 2005), pp. 3–6

ALTHUSSER, LOUIS, 'Ideology and Ideological State Apparatuses (Notes towards an Investigation)' (1970), in *Essays on Ideology* (London: Verso, 1984), pp. 1–60

ANDERSON, LINDA, *Autobiography* (London: Routledge, 2001)

ANDREWS, CHRIS, 'Hide and Seek: Autobiographical Secrets in the Work of Queneau and Perec', in *Soi-disant: Life-Writing in French*, ed. by Juliana De Nooy, Joe Hardwick and Barbara E. Hanna (Newark: University of Delaware Press, 2005), pp. 12–25

ANGREMY, ANNIE (ed.), *Nathalie Sarraute: portrait d'un écrivain* ([Paris]: Bibliothèque nationale de France, 1995)

ARCHAMBAULT, PAUL J., 'Autobiography and the Search for Transparency', *Symposium*, 51 (1998), 231–46

ASSO, FRANÇOISE, *Nathalie Sarraute: une littérature de l'effraction* (Paris: Presses Universitaires de France, 1995)

——'L'Insupportable', in *Nathalie Sarraute,* ed. by Françoise Asso, special edn of *Littérature*, 118 (June 2000), pp. 78–86

ASSO, FRANÇOISE (ed.), *Nathalie Sarraute*, special edn of *Littérature*, 118 (June 2000), pp. 1–127

ASTRO, ALAN, 'Allegory in Georges Perec's *W ou le souvenir d'enfance*', *MLN*, 102 (1987), 867–76

BACCHILEGA, CRISTINA, 'Feminine Voices Inscribing Sarraute's *Childhood* and Kingston's *The Woman Warrior*', *Textual Practice*, 6 (1992), 101–18

BAINBRIGGE, SUSAN, *Writing against Death: The Autobiographies of Simone de Beauvoir* (Amsterdam: Rodopi, 2005)

BAINBRIGGE, SUSAN (ed.), *Autothanatographies,* special edn of *Forum for Modern Language Studies*, 41.4 (October 2005), pp. 359–460

BAKER, FELICITY, 'Moral Death and Fictional Self-Portrayal', *Romance Studies*, 9 (Winter 1986), 35–51

BARBER, STEPHEN, *Jean Genet* (London: Reaktion Books, 2004)

BARBOUR, SARAH, *Nathalie Sarraute and the Feminist Reader: Identities in Process* (Lewisburg: Bucknell University Press; London: Associated University Presses, 1993)

BARTHES, ROLAND, *Mythologies* (Paris: Editions du Seuil, 1957)

——'La Mort de l'auteur' (1968), in *Essais Critiques*, IV: *Le Bruissement de la langue* (Paris: Editions du Seuil, 1984), pp. 61–67

——*Roland Barthes* (1975), 2nd edn (Paris: Editions du Seuil, coll. Ecrivains de toujours, 1995)

BARTLETT, NEIL, 'The Uses of Monotony: Repetition in the Language of Oscar Wilde,

Jean Genet, Edmund White and Juan Goytisolo', in *Flowers and Revolution: A Collection of Writings on Jean Genet*, ed. by Barbara Read (London: Middlesex University Press, 1997), pp. 113–27

Bataille, Georges, *La Littérature et le mal: Emily Brontë — Baudelaire — Michelet — Blake — Sade — Proust — Kafka — Genet* (Paris: Gallimard, 1957)

Battaglia, Anna Maria, 'Georges Perec: "L'Indicible vers quoi tend désespérément le désir d'écrire"', in *L'effetto autobiografico: scritture e letture del soggetto nella letteratura europea*, ed. by Edda Melon (Turin: Tirrenia, 1990), pp. 183–201

Baude, Jeannine, 'De l'improbable ou de l'autobiographie: Georges Perec, lire, écouter, voir...', *Cabinet d'amateur*, 7–8 (December 1998), 47–50

Beauvoir, Simone de, *Le Deuxième Sexe* (Paris: Gallimard, 1949)

—— *Mémoires d'une jeune fille rangée* (Paris: Gallimard, 1958)

Béhar, Stella, *Georges Perec: écrire pour ne pas dire* (New York: Peter Lang, 1995)

Bell, Sheila M., 'The Conjurer's Hat: Sarraute Criticism since 1980', *Romance Studies*, 23 (Spring 1994), 85–103

—— 'Endings in Autobiography: The Example of *Enfance*', in *Nathalie Sarraute ou le texte du for intérieur*, ed. by Lise Ouvrard and Monique Wittig, special edn of *Esprit créateur*, 36.2 (Summer 1996), pp. 21–36

—— 'Orchestrated Voices: Selves and Others in Nathalie Sarraute's *Tu ne t'aimes pas*', in *Narrative Voices in Modern French Fiction: Studies in Honour of Valerie Minogue*, ed. by Michael Cardy, George Evans and Gabriel Jacobs (Cardiff: University of Wales Press, 1997), pp. 13–35

Bellos, David, *Georges Perec: A Life In Words* (London: Harper Collins, 1993)

—— 'The "Third Dimension" of Georges Perec's *W ou le souvenir d'enfance*', *French Studies Bulletin*, 70 (Spring 1999), 1–3

Bénabou, Marcel, 'Perec et la judéité', *Cahiers Georges Perec*, 1 (1984), 15–30

Benmussa, Simone, *Entretiens avec Nathalie Sarraute* (Tournai: La Renaissance du Livre, 1999)

Benson, Peter, 'The Chiasmus of Mourning and Identification in Jean Genet', *Studies in Twentieth Century Literature*, 24 (2000), 205–24

Benstock, Shari, 'Authorizing the Autobiographical', in *The Private Self: Theory and Practice of Women's Autobiographical Writings*, ed. by Shari Benstock (London: Routledge, 1988), pp. 10–33

Benstock, Shari (ed.), *The Private Self: Theory and Practice of Women's Autobiographical Writings* (London: Routledge, 1988)

Bergen, Véronique, *Jean Genet: entre mythe et réalité* (Brussels: De Boeck Université, 1993)

Bern, Jeanne, 'La Mémoire, l'écriture et l'impossible à dire: Robert Antelme, Patrick Modiano, Georges Perec', *Colloquium Helveticum*, 27 (1998), 25–41

Bersani, Leo, 'Is the Rectum a Grave?', in *AIDS: Cultural Analysis, Cultural Activism*, ed. by Douglas Crimp (Cambridge, MA: MIT, 1988), pp. 198–222

—— *The Culture of Redemption* (Cambridge, MA: Harvard University Press, 1990)

—— 'Foucault, Freud, Fantasy and Power', *GLQ*, 2.1–2 (1995), 11–33

—— *Homos* (Cambridge, MA: Harvard University Press, 1995)

Blaise, Clark, 'Your Nearest Exit May Be behind You: Autobiography and the Post-Modernist Moment', in *The Seductions of Biography*, ed. by Mary Rhiel and David Suchoff (New York: Routledge, 1996), pp. 201–09

Blyth, Ian with Susan Sellers, *Hélène Cixous: Live Theory* (New York: Continuum, 2004)

Boswell, John, 'Revolutions, Universals and Sexual Categories', in *Hidden From History: Reclaiming the Gay and Lesbian Past*, ed. by Martin Bauml Duberman, Martha Vicinius and George Chauncey Jr. (Harmondsworth: Penguin, 1991), pp. 17–36

BOUCHARDEAU, HUGUETTE, *Nathalie Sarraute* (Paris: Flammarion, 2003)
BOUGON, PATRICE (ed.), *Jean Genet: littérature et politique (Literature and Politics)*, special edn of *Esprit créateur*, 35.1 (Spring 1995), pp. 1–88
BOYLE, CLAIRE, 'Relating to the Reader: Autobiographies by Sarraute, Perec, Genet and Cixous' (unpublished doctoral thesis, University of Cambridge, 2002)
——'Resisting The Whole Picture: The Gaze, and Reading Autobiographies by Nathalie Sarraute and Georges Perec', in *Seeing Things: Vision, Perception and Interpretation in French Studies*, ed. by Simon Kemp and Libby Saxton (Bern: Peter Lang, 2002), pp. 161–75
——'Writing Self-Estrangement: Possessive Knowledge and Loss in Cixous's Recent Autobiographical Work', in *Hybrid Voices, Hybrid Texts: Women's Writing at the Turn of the Millennium*, ed. by Gill Rye, special edn of *Dalhousie French Studies*, 68 (Fall 2004), 69–77
——'Friend or Foe? Misidentification and Genet's Queer Reception', in *Soi-disant: Life-Writing in French*, ed. by Juliana de Nooy, Joe Hardwick and Barbara E. Hanna (Newark: University of Delaware Press, 2005), pp. 26–40
——'Autobiography, The Dangers of Knowledge and Genet's Suspect Reader', *French Studies*, 59 (2005), 189–202
BRAY, ABIGAIL, *Hélène Cixous: Writing and Sexual Difference* (Basingstoke: Palgrave Macmillan, 2004)
BRÉE, GERMAINE, 'Autogynography', *Southern Review*, 22 (1986), 223–30
BRITTON, CELIA, *The 'Nouveau Roman': Fiction, Theory and Politics* (Basingstoke: Macmillan; New York: St Martin's Press, 1992)
BRODZKI, BELLA, 'Mothers, Displacement and Language in the Autobiographies of Nathalie Sarraute and Christa Wolf', in *Life/Lines: Theorizing Women's Autobiography*, ed. by Bella Brodzki and Celeste Schenk (Ithaca, NY: Cornell University Press, 1988), pp. 243–59
BRODZKI, BELLA and CELESTE SCHENK (eds), *Life/Lines: Theorizing Women's Autobiography* (Ithaca, NY: Cornell University Press, 1988)
BROUGHTON, T. L., 'Women's Autobiography: The Self at Stake?', in *Autobiography and Questions of Gender*, ed. by Shirley Neuman (London: Cass, 1991), pp. 76–107
BRUNER, JEROME, 'The Autobiographical Process', in *The Culture of Autobiography: Constructions of Self-Representation*, ed. by Robert Folkenflik (Stanford, CA: Stanford University Press, 1993), pp. 38–56
BRUSKE, HANS-GUNTHER, *'Verkehrtes Helduntum' und Absonderung in den Romanen Jean Genets* (Frankfurt am Main: Lang, 1980)
BRUSS, ELIZABETH W., *Autobiographical Acts: The Changing Situation of a Literary Genre* (Baltimore: Johns Hopkins University Press, 1976)
——'The Game of Literature and Some Literary Games', *New Literary History*, 9 (1977), 153–72
BULLARO, GRACE RUSSO, 'Genet: Gay Deceiver or Repressed Homosexual?', in *Flowers and Revolution: A Collection of Writings on Jean Genet*, ed. by Barbara Read (London: Middlesex University Press, 1997), pp. 73–84
BURGELIN, CLAUDE, 'Perec lecteur de Flaubert', *Revue des lettres modernes*, 703–06 (1984), 135–71
——'Perec et la cruauté', *Cahiers Georges Perec*, 1 (1985), 31–47
——*Georges Perec* (Paris: Editions du Seuil, 1988)
BURGELIN, CLAUDE, and GEORGES PÉREC [*sic*], 'Le Nouveau Roman et le refus du réel', *Partisans*, 3 (February 1962), 108–18
BURKE, SEÁN, 'Introduction: Reconstructing the Author', in *Authorship: From Plato to the Postmodern: A Reader*, ed. by Seán Burke (Edinburgh: Edinburgh University Press, 1995), pp. xv–xxx

BURKE, SEÁN, *The Death and Return of the Author: Criticism and Subjectivity in Barthes, Foucault and Derrida*, 2nd edn (Edinburgh: Edinburgh University Press, 1998)

BUTLER, JUDITH, *Gender Trouble: Feminism and the Subversion of Identity* (New York: Routledge, 1990)

——'Imitation and Gender Insubordination', in *Inside/Out: Lesbian Theories, Gay Theories*, ed. by Diana Fuss (New York: Routledge, 1991), pp. 13–31

——*Bodies That Matter: On the Discursive Limits of 'Sex'* (New York: Routledge, 1993)

——*The Psychic Life of Power: Theories in Subjection* (Stanford, CA: Stanford University Press, 1997)

BUTLER, REX, *Slavoj Žižek: Live Theory* (New York: Continuum, 2005)

BUTOR, MICHEL, *Essais sur le roman* (Paris: Editions de Minuit, 1964)

CALDERON, JORGE, 'Le Mot à l'œuvre: *Ouvrez* de Nathalie Sarraute', *Tropos*, 26 (Spring 2000), 65–76

CALLE-GRUBER, MIREILLE and HÉLÈNE CIXOUS, *Hélène Cixous: photos de racines* (Paris: Editions des femmes–Antoinette Fouque, 1994)

CALLE, MIREILLE (ed.), *Du féminin* (Grenoble: Presses Universitaires de Grenoble; Sainte-Foy, Quebec: Le Griffon d'argile, 1992)

CALLE-GRUBER, MIREILLE (ed.), *Hélène Cixous: croisées d'une œuvre: actes du colloque de Cérisy 22–30 juin 1998* (Paris: Galilée, 2000)

CARDY, MICHAEL, GEORGE EVANS and GABRIEL JACOBS (eds), *Narrative Voices in Modern French Fiction: Studies in Honour of Valerie Minogue* (Cardiff: University of Wales Press, 1997)

CARUTH, CATHY (ed.), *Trauma: Explorations in Memory* (Baltimore: Johns Hopkins University Press, 1995)

CASTRO MARTINS BAHIENSE, VERA LUCIA DE, 'Georges Perec: continuité et discontinuité de la mémoire culturelle', in *Genres as Repositories of Cultural Memory*, ed. by Hendrik van Gorp and Ulla Musarra-Schroeder (Amsterdam: Rodopi, 2000), pp. 189–96

CAWS, MARY ANN and OTHERS (eds), *Ecritures de femmes: nouvelles cartographies* (New Haven: Yale University Press, 1996)

CERTEAU, MICHEL DE, *L'Invention du quotidien*, I: *Arts de faire*, ed. by Luce Giard (Paris: Gallimard, coll. folio, 1990)

CHAMPAGNE, ROLAND A., 'Jean Genet in the Delinquent Colony of Mettray: The Development of an Ethical Rite of Passage', *French Forum*, 26.3 (Fall 2001), 71–90

CIXOUS, HÉLÈNE, *Dedans* (Paris: Grasset, 1969)

——*Neutre* (Paris: Grasset, 1972)

——'Le Rire de la méduse', *Arc*, 61 (1975), 39–54

——'Sorties', in Catherine Clément and Hélène Cixous, *La Jeune née* (Paris: Union Générale d'Editions, coll. 10/18, 1975), pp. 115–246

——'Fiction and its Phantoms: A Reading of Freud's *Das Unheimliche* (The "Uncanny")', trans. by Robert Dennomé, *New Literary History*, 7 (1976), 525–48

——*Vivre l'orange* (Paris: Editions des femmes, 1979)

——'The Laugh of the Medusa', trans. by K. and P. Cohen, in *The Routledge Language and Cultural Theory Reader*, ed. by Lucy Burke, Tony Crowley and Alan Girvan (London: Routledge, 2000), pp. 161–66 (first publ. in *New French Feminisims: An Anthology*, ed. by Elaine Marks and Isabel Courtivron (Brighton: Harvester Wheatsheaf, 1981), pp. 245–51)

——*Le Livre de Promethea* (Paris: Gallimard, coll. Blanche, 1983)

——*Jours de l'an* (Paris: des femmes-Antoinette Fouque, 1990)

——'De la scène de l'Inconscient à la scène de l'Histoire: chemin d'une écriture', in *Hélène Cixous: chemins d'une écriture*, ed. by Françoise van Rossum-Guyon and Myriam Díaz-Diocaretz (Paris: Presses Universitaires de Vincennes; Amsterdam: Rodopi, 1990), pp. 15–34

Cixous, Hélène, *Three Steps on the Ladder of Writing* (New York: Columbia University Press, 1993)

——'Mon Algériance', *Les Inrockuptibles*, 20 August 1997, pp. 70–74

——'Pieds nus', in *Une enfance algérienne*, ed. by Leïla Sebbar (Paris: Gallimard, 1997), pp. 53–63

——'My Algeriance, in Other Words: To Depart Not to Arrive from Algeria', in *Stigmata: Escaping Texts* (London: Routledge, 1998), pp. 153–72

——'What Is It O'Clock? Or the Door (We Never Enter)', in *Stigmata: Escaping Texts* (London: Routledge, 1998), pp. 57–83

——*Les Rêveries de la femme sauvage: scènes primitives* (Paris: Galilée, 2000)

——*Le Jour où je n'étais pas là* (Paris: Galilée, 2000)

Cixous, Hélène, and Mireille Calle-Gruber, *Hélène Cixous, Rootprints: Memory and Life Writing*, trans. by Eric Prenowitz (London: Routledge, 1997)

Clayton, Alan, *Nathalie Sarraute, ou, Le Tremblement de l'écriture* (Paris: Lettres modernes, 1989)

Coe, Richard N., *The Vision of Jean Genet* (London: Peter Owen, 1968)

Colonna, Vincent, '*W*, un livre blanc', *Cahiers Georges Perec*, 2 (1988), 15–24

——*Autofiction et autres mythomanies littéraires* (Auch: Tristram, 2004)

Compagnon, Antoine and Philippe Roger (eds), *Nathalie Sarraute ou l'usage de l'écriture*, special edn of *Critique*, 656/57 (Jan–Feb 2002), pp. 1–142

Conley, Verena Andermatt, *Hélène Cixous* (Hemel Hempstead: Harvester Wheatsheaf, 1992)

Consenstein, Peter, 'Memory and Oulipian Constraints', *Postmodern Culture*, 6.1 (September 1995) <http://www.infomotions.com/serials/pmc/pmc-v6n1-consenstein-memory.txt> [accessed 31 July 2006]

Cooke, Dervila, *Present Pasts: Patrick Modiano's (Auto)Biographical Fictions* (Amsterdam: Rodopi, 2005)

Cooper, Sarah, 'Genre and Sexuality: Cixous's and Derrida's Textual Performances', in *Powerful Bodies: Performance in French Cultural Studies*, ed. by Victoria Best and Peter Collier (Bern: Peter Lang, 1999), pp. 199–212

——'The Ethics of Rewriting the Loss of Exile in *Manne aux Mandelstams aux Mandelas*', in *Revisiting the Scene of Writing: New Readings of Cixous*, ed. by Julia Dobson and Gill Rye, special edn of *Paragraph*, 23.3 (November 2000), pp. 311–23

——*Relating to Queer Theory: Rereading Sexual Self-Definition with Irigaray, Kristeva, Wittig and Cixous* (Bern: Peter Lang, 2000)

Craig, George and Margaret McGowan, *Moy Qui Me Voy: The Writer and the Self from Montaigne to Leiris* (Oxford: Clarendon Press, 1989)

Creech, James, 'Outing Jean Genet', in *Genet: In the Language of the Enemy*, ed. by Scott Durham, special edn of *Yale French Studies*, 91 (1997), pp. 117–40

Culler, Jonathan, *Structuralist Poetics: Structuralism, Linguistics and the Study of Literature* (London: Routledge and Kegan Paul, 1975)

Darrieussecq, Marie, 'L'Autobiographie, un genre pas sérieux', *Poétique*, 107 (1996), 369–80

David, Nicolette, 'The Violence of Writing in Nathalie Sarraute's *Les Fruits d'Or* and *"disent les imbéciles"*', *French Studies*, 54 (2000), 163–76

Davis, Colin, 'Genet's *Journal du voleur* and the Ethics of Reading', *French Studies*, 48 (1994), 50–62

——*Levinas: An Introduction* (Cambridge: Polity, 1996)

——*Ethical Issues in Twentieth-Century French Fiction: Killing the Other* (Basingstoke: Macmillan, 2000)

De Man, Paul, 'Autobiography as De-Facement', *MLN*, 94 (1979), 919–30

——*Allegories of Reading: Figural Reading in Rousseau, Nietzsche, Rilke and Proust* (New Haven: Yale University Press, 1979)

DE NOOY, JULIANA, JOE HARDWICK and BARBARA E. HANNA (eds), *Soi-disant: Life-Writing in French* (Newark: University of Delaware Press, 2005)
DERRIDA, JACQUES, *Glas* (Paris: Galilée, 1974)
—— 'La Loi du genre', in *Parages* (Paris: Galilée, 1986), pp. 249–87 (first published in *Glyph*, 7 (1980), 176–201)
—— *L'Oreille de l'autre: otobiographies, transferts, traductions: textes et débats avec Jacques Derrida*, ed. by Claude Lévesque and Christie V. McDonald (Montreal: VLB, 1982)
—— *Otobiographies: l'enseignement de Nietzsche et la pratique du nom propre* (Paris: Galilée, 1984)
DICHY, ALBERT, 'Publishing Adventures', in *Flowers and Revolution: A Collection of Writings on Jean Genet*, ed. by Barbara Read (London: Middlesex University Press, 1997), pp. 198–200
DJEBAR, ASSIA, *L'Amour la fantasia* (Paris: Albin Michel, 1995)
DOBSON, JULIA and GILL RYE (eds), *Revisiting the Scene of Writing: New Readings of Cixous*, special edn of *Paragraph*, 23.3 (November 2000), pp. 243–352
DOLLIMORE, JONATHAN, *Sexual Dissidence: Augustine to Wilde, Freud to Foucault* (Oxford: Clarendon Press, 1991)
DOUBROVSKY, SERGE, *Autobiographiques: de Corneille à Sartre* (Paris: Presses Universitaires de France, 1988)
DUPUY-SULLIVAN, FRANÇOISE, 'Le lecteur et ses lectures dans *Les Fruits d'Or* (Nathalie Sarraute)', *Australian Journal of French Studies*, 27 (1990), 39–46
DURAS, MARGUERITE, *L'Amant* (Paris: Editions de Minuit, 1984)
—— *La Douleur* (Paris: P.O.L, 1985)
DURHAM, SCOTT (ed.), *Genet: In the Language of the Enemy,* special edn of *Yale French Studies*, 91, (1997), pp. 1–186
EAGLETON, TERRY, *Ideology: An Introduction* (London: Verso, 1991)
EAKIN, PAUL JOHN, 'Philippe Lejeune and the Study of Autobiography', *Romance Studies*, 8 (Summer 1986), 1–14
ECO, UMBERTO, *The Role of the Reader: Explorations in the Semiotics of Texts* (London: Hutchinson, 1981)
EDELSTEIN, MARILYN, 'Toward a Feminist Postmodern *Poléthique*: Kristeva on Ethics and Politics', in *Ethics, Politics and Difference in Julia Kristeva's Writing*, ed. by Kelly Oliver (New York: Routledge, 1993), pp. 196–214
EGAN, SUSANNA, *Mirror Talk: Genres of Crisis in Contemporary Autobiography* (Chapel Hill: University of North Carolina Press, 1999)
EKOTTO, FRIEDA, *L'Ecriture carcérale et le discours juridique chez Jean Genet* (Paris: L'Harmattan, 2001)
EL BASRI, AÏCHA, *L'Imaginaire carcérale de Jean Genet* (Paris: Harmattan, 1999)
ERNAUX, ANNIE, *Une femme* (Paris: Gallimard, 1987)
—— *L'Evénement* (Paris: Gallimard, 2000)
ERNAUX, ANNIE, and MARC MARIE, *L'Usage de la photo* (Paris: Gallimard, 2005)
EVANS, DYLAN, *An Introductory Dictionary of Lacanian Psychoanalysis* (London: Routledge, 1996)
FELMAN, SHOSHANA, *What Does A Woman Want? Reading and Sexual Difference* (Baltimore: Johns Hopkins University Press, 1993)
FELMAN, SHOSHANA, and DORI LAUB, *Testimony: Crises of Witnessing in Literature, Psychoanalysis, and History* (New York: Routledge, 1992)
FELSTINER, MARY LOWENTHAL, 'Taking Her Life/History: The Autobiography of Charlotte Salomon', in *Life/Lines: Theorizing Women's Autobiography*, ed. by Bella Brodzki and Celeste Schenk (Ithaca, NY: Cornell University Press, 1988), pp. 320–37
FINBURGH, CLARE, 'Jean Genet and the Poetics of Palestinian Politics: Statecraft as Stagecraft in "Quatre heures à Chatila"', *French Studies*, 56 (2002), 495–509

FINKIELKRAUT, ALAIN, 'From the Novelistic to Memory', in *Auschwitz and After: Race, Culture, and 'the Jewish Question' in France*, ed. by Lawrence D. Kritzman (New York: Routledge, 1995), pp. 83–97

FLETCHER, JOHN and ANDREW BENJAMIN (eds), *Abjection, Melancholia and Love* (London: Routledge, 1990)

FOLKENFLIK, ROBERT (ed.), *The Culture of Autobiography: Constructions of Self-Representation* (Stanford, CA: Stanford University Press, 1993)

FOUCAULT, MICHEL, 'Qu'est-ce qu'un auteur?' (1968), in *Dits et écrits 1954–1988*, ed. by Daniel Defer, François Ewart and Jacques Legrange (Paris: NRF-Gallimard, 1994), I: *1954–69*, pp. 789–821

—— *L'Ordre du discours: leçon inaugurale au Collège de France prononcée le 2 décembre 1970* (Paris: Gallimard, 1971)

—— *Surveiller et punir: naissance de la prison* (Paris: Gallimard, coll. tel, 1975)

—— *Histoire de la sexualité*, I: *La Volonté de savoir* (Paris: Gallimard, coll. tel, 1976)

—— *Discipline and Punish: The Birth of the Prison*, trans. by Alan Sheridan (London: Allen Lane, 1977)

—— *The History of Sexuality*, I: *An Introduction*, trans. by Robert Hurley (Harmondsworth: Penguin, 1990)

FOUTRIER, PASCALE, '*Enfance*: généalogie d'une écriture', in *Nathalie Sarraute ou l'usage de l'écriture*, ed. by Antoine Compagnon and Philippe Roger, special edn of *Critique*, 656/57 (Jan–Feb 2002), pp. 36–50

FOUTRIER, PASCALE (ed.), *Nathalie Sarraute: ethiques du tropisme: actes du colloque Nathalie Sarraute 7 mai 1999* (Paris: L'Harmattan, 2000)

FREDETTE, NATHALIE, 'A propos de la fiction biographique: lire Jean Genet aujourd'hui', *Etudes Françaises*, 26.1 (Spring 1990), 131–45

FREUD, SIGMUND, *The Standard Edition of the Complete Psychological Works of Sigmund Freud*, ed. by James Strachey and others, 24 vols (London: Hogarth Press, 1953–74)

—— 'Screen Memories' (1899), in *The Standard Edition*, III (1962), 299–322

—— *The Interpretation of Dreams* (1900), in *The Standard Edition*, IV and V (1953)

—— *Jokes and Their Relation to the Unconscious* (1905), in *The Standard Edition*, VIII (1960)

—— *Totem and Taboo* (1913), in *The Standard Edition*, XIII (1955), 1–162

—— 'The Uncanny' (1919), in *The Standard Edition*, XVII (1955), 217–52

—— *Beyond the Pleasure Principle* (1920), in *The Standard Edition*, XVIII (1955), 1–64

—— 'The Ego and The Id' (1923), in *The Standard Edition*, XIX (1961), 1–66

—— 'An Autobiographical Study' (1925), in *The Standard Edition*, XX (1959), 7–74

FRIEDMAN, SUSAN STANFORD, 'Women's Autobiographical Selves: Theory and Practice', in *The Private Self*, ed. by Shari Benstock (London: Routledge, 1988), pp. 34–62

FUSS, DIANA, *Essentially Speaking: Feminism, Nature and Difference* (London: Routledge, 1989)

—— *Identification Papers* (New York: Routledge, 1995)

GAITET, PASCALE, 'The Politics of Camp in Jean Genet's *Our Lady of the Flowers*', in *Jean Genet: Littérature et Politique (Literature and Politics)*, ed. by Patrice Bougon, special edn of *Esprit créateur*, 35.1 (Spring 1995), pp. 40–49

—— *Queens and Revolutionaries: New Readings of Jean Genet* (Newark: University of Delaware Press; London: Associated University Presses, 2003)

GASCOIGNE, DAVID, 'Dreaming the Self, Writing the Dream: The Subject in the Dream Narratives of Georges Perec', in *Subject Matters: Subject and Self in French Literature from Descartes to the Present*, ed. by Paul Gifford and Johnnie Gratton (Amsterdam: Rodopi, 2000), pp. 128–44

GASPARINI, PHILIPPE, *Est-il je? Roman autobiographique et autofiction* (Paris: Editions du Seuil, 2004)

GENET, JEAN, *Miracle de la rose* ([Lyons(?)]: Barbezat-L'Arbalète, coll. Gallimard folio, 1946)
——*Notre-Dame-des-Fleurs* ([Lyons(?)]: Barbezat-L'Arbalète, 1948)
——*Journal du voleur* (Paris: Gallimard, coll. folio, 1949)
——*Pompes funèbres* (Paris: Gallimard, coll. L'Imaginaire, 1953)
——'Ce qui est resté d'un Rembrandt déchiré en petits carrés et foutu aux chiottes', in *Œuvres complètes*, IV (Paris: Gallimard, 1968), pp. 19–31
——*Un captif amoureux* (Paris: Gallimard, 1986)
——*L'Ennemi déclaré: textes et entretiens*, ed. by Albert Dichy, *Œuvres complètes*, VI (Paris: Gallimard, 1991)
GENETTE, GÉRARD, *Seuils* (Paris: Editions du Seuil, 1987)
——*Fiction et diction* (Paris: Editions du Seuil, 1991)
GIDE, ANDRÉ, *Si le grain ne meurt* (1926) (Paris: Gallimard, 1955)
GIFFORD, PAUL and JOHNNIE GRATTON (eds), *Subject Matters: Subject and Self in French Literature from Descartes to the Present* (Amsterdam: Rodopi, 2000)
GILMORE, LEAH, *Autobiographics: A Feminist Theory of Women's Self-Representation* (Ithaca, NY: Cornell University Press, 1994)
GIRARD, RENÉ, *La Violence et le sacré* (Paris: Grasset, 1972)
GORP, HENDRIK VAN and ULLA MUSARRA-SCHROEDER, 'Introduction: Literary Genres and Cultural Memory', in *Genres as Repositories of Cultural Memory. Volume 5 of the Proceedings of the XVth Congress of the International Comparative Literature Association "Literature as Cultural Memory", Leiden 16–22 August 1997*, ed. by Hendrik van Gorp and Ulla Musarra-Schroeder (Amsterdam: Rodopi, 2000), pp. i–ix
GOSSELIN, MONIQUE, '*Enfance* de Nathalie Sarraute: les mots de la mère', *Revue des sciences humaines*, 222 (1991), 121–42
GRATTON, JOHNNIE, '*Roland Barthes par Roland Barthes*: Autobiography and the Notion of Expression', *Romance Studies*, 8 (Summer 1986), 57–65
——'Autobiography and Fragmentation: The Case of Nathalie Sarraute's *Enfance*', *Nottingham French Studies*, 34.2 (Autumn 1995), 31–40
——'Towards Narrativity: Nathalie Sarraute's *Enfance*', *Forum for Modern Language Studies*, 31 (1995), 300–11
GRAYBEAL, JEAN, 'Kristeva's Delphic Proposal: "Practice Encompasses the Ethical"', in *Ethics, Politics and Difference in Julia Kristeva's Writing*, ed. by Kelly Oliver (New York: Routledge, 1993), pp. 32–40
GREEN, MAY JANE, 'Structures of Liberation: Female Experience and Autobiographical Form in Quebec', in *Life/Lines: Theorizing Women's Autobiography*, ed. by Bella Brodzki and Celeste Schenk (Ithaca, NY: Cornell University Press, 1988), pp. 189–202
GRÜTER, DORIS, *Autobiographie und Nouveau Roman. Ein Beitrag zur literarischen Diskussion der Postmoderne* (Münster and Hamburg: Lit, 1994)
GUDMUNDSDÓTTIR, GUNNTHÓRUNN, *Borderlines: Autobiography and Fiction in Postmodern Life-Writing* (Amsterdam: Rodopi, 2003)
GUIBERT, HERVÉ, *A l'ami qui ne m'a pas sauvé la vie* (Paris: Gallimard, 1990)
GUSDORF, GEORGES, 'Conditions et limites de l'autobiographie', in *Formen der Selbstdarstellung. Analekten zu einer Geschichte des literarischen Selbstportraits. Festgabe für Fritz Neubert*, ed. by Günther Reichenkron and Erich Haase (Berlin: Duncker and Humblot, 1956), pp. 105–23
HALL, DONALD E., *Queer Theories* (Basingstoke: Palgrave Macmillan, 2003)
HALPERIN, DAVID, 'Sex before Sexuality: Pederasty, Power and Politics in Classical Athens', in *Hidden From History: Reclaiming the Gay and Lesbian Past*, ed. by Martin Bauml Duberman, Martha Vicinius and George Chauncey Jr. (Harmondsworth: Penguin, 1991), pp. 37–53

Hand, Seán, *Michel Leiris: Writing the Self* (Cambridge: Cambridge University Press, 2002)
Hanrahan, Mairéad, *Lire Genet: une poétique de la différence* (Montreal: Presses de l'Université de Montréal, 1997)
——'Of Altobiography', in *Revisiting the Scene of Writing: New Readings of Cixous*, ed. by Julia Dobson and Gill Rye, special edn of *Paragraph*, 23.3 (November 2000), pp. 282–95
——'Cixous's *Le Livre de Promethea*: A Diary in an Other Form', *French Studies*, 55 (2001), 195–206
——'Of Three-Legged Writing: Cixous's *Le Jour où je n'étais pas là*', *French Forum*, 28.2 (Spring 2003), 99–113
Hanrahan, Mairéad (ed.), *Genet*, special edn of *Paragraph*, 27.2 (July 2004), pp. 1–145
Harrison, Nick, 'Learning from Experience: Hélène Cixous's "Pieds nus"', *Paragraph*, 27 (2004), 21–32
Hartje, Hans, 'Georges Perec: des relais pour écrire', *Rivista di letterature moderne e comparate*, n.s. 51 (1998), 57–68
Harvey, Robert, 'Genet's Open Enemies: Sartre and Derrida', in *Genet: In the Language of the Enemy*, ed. by Scott Durham, special edn of *Yale French Studies*, 91 (1997), pp. 103–16
Hazlett, John Downton, *My Generation: Collective Autobiography and Identity Politics* (Madison: University of Wisconsin Press, 1998)
Hegel, G. W. F., *Phenomenology of Spirit* (1807), trans. by A. V. Miller (Oxford: Clarendon Press, 1977)
Henke, Suzette, *Shattered Subjects: Trauma and Testimony in Women's Life-Writing*, (Basingstoke: Macmillan, 1998)
Henrot, Geneviève, 'Distances dialogiques chez Nathalie Sarraute (*Les Fruits d'Or*)', *Poétique*, 97 (February 1994), 41–63
Hewitt, Leah D., *Autobiographical Tightropes: Simone de Beauvoir, Nathalie Sarraute, Marguerite Duras, Monique Wittig, and Maryse Condé* (Lincoln: University of Nebraska Press, 1990)
Heymann, Brigitte, *Textform und weibliches Selbstverständnis. Die Romane von Hélène Cixous und Chantal Chawaf* (Weinheim: Deutscher Studien Verlag, 1991)
Heymann, Jochen, 'Les Avatars de l'enfance dorée: Georges Perec et l'anthropologie du bonheur', in *Sehnsuchtsorte. Festschrift zum 60. Geburtstag von Titus Heydenreich*, ed. by Thomas Bremer and Jochen Heymann (Tubingen: Stauffenburg, 1999), pp. 359–71
Hoft-March, Eilene, 'For-Giving Death: Cixous's *Osnabrück* and *Le Jour où je n'étais pas là*', *Studies in Twentieth and Twenty-First Century Literature*, 28 (2004), 428–44
Horowitz, Irving Louis, 'Autobiography as the Presentation of Self for Social Immortality', *New Literary History*, 9 (1977), 173–79
Huffer, Lynne, 'From Lesbos to Montreal: Nicole Brossard's Urban Fictions', in *Same Sex/Different Text? Gay and Lesbian Writing in French*, ed. by Brigitte Mahuzier and others, special edn of *Yale French Studies*, 90 (1996), pp. 95–114
Hughes, Alex, *Heterographies: Sexual Difference in French Autobiography* (Oxford: Berg, 1999)
——'Autobiographical Desires: Repetition and Rectification in Serge Doubrovsky's *Laissé pour conte*', *French Studies*, 55 (2001), 179–93
Hughes, Edward J., *Writing Marginality in Modern French Literature: From Loti to Genet* (Cambridge: Cambridge University Press, 2001)
Jauvin, Lucie, 'L'Autoportrait virtuel et universel de Nathalie Sarraute', *Etudes Françaises*, 29.3 (Winter 1993), 181–91
Jefferson, Ann, *The 'Nouveau Roman' and the Poetics of Fiction* (Cambridge: Cambridge University Press, 1980)
——'Beyond Contract: The Reader of Autobiography and Stendhal's *Vie de Henry Brulard*', *Romance Studies*, 9 (Winter 1986), 53–69

JEFFERSON, ANN, 'Nathalie Sarraute: Criticism and the Terrible Desire to Establish Contact', in *Narrative Voices in Modern French Fiction: Studies in Honour of Valerie Minogue*, ed. by Michael Cardy, George Evans and Gabriel Jacobs (Cardiff: University of Wales Press, 1997), pp. 37–56

——*Nathalie Sarraute, Fiction and Theory: Questions of Difference* (Cambridge: Cambridge University Press, 2000)

JELINEK, ESTELLE C., 'Introduction: Women's Autobiography and the Male Tradition', in *Women's Autobiography: Essays in Criticism*, ed. by Estelle C. Jelinek (Bloomington: Indiana University Press, 1980), pp. 1–20

JONES, DAVID HOUSTON, *The Body Abject: Self and Text in Jean Genet and Samuel Beckett* (Bern: Peter Lang, 2000)

KAMUF, PEGGY, 'To Give Place: Semi-Approaches to Hélène Cixous', in *Another Look, Another Woman: Retranslations of French Feminism*, ed. by Lynne Huffer, special edn of *Yale French Studies*, 87 (1995), pp. 68–89

KAUFMAN, ELEANOR, 'Falling from the Sky: Trauma in Perec's *W* and Caruth's *Unclaimed Experience*', *Diacritics*, 28.4 (Winter 1998), 44–53

KAWAKAMI, AKANE, 'Nathalie Sarraute's Accent: The Poetry of *Tropismes*', *French Studies*, 58 (2004), 499–512

KEEFE, TERRY and EDMUND SMYTH (eds), *Autobiography and the Existential Self: Studies in Modern French Writing* (Liverpool: Liverpool University Press, 1995)

KNAPP, BETTINA, *Nathalie Sarraute* (Amsterdam: Rodopi, 1994)

KRISTEVA, JULIA, *La Révolution du langage poétique: l'avant-garde à la fin du XIXe siècle: Lautréamont et Mallarmé* (Paris: Editions du Seuil, 1974)

——*Polylogue* (Paris: Editions du Seuil, 1977), pp. 55–106

——*Pouvoirs de l'horreur: essai sur l'abjection* (Paris: Editions du Seuil, coll. Points, 1980)

——*Desire in Language: A Semiotic Approach to Literature and Art*, ed. by Leon S. Roudiez (Oxford: Blackwell, 1980)

——*Powers of Horror: An Essay on Abjection*, trans. by Leon S. Roudiez (New York: Columbia University Press, 1982)

——*Revolution in Poetic Language*, trans. by Margaret Waller (New York: Columbia University Press, 1984)

——*Soleil noir: dépression et mélancholie* (Paris: Gallimard, 1987)

——*Etrangers à nous-mêmes* (Paris: Fayard, 1988)

KRITZMAN, LAWRENCE D., 'Remembrance of Things Past: Trauma and Mourning in Perec's *W ou le souvenir d'enfance*', in *Cultural Memory in France: Margins and Centres, Part II*, ed. by Aimée Boutin and others, special edn of *Journal of European Studies*, 35.2 (June 2005), pp. 187–200

KRITZMAN, LAWRENCE D. (ed.), *Auschwitz and After: Race, Culture, and 'the Jewish Question' in France* (New York: Routledge, 1995)

LACAN, JACQUES, *Ecrits* (1966), ed. by Jacques-Alain Miller, 2nd edn, 2 vols (Paris: Editions du Seuil, coll. Points, 1999)

——*Le Séminaire, Livre XI: Les Quatre Concepts fondamentaux de la psychanalyse*, ed. by Jacques-Alain Miller (Paris: Editions du Seuil, coll. Le Champ freudien, 1973)

——*The Four Fundamental Concepts of Psycho-Analysis*, ed. by Jacques-Alain Miller, trans. by Alan Sheridan (London: Vintage, 1998)

——'Le Stade du miroir comme formateur de la fonction du Je' (1949), in *Ecrits*, I, 92–99

——'L'Instance de la lettre dans l'inconscient ou la raison depuis Freud' (1957), in *Ecrits*, I, 490–527

——'Subversion du sujet et dialectique du désir dans l'inconscient freudien' (1960), in *Ecrits*, II, 273–308

Laforgue, Pierre, *'Notre-Dame-des-Fleurs' ou la symphonie carcérale* (Toulouse: Presses Universitaires du Mirail, 2002)

Lancelot, Bernard-Olivier, 'Présentation en forme de montage ou l'état de manque', *Littératures*, n.s. 7 (1983), 23–30

Lane, Christopher, 'The Voided Role: On Genet', *MLN*, 112 (1997), 876–908

Lane, Jeremy, 'Towards a Poetics of Consumerism: Gaston Bachelard's "Material Imagination" and Narratives of Post-War Modernisation', *French Cultural Studies*, 17.1 (February 2006), 19–34

Laouyen, Mounir (ed.), *Les Nouvelles Autobiographies/New Autobiographies*, special edn of *Esprit créateur*, 42.4 (Winter 2002), pp. 1–96

Laub, Dori, 'Bearing Witness or the Vicissitudes of Listening', in Shoshana Felman and Dori Laub, *Testimony: Crises of Witnessing in Literature, Psychoanalysis, and History* (New York: Routledge, 1992)

Leak, Andy, '*W* dans un réseau de lignes entrecroisées: souvenir, souvenir-écran et construction dans *W ou le souvenir d'enfance*', in *Parcours Perec*, ed. by Mireille Ribière (Paris: Presses Universitaires de Lyon, 1990), pp. 75–90

Lecarme, Jacques and Eliane Lecarme-Tabone, *L'Autobiographie*, 2nd edn (Paris: Colin, 1999)

Leibacher-Ouvrard, Lise and Monique Wittig (eds), *Nathalie Sarraute ou le texte du for intérieur*, special edn of *Esprit créateur*, 36.2 (Summer 1996), pp. 1–126

Leiris, Michel, *L'Age d'homme* (Paris: Gallimard, 1939)

Lejeune, Philippe, *L'Autobiographie en France* (Paris: Colin, 1971)

——*Le Pacte autobiographique* (Paris: Editions du Seuil, 1975)

——*Je est un autre: l'autobiographie, de la littérature aux médias* (Paris: Editions du Seuil, 1980)

——*Moi aussi* (Paris: Editions du Seuil, 1986)

——*On Autobiography*, ed. by Paul John Eakin, trans. by Katherine Leary (Minnesota: University of Minnesota Press, 1989)

——'Paroles d'enfance', *Revue des sciences humaines*, 217 (1990), 23–38

——*La Mémoire et l'oblique: Georges Perec autobiographe* (Paris: P.O.L., 1991)

Levinas, Emmanuel, *Totalité et infini: essai sur l'exteriorité* (Paris: Livre de poche, 1971)

Lionnet, Françoise, *Autobiographical Voices: Race, Gender, Self-Portraiture* (Ithaca, NY: Cornell University Press, 1989)

Lockridge, Larry, 'The Ethics of Biography and Autobiography', in *Critical Ethics: Text, Theory and Responsibility*, ed. by Dominic Rainsford and Tim Woods (Basingstoke: Macmillan, 1999), pp. 125–40

Loftus, Brian, 'Speaking Silence: The Strategies and Structures of Queer Autobiography', *College Literature*, 24.1 (February 1997), 28–44

Lucey, Michael, 'Genet's *Notre-Dame-des-Fleurs*: Fantasy and Sexual Identity', in *Genet: In the Language of the Enemy*, ed. by Scott Durham, special edn of *Yale French Studies*, 91 (1997), pp. 80–102

Lydon, Mary, 'Re-Translating no Re-Reading no, rather: Rejoycing (with) Hélène Cixous', in *Another Look, Another Woman: Retranslations of French Feminism*, ed. by Lynne Huffer, special edn of *Yale French Studies*, 87 (1995), pp. 90–102

Magedera, Ian H., '*Seing* Genet, Citation and Mourning; a propos *Glas* by Jacques Derrida', *Paragraph*, 21 (1998), 28–44

Magné, Bernard, 'Les Sutures dans *W ou le souvenir d'enfance*', *Cahiers Georges Perec*, 2 (1988), 39–55

Mahuzier, Brigitte and others (eds), *Same Sex/Different Text? Gay and Lesbian Writing in French*, special edn of *Yale French Studies*, 90 (1996), pp. 1–255

Marcus, Laura, *Auto/Biographical Discourses: Theory, Criticism, Practice* (Manchester: Manchester University Press, 1994)

Marks, Elaine, 'The Dream of Love: A Study of Three Autobiographies', in *Twentieth Century French Fiction: Essays for Germaine Brée*, ed. by George Stambolian (New Brunswick: Rutgers University Press, 1975), pp. 72–88

——'*Cendres juives*: Jews Writing in French "after Auschwitz"', in *Auschwitz and After: Race, Culture and 'the Jewish Question' in France*, ed. by Lawrence D. Kritzman (New York: Routledge, 1995), pp. 35–46

Marson, Susan, *Le Temps de l'autobiographie: Violette Leduc ou la mort avant la lettre* (Saint-Denis: Presses Universitaires de Vincennes, 1998)

Marson, Susan, 'The Empty Crypt: Autobiographical Identity in Genet's *Journal du Voleur*', *Romance Studies*, 19 (2001), 29–39

Martinez, Odile, 'Un trompe-l'œil photographique dans *W ou le souvenir d'enfance*', in *Il senso del nonsenso: scritti in memoria di Lynn Salkin Sbiroli*, ed. by Monique Streiff Moretti, Mireille Revol Cappelletti and Odile Martinez (Naples: Edizioni Scientifiche Italiane, 1994), pp. 531–48

Mason, Mary G., 'The Other Voice: Autobiographies of Women Writers', in *Autobiography: Essays Theoretical and Critical*, ed. by James Olney (Princeton, NJ: Princeton University Press, 1980), pp. 207–35

Masters, Bernadette, *Esthétique et manuscripture* (Heidelberg: Winter, 1992)

May, Georges, *L'Autobiographie* (Paris: Presses Universitaires de France, 1979)

Maynard, Jessica, 'I Remember... (Points of Suspension)', in *The French Connections of Jacques Derrida*, ed. by Julian Wolfreys, John Brannigan and Ruth Robbins (Albany: State University of New York Press, 1999), pp. 101–18

Meitinger, Serge, 'L'Irréel de jouissance dans le *Journal du Voleur* de Genet', *Littérature*, 62 (May 1986), 65–74

Merck, Mandy, 'Savage Nights', in *Coming Out of Feminism?*, ed. by Mandy Merck, Naomi Segal and Elizabeth Wright (Oxford: Blackwell, 1998), pp. 214–43

Miller, Nancy, 'Writing Fictions: Women's Autobiography in France', in *Life/Lines: Theorizing Women's Autobiography*, ed. by Bella Brodzki and Celeste Schenk (Ithaca, NY: Cornell University Press, 1988), pp. 45–61

Millett, Kate, *Sexual Politics* (London: Virago, 1977), pp. 338–61

Minogue, Valerie, *Nathalie Sarraute and the War of the Words: A Study of Five Novels* (Edinburgh: Edinburgh University Press, 1981)

——'Fragments of a Childhood: Nathalie Sarraute's *Enfance*', *Romance Studies*, 9 (Winter 1986), 71–83

——'Nathalie Sarraute's *Enfance*: From Experience of Language to the Language of Experience', in *Studies in French Fiction in Honour of Vivienne Mylne*, ed. by Robert Gibson ([London]: Grant and Cutler, 1988), pp. 209–24

Misch, Georg, *Geschichte der Autobiographie* (Leipzig: Teubner, 1907–[never completed]), i: *Das Altertum* (1907)

——*Geschichte der Autobiographie*, 3rd expanded edn, 8 vols (Frankfurt-am-Main: Schulte-Bulmke, 1949–69)

——*A History of Autobiography in Antiquity*, trans. by E. W. Dickes, 2 vols (London: Routledge and Kegan Paul, 1950)

Misrahi, Robert, '*W*, un roman réflexif', *Arc*, 76 (1979), 81–86

Modiano, Patrick, *Dora Bruder* (Paris: Gallimard, 1997)

Moi, Toril, *Sexual/Textual Politics* (1985), 2nd edn (London: Routledge, 2002)

Montandon, Alain (ed.), *De soi à soi: l'écriture comme autohospitalité* (Clermont-Ferrand: Presses Universitaires Blaise Pascal, 2004)

Montfrans, Manet van, *Georges Perec: la contrainte du réel* (Amsterdam: Rodopi, 1999)

Moraly, Jean-Bernard, *Jean Genet: la vie écrite* (Paris: Editions de la Différence, 1988)

Motard-Noar, Martine, *Les Fictions d'Hélène Cixous: une autre langue de femme* (Lexington: French Forum, 1991)

MOTTE, WARREN F., *The Poetics of Experiment: A Study of the Work of Georges Perec* (Kentucky: French Forum, 1984)

MOTTE, WARREN, 'Georges Perec and the Broken Book', in *Auschwitz and After: Race, Culture, and 'the Jewish Question' in France*, ed. by Lawrence D. Kritzman (New York: Routledge, 1995), pp. 235–49

——'The Work of Mourning', in *Pereckonings: Reading Georges Perec*, ed. by Warren Motte and Jean-Jacques Poucel, special edn of *Yale French Studies*, 105 (2004), pp. 56–71

MULVEY, LAURA, 'Visual Pleasure and Narrative Cinema' (1975), in *Visual and Other Pleasures* (Basingstoke: Macmillan, 1989), pp. 14–26

MYATT, ANNA, 'Roland Barthes: Role Play in Autobiography and Photography', in *Powerful Bodies: Performance in French Cultural Studies*, ed. by Victoria Best and Peter Collier (Bern: Peter Lang, 1999), pp. 83–96

NDIAYE, MARIE, *Autoportrait en vert* ([Paris?]: Mercure de France, 2005)

NEGRON MARRERO, MARA, 'Comment faire pour écrire l'histoire poétiquement/ou comment faire pour ne pas oublier...', in *Hélène Cixous: chemins d'une écriture*, ed. by Françoise Rossum-Guyon and Myriam Díaz-Diocaretz (Paris: Presses Universitaires de Vincennes; Amsterdam: Rodopi, 1990), pp. 205–12

NEUMAN, SHIRLEY (ed.), *Autobiography and Questions of Gender* (London: Cass, 1991)

New Literary History, 9 (1977)

NORA, PIERRE, *Les Lieux de mémoire*, 3 vols (Paris: Gallimard, 1984–92)

O'BEIRNE, EMER, *Reading Nathalie Sarraute: Dialogue and Distance* (Oxford: Clarendon Press, 1999)

O'CALLAGHAN, RAYLENE, 'Voice(s) in Nathalie Sarraute's *Enfance*', *New Zealand Journal of French Studies*, 9 (1988), 83–94

——'La Nouvelle Autobiographie de Nathalie Sarraute et la question du sexe du texte', *Degré second*, 13 (December 1992), 51–58

OLIVER, KELLY (ed.), *Ethics, Politics and Difference in Julia Kristeva's Writings* (New York: Routledge, 1993)

OLNEY, JAMES, *Metaphors of Self: The Meaning of Autobiography* (Princeton, NJ: Princeton University Press, 1972)

——'Some Versions of Memory, Some Versions of *Bios*: The Ontology of Autobiography', in *Autobiography: Essays Theoretical and Critical*, ed. by James Olney (Princeton, NJ: Princeton University Press, 1980), pp. 236–67

OLNEY, JAMES (ed.), *Autobiography: Essays Theoretical and Critical* (Princeton, NJ: Princeton University Press, 1980)

ORTIZ, MARIA CONSUELO, 'L'Autobiographie chez Georges Perec: le cas d'*Espèces d'espaces*', *Romanische Forschungen*, 107 (1995), 157–62

PADGUG, ROBERT, 'Sexual Matters: Rethinking Sexuality in History', in *Hidden From History: Reclaiming the Gay and Lesbian Past*, ed. by Martin Bauml Duberman, Martha Vicinius, and George Chauncey Jr. (Harmondsworth: Penguin, 1991), pp. 54–64

PAGANINI, MARIA, 'Ecriture carcérale: l'échappée belle', *Esprit créateur*, 38.3 (Fall 1998), 40–50

PASCAL, ROY, *Design and Truth in Autobiography* (London: Routledge and Kegan Paul, 1960)

PAULY, REBECCA N., *Le Berceau et la bibliothèque: le paradoxe de l'écriture autobiographique* (Saratoga: Anma Libri, 1989)

PAWLIKOWSKA, EWA, 'La colle bleue de Gaspard Winckler', *Littératures*, n.s. 7 (Spring 1983), 79–87

——'Insertion, recomposition dans *W ou le souvenir d'enfance* de Georges Perec', in *Penser, classer, écrire de Pascal à Perec*, ed. by Béatrice Didier and Jacques Neefs (Saint-Denis: Presses Universitaires de Vincennes, 1990)

PEREC, GEORGES, *La Disparition* (Paris: Denoël, coll. Gallimard Imaginaire, 1969)
——*La Boutique obscure: 124 rêves* (Paris: Denoël, 1973)
——*Espèces d'espaces* (1974), 2nd edn (Paris: Galilée, 2000)
——*W ou le souvenir d'enfance* ([Paris]: Denoël, coll. Gallimard Imaginaire, 1975)
——*Je me souviens: les choses communes*, I (Paris: Hachette, coll. Textes du XXe siècle, 1978)
——*Penser/Classer* (Paris: Hachette, 1985)
——'Conférence inédite: pouvoirs et limites du romancier contemporain', ed. by Leslie Hill, in *Parcours Perec*, ed. by Mireille Ribière (Lyons: Presses Universitaires de Lyon, 1990), pp. 31–40
——'Tentative d'inventaire des aliments liquides et solides que j'ai ingurgités au cours de l'année 1974', in *L'Infra-ordinaire* (Paris: Editions du Seuil, coll. La Librairie du XXe siècle, 1989), pp. 113–30
——*Je suis né* (Paris: Editions du Seuil, coll. La Librairie du XXe siècle, 1990)
——'Notes sur ce que je cherche', in *Penser/Classer*, pp. 9–12
——'Lettre à Maurice Nadeau', in *Je suis né*, pp. 51–66
——'Les Gnocchis de l'automne, où réponse à quelques questions me concernant', in *Je suis né*, pp. 67–74
——'Le Rêve et le texte', in *Je suis né*, pp. 75–79
——'Le Travail de la mémoire', in *Je suis né*, pp. 81–93
——'Ellis Island: description d'un projet', in *Je suis né*, pp. 95–103
PEREC, GEORGES and ROBERT BOBER, *Récits d'Ellis Island: histoires d'errance et d'espoir* (1980), 2nd edn (Paris: P.O.L, 1994)
PHILLIPS, JOHN, *Nathalie Sarraute: Metaphor, Fairy-Tale and the Feminine of the Text* (New York: Peter Lang, 1994)
PIERROT, JEAN, *Nathalie Sarraute* (Paris: Corti, 1990)
PORTUGUES, CATHERINE, 'Seeing Subjects: Women Directors and Cinematic Autobiography', in *Life/Lines: Theorizing Women's Autobiography*, ed. by Bella Brodzki and Celeste Schenk (Ithaca, NY: Cornell University Press, 1988), pp. 338–50
RAFFY, SABINE, *Sarraute romancière: espaces intimes* (New York: Peter Lang, 1988)
——'Une lecture paranoïaque de l'œuvre de Nathalie Sarraute', in *Nathalie Sarraute ou l'usage de l'écriture*, ed. by Antoine Compagnon and Philippe Roger, special edn of *Critique*, 656/57 (Jan–Feb 2002), pp. 12–21
RAINSFORD, DOMINIC and TIM WOODS (eds), *Critical Ethics: Text, Theory and Responsibility* (Basingstoke: Macmillan, 1999)
RAMSAY, RAYLENE, 'The Unself-loving Woman in Nathalie Sarraute's *Tu ne t'aimes pas*', *French Review*, 67 (1994), 793–802
RAMSAY, RAYLENE L., *The French New Autobiographies: Sarraute, Duras, and Robbe-Grillet* (Gainesville: University Press of Florida, 1996)
READ, BARBARA (ed.), *Flowers and Revolution: A Collection of Writings on Jean Genet* (London: Middlesex University Press, 1997)
REDONNET, MARIE, *Jean Genet, le poète travesti: portrait d'une œuvre* (Paris: Grasset, 2000)
REED, JEREMY, 'Gender in Genet's Poetry', in *Flowers and Revolution: A Collection of Writings on Jean Genet*, ed. by Barbara Read (London: Middlesex University Press, 1997)
RENZA, LOUIS A., 'The Veto of the Imagination: A Theory of Autobiography', *New Literary History*, 9 (1977), 1–26
REUTER, YVES, 'Construction/déconstruction du personnage dans *Un homme qui dort* de Georges Perec', *Roman 20–50*, 17 (June 1994), 209–23
RIBIÈRE, MIREILLE (ed.), *Parcours Perec* (Lyons: Presses Universitaires de Lyon, 1990)
RICŒUR, PAUL, *Soi-même comme un autre* (Paris: Editions du Seuil, 1990)
——*La Mémoire, l'histoire, l'oubli* (Paris: Editions du Seuil, 2000)
ROBBE-GRILLET, ALAIN, *Pour un nouveau roman* (Paris: Editions de Minuit, 1963)
——*Le Miroir qui revient* (Paris: Editions de Minuit, 1984)

ROBINSON, CHRISTOPHER, *Scandal in the Ink: Male and Female Homosexuality in Twentieth-century French Literature* (London: Cassell, 1995)
ROBINSON, PAUL, *Gay Lives: Homosexual Autobiography from John Addington Symonds to Paul Monette* (Chicago: University of Chicago Press, 1999)
ROBINSON, SALLY, 'The "Anti-Logos Weapon": Multiplicity in Women's Texts', *Contemporary Literature*, 29 (1988), 105–24
ROBSON, KATHRYN, *Writing Wounds: The Inscription of Trauma in Post-1968 French Women's Life-Writing* (Amsterdam: Rodopi, 2004)
ROCHE, ANNE, 'L'Auto(bio)graphie', *Cahiers Georges Perec*, 1 (1985), 65–80
ROEY-ROUX, FRANÇOISE VAN, '*Enfance* de Nathalie Sarraute ou de la fiction à l'autobiographie', *Etudes littéraires*, 17 (1984), 273–82
ROSE, JACQUELINE, 'Julia Kristeva — Take Two', in *Ethics, Politics and Difference in Julia Kristeva's Writing*, ed. by Kelly Oliver (New York: Routledge, 1993), pp. 41–61
ROTHENBERG, JOHN, 'Nathalie Sarraute Changing Genres: From *"disent les imbéciles"* to *Elle est là*', *Australian Journal of French Studies*, 35 (1998), 215–27
ROUSSEAU, JEAN-JACQUES, *Les Confessions* (1782), in *Œuvres complètes*, I: *Les Confessions; autres textes autobiographiques*, ed. by Bernard Gagnebin and Marcel Raymond (Paris: Gallimard, coll. Bibliothèque de la Pléiade, 1959), pp. 1–656
RUNNING-JOHNSON, CYNTHIA, 'The Medusa's Tale: Feminine Writing and "La Genet"', *Romanic Review*, 80 (1989), 483–95
RYE, GILL, 'Agony or Ecstasy? Reading Cixous's Recent Fiction', in *Revisiting the Scene of Writing: New Readings of Cixous*, ed. by Julia Dobson and Gill Rye, special edn of *Paragraph*, 23.3 (November 2000), pp. 296–310
RYKNER, ARNAUD, *Nathalie Sarraute* (Paris: Editions du Seuil, coll. Les Contemporains,1991)
SALINO, BRIGITTE, 'Sami Frey se souvient, encore une fois', *Le Monde*, 23 September 2003, p. 23
SARKONAK, RALPH, 'Traces and Shadows: Fragments of Hervé Guibert', in *Same Sex/Different Text? Gay and Lesbian Writing in French*, ed. by Brigitte Mahuzier and others, special edn of *Yale French Studies*, 90 (1996), pp. 172–202
SARRAUTE, NATHALIE, 'De Dostoïevski à Kafka' (1947), in *L'Ere du soupçon*, pp. 1557–77
——'L'Ere du soupçon' (1950), in *L'Ere du soupçon*, pp. 1577–87
——*L'Ere du soupçon: essais sur le roman*, 2nd edn, in *Œuvres complètes*, pp. 1551–1620
——*Le Planétarium* (1959), in *Œuvres complètes*, pp. 339–519
——*Les Fruits d'or* (1963), in *Œuvres complètes*, pp. 521–620
——*Entre la vie et la mort* (1968), in *Œuvres complètes*, pp. 621–734
——'Ce que je cherche à faire' (1972), in *Œuvres complètes*, pp. 1694–1706
——*Enfance* (1983), in *Œuvres complètes*, pp. 987–1145
——*Pour un oui ou pour un non* (1986), in *Œuvres complètes*, pp. 1495–1515
——*Tu ne t'aimes pas* (1989), in *Œuvres complètes*, pp. 1147–1291
——*Œuvres complètes*, ed. by Jean-Yves Tadié and others (Paris: Gallimard, coll. Bibliothèque de la Pléiade, 1996)
——*Ouvrez* (Paris: Gallimard, coll. Blanche, 1997)
SARTRE, JEAN-PAUL, 'Le Regard', in *L'Etre et le néant: essai d'ontologie phénoménologique*, ed. by Arlette Elkaïm-Sartre, rev'd edn (Paris: Gallimard, coll. tel, 1943), pp. 292–341
——*Saint Genet: comédien et martyr*, published as *Œuvres complètes de Jean Genet*, I (Paris: Gallimard, 1952)
——*Les Mots* (Paris: Gallimard, 1964)
SAVONA, JEANNETTE LAILLOU, 'Théâtre et univers carcéral: Jean Genet et Michel Foucault', *French Forum*, 10.2 (May 1985), 201–13
SCHIPA, MARY E., 'Hélène Cixous: sur la piste d'une autobiographie féministe', *Romance Review*, 5.1 (Spring 1995), 29–37

SCHMUTZ, MARIANNE, *'Enfance' de Nathalie Sarraute comme autobiographie* (Lyons: Aldrui, 1999)

SCHNITZER, DAPHNÉ, 'A Drop in Numbers: Deciphering Georges Perec's Postanalytic Narratives', in *Pereckonings: Reading Georges Perec,* ed. by Warren Motte and Jean-Jacques Poucel, special edn of *Yale French Studies*, 105 (2004), pp. 110–26

SCHWARTZ, PAUL, *Georges Perec: Traces of his Passage* (Alabama: Summa Publications Inc., 1988)

SEDGWICK, EVE KOSOFSKY, *Tendencies* (Durham, NC: Duke University Press, 1993)

——*Epistemology of the Closet* (Harmondsworth: Penguin, 1994)

SEIDMAN, STEVEN, 'Identity and Politics in a "Postmodern" Gay Culture: Some Historical and Conceptual Notes', in *Fear of a Queer Planet: Queer Politics and Social Theory*, ed. by Michael Warner (Minneapolis: University of Minnesota Press, 1993), pp. 105–42

SELLERS, SUSAN, *Hélène Cixous: Authorship, Autobiography and Love* (Cambridge: Polity Publishers, 1996)

SELLERS, SUSAN (ed.), *Writing Differences: Readings from the Seminar of Hélène Cixous* (Milton Keynes: Open University Press, 1988)

SHERINGHAM, MICHAEL, 'Narration and Experience in Genet's *Journal du voleur*', in *Studies in French Fiction in Honour of Vivienne Mylne*, ed. by Robert Gibson (London: Grant and Cutler, 1988), pp. 289–306

——'Ego Redux? Strategies in New French Autobiography', in *Dalhousie French Studies*, 17 (Fall–Winter 1989), 27–35

——*French Autobiography: Devices and Desires: Rousseau to Perec* (Oxford: Clarendon Press, 1993)

——'Changing the Frame: Women Writers and the Rise of Autobiography', in *A History of Women's Writing in France*, ed. by Sonya Stephens (Cambridge: Cambridge University Press, 2000), pp. 185–203

——'Attending to the Everyday: Blanchot, Lefebvre, Certeau, Perec', *French Studies*, 54 (2000), 187–99

SHIACH, MORAG, *Hélène Cixous: A Politics of Writing* (London: Routledge, 1991)

SINGER, LINDA, 'True Confessions: Cixous and Foucault on Sexuality and Power', in *The Thinking Muse: Feminism and Modern French Philosophy*, ed. by Jeffner Allen and Iris Marion Young (Bloomington: Indiana University Press, 1989), pp. 136–55

SIRVENT, MICHEL, 'Blanc, coupe, énigme: 'Auto(bio)graphies': *W ou le souvenir d'enfance* de Georges Perec', *Littérature*, 98 (May 1995), 3–23

——'An Auto-Bio-Graphy: *W ou le souvenir d'enfance* or the Space of the Double Cover', *Sites*, 1 (1997), 461–80

——'Reader-Investigators in the Post-Nouveau Roman: Lahougue, Peeters, and Perec', *Romanic Review*, 88 (1997), 315–35

SMITH, KAREN R., 'Allegory and Autobiography: Georges Perec's Narrative Resistance to Nostalgia', *Journal of Narrative Technique*, 23 (1993), 201–10

SMITH, ROBERT, *Derrida and Autobiography* (Cambridge: Cambridge University Press, 1995)

SMITH, SIDONIE, *A Poetics of Women's Autobiography: Marginality and the Fictions of Self-Representation* (Bloomington: Indiana University Press, 1987)

——'The Autobiographical Manifesto: Ideas, Temporalities, Politics', in *Autobiography and Questions of Gender*, ed. by Shirley Neuman (London: Cass, 1991), pp. 186–212

——*Subjectivity, Identity and the Body: Women's Autobiographical Practices in the Twentieth Century* (Bloomington: Indiana University Press, 1993)

STANTON, DOMNA C., 'Autogynography: Is the Subject Different?', in *The Female Autograph: Theory and Practice of Autobiography from the Tenth to the Twentieth Century*, ed. by Domna C. Stanton (Chicago: University of Chicago Press, 1987), pp. 3–20

STAROBINSKI, JEAN, 'Le Style de l'autobiographie', *Poétique*, 1 (1970), 255–65

STEPHENS, ELIZABETH, 'Disseminating Phallic Masculinity: Seminal Fluidity in Genet's Fiction', in *Genet*, ed. by Mairéad Hanrahan, special edn of *Paragraph*, 27.2 (July 2004), pp. 85–97

——'"Je suis un mensonge qui dit toujours la vérité": Genet's Queer Subjectivities', in *Soi-disant: Life-Writing in French*, ed. by Juliana De Nooy, Joe Hardwick and Barbara E. Hanna (Newark: University of Delaware Press, 2005), pp. 41–52

STEVENS, CHRISTA, *L'Ecriture solaire d'Hélène Cixous: travail du texte et histoire du sujet dans 'Portrait du soleil'* (Amsterdam: Rodopi, 1999)

——'Judéités, à lire dans l'œuvre d'Hélène Cixous', *International Journal of Francophone Studies*, 7 (2004), 81–93

STEWART, HARRY E. and ROB ROY MCGREGOR, *Jean Genet: A Biography of Deceit 1910–1951* (New York: Peter Lang, 1989)

STURROCK, JOHN, 'The New Model Autobiographer', *New Literary History*, 9 (1977), 51–63

——'Theory Versus Autobiography', in *The Culture of Autobiography: Constructions of Self-Representation*, ed. by Robert Folkenflik (Stanford, CA: Stanford University Press, 1993), pp. 21–37

——*The Language of Autobiography: Studies in the First Person Singular* (Cambridge: Cambridge University Press, 1993)

STUMP, JORDAN, '*Un homme qui dort* et ses doubles', *French Review*, 67 (1994), 609–18

SULEIMAN, SUSAN RUBIN, 'War Memories: On Autobiographical Reading', in *Auschwitz and After: Race, Culture, and 'the Jewish Question' in France*, ed. by Lawrence D. Kritzman (New York: Routledge, 1995), pp. 47–62

SWINDELLS, JULIA (ed.), *The Uses of Autobiography* (London: Taylor and Francis, 1995)

THODY, PHILIP, *Jean Genet: A Study of his Works and Plays* (London: Hamish Hamilton, 1968)

——'Sartre and White: Biographers of a Contrary Child', in *Flowers and Revolution: A Collection of Writings on Jean Genet*, ed. by Barbara Read (London: Middlesex University Press, 1997), pp. 25–32

TIDD, URSULA, *Simone de Beauvoir: Gender and Testimony* (Cambridge: Cambridge University Press, 1999)

TOONDER, JEANETTE DEN, 'Le Rôle de la mémoire dans l'écriture autobiographique', in *Genres as Repositories of Cultural Memory: Volume 5 of the Comparative Literature Association 'Literature as Cultural Memory' Leiden 16–22 August 1997*, ed. by Hendrik van Gorp and Ulla Musarra-Schroeder (Amsterdam: Rodopi, 2000), pp. 323–32

TOONDER, JEANETTE M. L. DEN, *'Qui est-je?' L'Ecriture autobiographique des nouveaux romanciers* (Bern: Peter Lang, 1999)

TYLER, CAROLE-ANNE, 'Desiring Machines? Queer Re-visions of Feminist Film Theory', in *Coming Out of Feminism?*, ed. by Mandy Merck, Naomi Segal and Elizabeth Wright (Oxford: Blackwell, 1998), pp. 154–93

VAN ROSSUM-GUYON, FRANÇOISE and MYRIAM DÍAZ-DIOCARETZ, *Hélène Cixous: chemins d'une écriture* (Paris: Presses Universitaires de Vincennes; Amsterdam: Rodopi, 1990)

VERCIER, BRUNO, '(Nouveau) Roman et autobiographie: *Enfance* de Nathalie Sarraute', *French Literature Series*, 12 (1985), 162–70

WAGSTAFF, PETER, 'Utopia and Autobiography: George [*sic*] Perec's *W ou le souvenir d'enfance*', *Utopian Studies*, 8.2 (1997), 87–103

WALKER, DAVID, 'Antecedents for Genet's Persona', in *Autobiography and the Existential Self: Studies in Modern French Writing*, ed. by Terry Keefe and Edmund Smyth (Liverpool: Liverpool University Press, 1995), pp. 147–68

WATSON, JULIA, 'Toward An Anti-Metaphysics of Autobiography', in *The Culture of Autobiography: Constructions of Self-Representation*, ed. by Robert Folkenflik (Stanford, CA: Stanford University Press, 1993), pp. 57–79

Watson-Williams, Helen, *The Novels of Nathalie Sarraute: Towards an Aesthetic* (Amsterdam: Rodopi, 1981)

Webb, Richard and Webb, Suzanne, *Jean Genet and his Critics: An Annotated Bibliography 1943–1980* (London: Scarecrow Press, 1982)

White, Edmund, *Genet* (London: Chatto and Windus, 1993)

—— 'Genet and Europe', in *Jean Genet: Littérature et Politique (Literature and Politics)*, ed. by Patrice Bougon, special edn of *Esprit créateur*, 35.1 (Spring 1995), pp. 5–10

—— 'Once a Sodomite, Twice a Philosopher', *Harvard Gay and Lesbian Review*, 3.1 (1996) <http://semgai.free.fr/doc_et_pdf/pdf_these_articles_externes/White_Genet.pdf> [accessed 1 August 2006]

White, Nicholas, *The Family in Crisis in Late Nineteenth-Century French Fiction* (Cambridge: Cambridge University Press, 1999)

Wilcox, Helen (ed.), *The Body and the Text: Hélène Cixous and Reading and Teaching* (New York: St Martin's Press; Hemel Hempstead: Harvester Wheatsheaf, 1990)

Willging, Jennifer, 'Partners in Slime: The Liquid and the Viscous in Sarraute and Sartre', *Romanic Review*, 92 (2001), 277–96

Wilson, Emma, 'Hélène Cixous: An Erotics of the Feminine', in *French Erotic Fiction: Women's Desiring Writing, 1880–1990*, ed. by Alex Hughes and Kate Ince (Oxford: Berg, 1996), pp. 121–45

—— *Sexuality and the Reading Encounter: Identity and Desire in Proust, Duras, Tournier and Cixous* (Oxford: Clarendon Press, 1996)

—— 'Identification and Melancholia: The Inner Cinema of Hélène Cixous', in *Revisiting the Scene of Writing: New Readings of Cixous*, ed. by Julia Dobson and Gill Rye, special edn of *Paragraph*, 23.3 (November 2000), pp. 258–69

Wilson, Suzanne, 'Auto-bio-graphie: vers une théorie de l'écriture féminine', *French Review*, 63 (1990), 617–22

Wittig, Monique, 'Le Déambulatoire: entretien avec Nathalie Sarraute', in *Nathalie Sarraute ou le texte du for intérieur*, ed. by Lise Leibacher-Ouvrard and Monique Wittig, special edn of *Esprit créateur*, 36.2 (Summer 1996), pp. 3–8

—— 'Avatars', in *Nathalie Sarraute ou le texte du for intérieur*, ed. by Lise Leibacher-Ouvrard and Monique Wittig, special edn of *Esprit créateur*, 36.2 (Summer 1996), pp. 109–16

Yee, Jennifer, 'The Colonial Outsider: "Malgérie" in Hélène Cixous' Novel *Les Rêveries de la femme sauvage*', *Tulsa Studies in Women's Literature*, 20 (2001), 189–200

Ziarek, Ewa, 'Kristeva and Levinas: Mourning, Ethics and the Feminine', in *Ethics, Politics and Difference in Julia Kristeva's Writing*, ed. by Kelly Oliver (New York: Routledge, 1993), pp. 62–78

Žižek, Slavoj, *Looking Awry: An Introduction to Jacques Lacan through Popular Culture* (Cambridge, MA: MIT, 1991)

—— 'Fantasy as a Political Category: A Lacanian Approach' (1996), in *The Žižek Reader*, ed. by Elizabeth Wright and Edmond Wright (Oxford: Blackwell, 1999), pp. 87–101

—— '"I Hear You with My Eyes"; or, The Invisible Master', in *Gaze and Voice as Love Objects*, ed. by Renata Salecl and Slavoj Žižek (Durham, NC: Duke University Press, 1996), pp. 90–126

INDEX

❖